The fall and rise of the PDS in eastern Germany

The New Germany in Context

Series editors: Jonathan Grix (Birmingham), Paul Cooke (University of Wales, Aberystwyth) and Lothar Funk (University of Trier)

The *New Germany in Context* provides a forum for original research into the state of post-unity German society from a wide range of disciplinary perspectives. Since unification, Germany, and its place in the world, has undergone a period of rapid development and change. This series brings together academics from political science, economics, history and cultural studies in order to explore the legacies and debates which shape the new Federal Republic.

Other titles in the series include:

Published:
The new regulatory state in Germany
Markus M. Müller

Ten years of German unification: transfer, transformation, incorporation?
Edited by Jörn Leonhard and Lothar Funk

Economic transition, unemployment and Active Labour Market Policy
Corinne Nativel

Forthcoming:
Identity creation and the culture of contrition: reconfiguring national identity in the Berlin Republic
Karl Wilds

Unification, collective bargaining and the German model of industrial relations
Steve French

East German distinctiveness in a unified Germany
Edited by Jonathan Grix and Paul Cooke

Approaches to the study of contemporary Germany: research methodologies in German Studies
Edited by Jonathan Grix

The making of the Berlin Republic
Edited by William Paterson and Jonathan Grix

The fall and rise of the PDS in eastern Germany

Dan Hough, University of Birmingham

THE UNIVERSITY
OF BIRMINGHAM

UNIVERSITY PRESS

First published in the United Kingdom by The University of Birmingham Press, Edgbaston, Birmingham, BI5 2TT, UK.

ISBN 1-902459-14-8 √

British Library Cataloguing in Publication data
A CIP catalogue record for this book is available from the
British Library

Printed & bound by Antony Rowe Ltd, Eastbourne

Typeset by Book Production Services, London,

Contents

Acknowledgements

This book could not have been written without the help of a number of people and institutions. Firstly, I thank the Institute for German Studies (IGS) at the University of Birmingham, and the Economic and Social Research Council, for funding the research from which this monograph stems. My sincere thanks go to Professor Charlie Jeffery of the IGS for his constant coaxing, cajoling and prompting: without his input this book would undoubtedly be much the poorer. A similar tribute is due to Professor Stephen Padgett and Professor William Paterson, whose insightful comments also improved the quality of my work immeasurably.

I owe a considerable debt to the other staff and students of the IGS. Since its opening in 1994 it has developed into a flourishing academic community, and I am proud to have been a part of it. In this regard, and in no particular order, Andy McLintock, Hannah Tooze, Helen Miller, Jonathan Grix, Simon Green, Emma Gittus, Kerry Longhurst, Vanda Knowles and Rosanne Palmer all deserve special mention for sharing, at one time or another, an office with me and for putting up with my excessive enthusiasm for Shrewsbury Town FC, my smelly football kit, anti-social working hours and other bad or annoying habits! Their contribution to keeping me somewhere near sane should not be underestimated.

When in Germany I never ceased to be amazed by the enthusiasm and helpfulness shown by members of the PDS in supplying me with material and information on their party. In this regard I would particularly thank Dr Christian Westphal of the PDS in Rostock for his stimulating comments and observations on the PDS and on politics in general, as well as for his assistance in gathering information on the party in Mecklenburg Western Pomerania. I must also thank the members of the PDS *Landesgeschäftstelle* in Schwerin for making my short stay with them in May 1999 so pleasurable.

Finally, eight people deserve my special thanks, for very different reasons. My academic interest in the PDS would never have become as pronounced if I had not met Frau Renate Vogt in Leipzig in 1995. Her willingness to assist me in my quest for information has been an inspiration, and I deeply appreciate the time and effort she put in on my behalf. Secondly, I must thank the *'Oberkrautfresser'* himself, Felix Lange, for his ongoing interest in all things political and for the many conversations, discussions, disputes and slanging matches we enjoyed on the topic of the PDS, whether they took place in Leipzig, Wagenfeld, Berlin, Lyon, Salt Lake City, Tehran, Trabzon or Sofia! Thirdly I owe a special debt to the series editors of *The New Germany in Context*, Jonathan Grix, Paul Cooke and Lothar Funk, and Alec McAulay of the University of Birmingham Press, for helping me convert my thesis into a half-way readable book. Their patience and thoroughness have undoubtedly helped make the final version more accessible and engaging. Finally, I thank my parents for their support and assistance throughout the course of my research, and it is to them that I dedicate this book.

List of tables and figures

Figures

Introduction:
the fall and rise of the PDS

The stabilisation of the *Partei des Demokratischen Sozialismus* (Party of Democratic Socialism – PDS) in the German party system has been one of the most surprising outcomes of the unification process. Whereas the PDS was once perceived as unlikely to have any future at all in unified Germany,[1] developments over the last decade have seen the party stabilise and even prosper. The spectrum of political and academic opinion expressed on the PDS remains, however, broad and diverse. At the one extreme, notably in conservative circles, the PDS is viewed as an extremist, undemocratic and disruptive force that should be regarded as a pariah, and a threat to the democratic stability of the German state. At the other, the PDS is regarded as a broad church of socialist opinion, aiming to alter fundamentally the economic inequalities in German society by reversing the trend towards neo-liberalism and social inequality. Positions between the extremes are equally fervently espoused. This book attempts to analyse the PDS from a perspective that avoids partisan alignments and value judgements. For this reason the ideological contradictions within the PDS's programme are given markedly less attention than is perhaps the case in other works. It seeks to explain the reasons for the fall and rise of the PDS since unification by illustrating how it has established itself as an eastern German regional party. It explains how the PDS has become a relevant political actor and why it has succeeded in articulating *regionally specific* interests.

The continuing vigour of the PDS should not be allowed to obscure the belief that most politicians and political scientists espoused in the early 1990s – that the PDS was a transitory phenomenon that would be unable to hold its place in the German party system. Following the collapse of the state socialist regimes of central and eastern Europe it was expected that the PDS would, perhaps after an interim period representing the apparatchiks of the GDR state, disappear as all anachronisms should. Hence, although the PDS was widely expected to enter the 12th *Bundestag* in 1990, largely as a result of a relaxation of the entry requirements, few analysts expected it to return in

1994. In fact, the PDS confounded its critics by building on its strength in eastern Berlin to win four seats (*Direktmandate*), thus ensuring parliamentary representation in the 13th *Bundestag*.[2] Although the PDS was (perhaps paradoxically) generally given a much better chance of survival in 1998 than was the case in 1994, it was also not until the final few results were received that the PDS knew it had cleared the 5 per cent barrier – so entering the *Bundestag* for the first time as a *Fraktion* rather than as a *Bundestagsgruppe*. Given that it has retained its place in eastern German legislatures and the *Bundestag* for a whole decade, it seems high time for an analysis of the reasons that lie at the base of its improbable success.

Structure of the book

This book is divided into six chapters. Chapter one briefly outlines the PDS's development in the first ten years since unification. Having witnessed the implosion of the GDR, the SED realised that it needed to take drastic action if it were to secure a role for itself in post-unification Germany. While this was anything but straightforward, the transformation of the SED into the PDS was the first step towards finding a new function within post-unification politics. Chapter one highlights how the PDS has skilfully steered a path between outright continuity with its SED past and clear-cut ideological and programmatic change. Chapter two illustrates that the painful process of change outlined in chapter one has led authors to adopt a variety of approaches when discussing the PDS. The traditional approaches highlight different parts of the PDS's complex nature, and it is for this reason that they each contribute something to an understanding of the party's development, ideological orientation and inner contradictions. Chapter two also illustrates that a specifically regionalist approach has been lacking, and that there has been remarkably little scholarly analysis of the PDS's parallels with other regional parties.

The third chapter develops the analytical framework that is to be employed in chapters four, five and six. The PDS, like other regional parties of the democratic world, is most at home in its own cultural and social environment, articulating specifically regional sentiments and interests. This is in spite of strenuous efforts to broaden its electoral base nationwide. Some of the reasons why so little academic analysis has been conducted on the PDS as a regional party – comparable though it is to other regional movements[3] – are clarified in chapter three, which introduces a systematic classification of the foundations of regional party success that has, until now, been lacking in the broader literature on regional parties. The analytical tool that enables the political scientist to comprehend the complex nature of regional party success is a typology of regional parties. The first part of the typology broadly outlines the structural and causal factors inherent in political regionalism. This enables the existence of an eastern German *Trotzidentität* (identity of defiance) to be analysed in chapter four. The cultural and socioeconomic variables selected form the cornerstones of the development of regional identities: without these, regional parties will not succeed in the political arena. The complex interaction of a regional identification[4] and other important cleavages (class, economic difference, religion and so forth) dictate, in each case, exactly what constellation of political forces exists within a region. The second part of the typology then sets out three factors which are important in the mobilisation of regionalism by regional parties: leadership, political organisation and a coherent set of core policies.

The first part of the typology is applied to the eastern German case in chapter four, discussing how eastern Germany is a distinct and unique political and cultural space. It helps to reveal the processes of identity creation that have taken (and are still taking) place there, leading to the establishment of a *Trotzidentität*. The transformation process has lent itself to a re-identification of many eastern Germans with 'their' territorial space, and a consequent orientation towards regional feelings and sentiments. Both the legacy of combined experience within the GDR and the socialisation processes that this entailed, coupled with the unique and complex transformation processes that unification set in motion, have enabled eastern Germans to collectively re-identify with one another (if not the state where they used to live) in a way that would have been unthinkable as the Berlin Wall came down. These complex developments have created a territorial cleavage along the former East–West border, cross-cutting other more long-standing social cleavages in Germany. The typology helps to highlight the clear differences that exist in the *Weltanschauungen* of eastern and western Germans – and the advantageous climate that has been created for a party mobilising specifically eastern German concerns within local, *Land* and national political arenas.

The second part of the typology is applied to the PDS in chapters five and six. The fifth chapter illustrates how the PDS has developed the capacity to mobilise easternness, while the sixth chapter dissects the PDS's policy package in detail, illustrating how the PDS attempts to make policy for eastern Germany. These are powerful preconditions of the PDS's success in the eastern states, enabling it to be successful as a result of the East/West divide and the processes of identity creation that this has spawned. Chapter six turns specifically to the policy approaches of the PDS, illustrating how its policy package and parliamentary work is based on issues and policies that are of particular resonance in the eastern states: in other words, the PDS remains strong and vociferous on exactly the issues where eastern German self-perceptions and attitudes vary from their western equivalents. The final chapter discusses, in view of the findings outlined through the course of this book, what this may mean for the future of the PDS as well as the ramifications this is likely to have on the (eastern) German party system as a whole.

Notes

1 See Bortfeldt, 1992, p.295; Smith, 1992, p.100; Moreau, 1992, p.459; Gerner, 1994, p.59.
2 Although the PDS did indeed return to the *Bundestag* in 1994, it did so despite only registering 4.4 per cent of the vote. The PDS made use of a clause allowing parties obtaining three directly elected members to take their place in Parliament as a *Bundestagsgruppe* rather than a *Bundestagsfraktion*. Although this prevented the PDS from enjoying the same rights as the parties who did achieve 5 per cent, it none the less enabled it to register 30 members of the Federal Parliament.
3 The only study that has attempted to place the PDS in a cross-national, regional perspective is that conducted by David Patton, and he limits himself to a comparison with the *Lega Nord*, the SNP in Scotland and the Reform Party in Canada. While enlightening, Patton's article only touches the surface of successful territorial mobilisation, and leaves scope for a broader analysis on the, as he concludes, similarities in political manner between these parties. See Patton, 1998, pp.500–26.
4 It is worth clarifying here what is exactly meant by the term 'identity'. In the context of this book 'identity' is taken to mean the distinct norms, beliefs and values of an individual (or group) that can be regarded as a persisting entity. Further to this, and particularly within the context of larger communities, identity can also be understood as a set of behavioural or personal characteristics by which an individual is recognisable as a member of a certain group. For a broader discussion on the definitional problems that one is inevitably faced with when discussing the phenomena of social identity see Knight, 1982, pp.514–31; Gellner, 1987; Keith and Pile, 1993.

1

From SED to PDS: the uneasy path between continuity and change

The PDS's strong and consistent showing in the late 1990s in eastern Germany should not disguise the traumatic and schizophrenic early period of the party's development. The PDS grew out of a dictatorial and inherently anti-democratic predecessor –the *Sozialistische Einheitspartei Deutschlands* (Socialist Unity Party: SED) – and its starting position in 1990 was, therefore, not at all advantageous. Over forty years the SED had proved itself to be one of the most hard-line and dogmatic Communist parties in eastern Europe, and, as the GDR collapsed, it was only at the last moment that its leaders appeared to realise the true severity of the crisis affecting their party and their state. Only as the GDR imploded in the weeks and months after the fall of the Berlin Wall did the party leaders grasp that radical changes in ideology, organisation and policy were necessary if the SED were to survive in post-Wall Germany. In late 1989 and early 1990, therefore, the SED set out on an uneasy and disjointed process of reform. The stumbling nature of the reform process stemmed from the nature of the dilemma which the SED leadership faced. Once it became clear that unification was highly likely to take place, the party needed to make rapid and quantifiable progress in aligning itself with the structures enshrined in the West German Basic Law and in shaping a party programme with which it could plausibly go to the electorate. Yet, at the same time, the leaders of the SED realised that wholesale reforms were completely out of the question. The SED needed to stay true to the core of its rapidly shrinking membership base, otherwise it was faced with the prospect of disintegrating altogether.[1]

After initially attempting to take up a position on the left of the political spectrum, as a counterweight to the conservative coalition led by Helmut Kohl, the leaders of the SED realised that the party was still suffering from a chronic lack of legitimacy and that it had to attempt to re-invent itself. Disbanding the SED was the obvious option, so as to create space for a left-wing organisation as free as possible of ideological taint from the GDR, and able to propagate a newly defined socialism based on democratic principles. But, for a number of reasons, this was a route that both the SED leadership and the membership were highly unlikely ever to support: if the SED were to disband it would find it very difficult to retain the assets and organisational strength that it still possessed, hence the party opted for financial and organisational continuity in the form of a name change. Indeed, without the advantages that this offered the party in terms of connections, networks and resources,[2] it is doubtful that the SED, SED/PDS or PDS would have been able to survive beyond the initial months of the unification period.[3]

On 17 December 1989, therefore, the party chose to adopt a new, transitional, name – the SED/PDS.[4] Following the formation of the SED/PDS, Gregor Gysi, the new party leader, continued to champion a further name change that would lead to 'SED' being dropped altogether, in order (he hoped) to signal a clear and definitive break with the past. The life-span of the SED/PDS, therefore, was short: at the Executive meeting of 4 February 1990 the decision was taken to re-name the party once again – this time simply to the PDS. This, so the leadership hoped, would indicate to the wider world that a break had indeed been made and that the PDS was to be a new, democratic, political actor. Unsurprisingly, the vast majority of citizens saw through the smokescreen and remained unconvinced by the PDS's apparent metamorphosis. Only in later years, and largely for reasons that few envisaged in early 1990, as we shall see, did the PDS gain acceptance in eastern Germany.

Internal reforms such as the denunciation of democratic centralism and the introduction of more transparent internal procedures could not prevent the party losing over two million members between mid 1989 and December 1991, with only the ideologically convinced former SED cadre remaining loyal to the party. Policy reform remained equally problematic and necessarily piecemeal. The change of name could not disguise the fact that the PDS remained tied to much of the ideological rhetoric it had espoused in the GDR.[5] The party appeared unable to embrace wholeheartedly the democratic structures of the Federal Republic, and it experienced enormous difficulties in particular in attempting to clarify its position towards the GDR. Indeed, it was only in the late 1990s that the PDS genuinely attempted to come to terms with what the GDR was, what it stood for and what exactly was wrong with it; indeed, many commentators argue that the PDS still has work to do on this issue today. The PDS also needed to redefine its whole raison d'être: what exactly did it want to achieve? If this was to be a form of socialism, what would it look like? How would the PDS avoid the mistakes made in socialism's name in the past? All of these complex issues caused much consternation in the party, and prevented reform from taking place at more than snail's pace.

In the years immediately following unification, the PDS was consequently written off as an anachronism that, over the course of time, would disappear from the party political map.[6] It had no coherent political agenda and appeared unable to influence the wider political environment around it. Furthermore, who, apart from a small band of disaffected SED stalwarts, was ever likely to support a party that had presided over a state with a moribund economy, a state that had consistently trampled on the democratic rights of its citizens and a state that had shown a blatant disregard for human life – as the shootings at the Berlin Wall and other border crossings amply testified? The answer, surely, would be hardly anyone. It therefore seems plausible that had eastern Germany blossomed into the 'flourishing economic landscape' that Federal Chancellor Helmut Kohl had promised, the PDS would have drifted, as the cadre gradually died away, into non-existence. Yet, by the end of 1991, and increasingly thereafter, the fallout from unification was beginning to disillusion many eastern Germans, and new and unexpected electoral potential was developing for the PDS. The perceived arrogance of western politicians, the apparent annexation (although initially approved of) of eastern Germany, and the blatant lack of regard for most things 'East German' led many to feel like strangers in their own land.[7] The PDS sensed that things might not be as bleak as was first believed, and sought to develop a new role for itself as the articulator of dissatisfied sections of the eastern German electorate. Those who perceived themselves as being subjectively worse off, or were uneasy at the social and economic fallout from unification, consequently expressed themselves politically in increasing numbers with a vote for the PDS. The enduring material and psychological differences between eastern and western Germany ensured that the PDS was able to develop and expand on its steady bedrock of former functionary support (see chapter two).

Continuities between the PDS and the SED

Despite its stabilisation in all of the eastern German *Landtage* and in the *Bundestag*, and despite its protestations to the contrary, the PDS is still no 'ordinary' political party. For opponents and supporters alike, the PDS represents an element of continuity with the GDR in the 'new' party system. The bedrock of the party's 85,000 membership remains the loyal functionaries and supporters of the SED regime. Indeed, it was only their continued support and loyalty that ensured, in the immediate post-unification period, that the party did not disintegrate and was able to gain parliamentary representation in unified Germany. If it had failed in this then the party would not have been in a position to rebuild its electoral base in later years. In many ways the PDS owes its survival to the sustained loyalty of those GDR citizens who most fervently believed in the SED – even after all that it stood for had ceased to exist. The element of continuity that the PDS provides for those who saw the end of the GDR in negative terms is self-evident. Although it came as no surprise that the PDS was able to mobilise this vote in the immediate post-1989 elections, these supporters have also remained vitally important in dictating both the speed and extent of reform in the late 1990s. When coupled with the inability of the PDS to attract new members, it is clear that the overwhelming numerical dominance of traditionalists within the party has ensured that changes in the party programme have been slow and incremental.

Programmatically, the PDS has not been able to throw off all the Communist shackles that it inherited. Although it remains unique amongst political parties in Germany in that it is home to an almost impracticably broad church of members, with strikingly differing ideological beliefs, the common goal of a socialist German state does not prevent hardline Communists from taking their place in the party's rank and file. Communist rhetoric and beliefs are therefore part of everyday discourse within the PDS. Stout and dogged defence of the socialism/communism of the GDR, although not aggressively deployed by most of the PDS leadership, is also a cause dear to considerable sections of the PDS membership.[8] The existence of the Communist Platform (KPF), around which outspoken critics of the capitalist societal system gather, as well as the Marxist Forum and various other extreme left groups, illustrate that within the PDS there exists what can be best described as a strong current of communist support. Deprived of leadership positions and small in number they may be, it is none the less undeniable that they enjoy considerable popular support among the party 'grass-roots' and, despite the considerable pressure to cleanse the party of such elements, it is inconceivable that any party leader would wish to antagonise such a large portion of the party membership. Hence, their continued existence within the party appears to be secure – although it is worth remembering that many are members of the *Aufbaugeneration* (the generation that helped to create the GDR out of the rubble of the Second World War) and are therefore likely to be relatively old.

The existence of such groups is often taken as evidence that a reconciliation with the GDR past has not been carried out; only when the PDS undertakes such a thorough self-evaluation, as even members of the KPF like Michael Benjamin[9] admitted, will the party be able to de-couple itself from its SED heritage. Expelling the KPF alone would not resolve this problem: the party has to go past symbolic gestures and declarations (like those condemning Stalinism) and conduct its own process of *Vergangenheitsbewältigung* (coming to terms with the past) or else condemn itself to a permanent state of *Politikunfähigkeit* (lacking political credibility). This is an issue addressed in the next chapter; suffice it to say here that if the party is to demonstrate that it has truly changed, a clear evaluation of what exactly was wrong with the GDR, why, and what this means for the future of socialism, will be necessary.

Processes of change and adaptation within the PDS

The elements of continuity evident within the PDS are widely known, and widely publicised by politicians from other parties and in the popular media. This is often done at the expense of recognising the changes, many of them drastic, that the PDS has undergone since it officially came into being in February 1990. In order to merit a place in the 'new' party system, it had to undertake considerable pragmatic change, particularly in areas of policy formulation, party structure and *Weltanschauung*. Subsequently, it has developed into a post-communist party of the type much in evidence across central and eastern Europe, while simultaneously articulating the interests of its eastern German clientele, much as the other 'regional' parties in western Europe represent territorially based groups in the political process. The result of this is a complex, sometimes contradictory, party that competes ably and effectively with the other 'western' parties for votes and influence within the five eastern *Länder* and Berlin, as well as at the federal level.

Despite the inability and/or unwillingness of the party's leadership to distance itself completely from its SED past, it is indisputable that the PDS has moved away from the rigid internal structures that existed in the SED. No votes are contrived (or at least no more than in any other party where leaders attempt to impose their will on members), any member is free to stand for election and, as the resignation of leading lights like André Brie and Gregor Gysi and the fiery confrontations seen at the Münster Party Conference of April 2000 have illustrated, the party grass-roots does not always act as the leadership expects, or hopes, it will. In this sense, the democratic changes and healthy debates that have come to characterise conferences since 1989 represent a distinct metamorphosis.

The all-encompassing Marxist-Leninist ideology of the SED has been replaced, and the PDS now attempts to portray itself as a broad socialist party to the left of the SPD, having denied the importance of the leading role of the working class and chosen, even if in a guarded way, to admit that the market may have a role to play in its future ideal world. The party is therefore nowhere near as 'extreme' as it once was. It welcomes anyone who wishes to oppose capitalism and the societal relationships that it fosters, and although definitive statements of what the party hopes to achieve, and how it plans to pay for it, are lacking, it is clear that the PDS has moved towards being a broad left-wing alternative to the SPD.

Despite the uniqueness born of its heritage and political development, it is clear that the PDS is not an irrelevant extra within the German party system. It has undertaken a process of reform, even if this has not been as thorough and convincing as many would have liked. But it has been enough to cement the PDS into eastern German state parliaments, and it remains an energetic advocate of wholesale reform of the prevailing social market structures of contemporary Germany. Chapter two discusses the mechanics of this development in greater detail, and highlights errors in the ways other academic studies of the PDS have tended to characterise the party. It explains why the particular analytical approach adopted in this study has been chosen and why, contrary to the conclusions of much of the academic discourse of the 1990s, the PDS may have a long future in German political life.

Notes

1   Hough, 2000a, p.124.
2   One source has claimed that in 1992 the SPD had assets amounting to DM 276.8 million, while the PDS could register a remarkable DM 438.7 million. *This Week in Germany*: 20 January 1995, p.5.
3   Neugebauer, in Brie, Herzig and Koch (eds.), 1995, p.41.
4   For a detailed analysis of the PDS's development out of the SED, see Barker, 1998, pp.1–17.
5   For a particularly critical analysis of the PDS's development see the work of Patrick Moreau, Jürgen Lang and/or Viola Neu: Moreau, 1992; Moreau and Lang, 1994; Moreau and Neu, 1994; Moreau and Lang, 1996a; Moreau, 1996, pp.27–42; Neu, 1998; Moreau, 1998; Neu, 1999.
6   Gerner, 1994, p.242.
7   Pulzer, 1993, p.325.

7 See, for instance, Modrow, 1991; Bisky, Heuer and Schumann, 1993; Modrow, 1998. For evidence of a willingness on the part of a small minority of PDS members to defend much more controversial parts of the GDR's history, such as the building of the Berlin Wall see, for example, 'PDS Vorstandsmitglied verteidigt Mauerbau', in *Schweriner Volkszeitung*, 25 January 1999, p.1; Michael Benjamin: '7. Oktober – war da nicht was?', in *Junge Welt*, 7 October 1999, p.2.

8 Benjamin in Bisky *et al.* (eds.), 1996, p.230.

2

The PDS: broad church or bundle of contradictions?

In the first years after unification, as chapter one has indicated, the PDS was largely taken to be a transitory political phenomenon. Despite such characterisations there has been a surprisingly large amount of literature published on the PDS.[1] Most commentators have tended to discuss the subject of the PDS's longevity by broadly adopting one of four approaches:

* The protest party approach
* The socialist reform party approach
* The anti-System, extremist party approach
* The milieu party approach

Each of the four approaches is generally employed within the framework of two main schools of thought on the PDS and its role in Germany today. The first sees the PDS as a dysfunctional, disruptive element within the German political system, often bordering on the extremist fringe, contributing to a destabilising of political life;[2] the second sees the PDS more as a stabilising, reforming, corrective influence, stressing its integrative and representative functions. However, each approach should not be taken to be absolutely individual and distinct – significant degrees of overlap and co-ordination are evident in all the literature on the PDS, as the analysis in this chapter will illustrate.

The protest party approach

Almost every analysis of the PDS acknowledges, in some shape or form, that the party represents disparate feelings of eastern German protest. In this sense, a vote for the PDS is seen as an articulation of disruptive, non-institutionalised feelings of disenchantment, brought on by conceptions of subjective or material dissatisfaction with one or more of the social, economic and political changes invoked in eastern Germany since the collapse of the GDR.[3] Such protest does not have to be based on material disadvantage, although, in certain circumstances, this may play a major role. Instead, a complex mixture of economic, political and socio-psychological dissatisfaction has been perceived as the basis of a vote for the PDS, and it has been argued that as the eastern *Länder* become further integrated into German society, and as, in particular, the economic environment in the new *Länder* improves, then the reasons for protest voting will subside.

Hence the claim made in the mid 1990s by Hans-Georg Betz and Ann L. Phillips that the PDS represented a 'reservoir for protest voters'[4] has some validity. In eastern Germany the PDS proved itself to be the principal vehicle through which dissatisfaction with socioeconomic and political change in the region was articulated. This form of protest voting is based on the *subjective, psychological* dissatisfaction of easterners with the social, economic and political realities of contemporary German life. However, this has not stopped a number of authors from stressing the *material* differences between eastern and western Germans, and they have tried to ground the PDS's political stabilisation in the successful articulation of material disadvantages that eastern Germans still experience. These two sub-approaches have differing levels of validity, as the analysis below reveals.

Material protest

In the 1990s material protest, based on the weaker economic position of the eastern states and the weaker financial position of easterners in general, was believed to be a key variable in explaining PDS support in eastern Germany. At the 1999 state election in Saxony, for example, voters for the PDS viewed both their own personal economic situation and the general economic environment in the eastern states as worse than supporters of the SPD or CDU did – sentiments that were consistently repeated through the 1990s across eastern Germany.[5]

Such feelings of material disadvantage are based on a number of assumptions. Many eastern Germans who had not been functionaries of the SED regime believed that after 1989 they were going to have the opportunity to take part in the economic success story that they (largely correctly) perceived West Germany to be. But as the economic and social difficulties of the transformation from a command economy to a capitalist economy unfolded, many easterners grew disillusioned with the inability of the eastern economy to 'catch up' with that of the West. Unemployment rose, job insecurity increased and the state no longer appeared able or willing to support the poor and weak in society. General disenchantment with the inequalities and contradictions of the social market economy increased rapidly. Easterners grew aware of their disadvantageous economic position vis-à-vis westerners and sought, it is argued, to express their dissatisfaction through the ballot box by supporting the non-establishment, left-wing PDS.[6]

Persuasive though this argument may appear at first glance, it does not correspond to the reality of the PDS's support base in the eastern states. The socio-economic profile of both the PDS's electorate and its membership are *not* characterised by particular economic hardship (see tables 2.1. and 2.2.). =n 1996, a mere 12 per cent of members of the PDS were either *Vorruheständler* (citizens who had taken early retirement) or unemployed (and so theoretically most likely to suffer material disadvantage).[7] At the 1994 election Jürgen W. Falter and Markus Klein described the areas of high unemployment in eastern Germany as the PDS *Wahltiefburgen* (electoral wastelands),[8] and the over-representation of civil servants and white-collar workers as disproving the theory that the PDS was singularly a party of the materially disadvantaged.[9]

Statistics referring to the 1998 election illustrate clearly the heterogeneous nature of the PDS electorate. The young and the old, men and women, the well educated and those with no or few qualifications all vote for the PDS in relatively large and consistent numbers.[10] It is especially noteworthy that voters from all age categories supported the PDS. This is in sharp contrast to the membership structure of the party, which is dominated by people over 60 years of age.[11] Such a heterogeneous support base has now ensured that the majority position within the scholarly literature on the PDS no longer attributes the party's success primarily to 'materially based protest'. Proponents of the protest hypothesis have moved to attribute the PDS's electoral success to a subjective, rather than objective, deprivation inside the 'new' Federal German Republic.

Sociopsychological protest

When discussing the importance of sociopsychological protest in explaining PDS success in eastern Germany, it is important to differentiate between the motives of the *membership* of the party and those of the PDS's *broader electoral base*. This is because these two groups support the party for very different reasons. Wilfred Barthel *et al.*, in their comprehensive survey of the values, opinions and motivations of the PDS membership, firmly concluded that 'unification losers have congregated in large masses in the PDS'.[12] Many PDS members worked for long periods of their life in the ultimately vain attempt to make the GDR a successful political, economic and social project. Members of the *Aufbaugeneration* genuinely believed that the GDR was the first attempt to create a just, socialist state on German soil. Its failure represented the failure of their hopes and ambitions. Slightly younger former SED functionaries who remain in the PDS are now deprived of the power and prestige that they were once accorded in the GDR. Although they remain materially better off than they were before 1989, their loss of status causes feelings of disenchantment with the FRG. They owed their career development to the GDR system, and with its abolition went the legitimisation for their chosen career path. Hence, both of these segments of the PDS membership can be termed socio-psychological protesters.

Viola Neu, talking of the PDS's base of support in the wider electorate, also asserts that 'the PDS electorate is largely made up of the "losers" from 1989'.[13] This observation is more questionable than the conclusions that Barthel *et al.* came to concerning the motives for the membership's support of the party. Tables 2.1 and 2.2 illustrate that the PDS's base in the *electorate* is much broader and heterogeneous than that of its membership.[14] This paradox is not lost on PDS party elites, who have to tread a careful line between the wants and desires of an ageing, conservative rank and file, and those of a much more heterogeneous electorate. Hence although an element of protest certainly encourages easterners to support the PDS, as it represents their feelings of dissatisfaction with the contemporary German economy, society and political system, the view that this is purely a diffuse form of protest misses the point that such sentiment is expressly territorial in nature.

Sociopsychological protest is something that has also been evident in the sectors of the electorate who had most *to gain* from unification. Easterners remain critical of the way that the GDR (and their lives and achievements within it) is handled in popular discourse. They also remain highly critical of politicians who make promises that they appear unable to keep. Broad-based feelings of second-class citizenship exist across all of the eastern states, as westerners continue to dominate politics and economics in the united Germany. 'Perceptions of collective inferiority', argue Beverly Crawford and Arendt Lijphart, 'have created a culture of victimisation and political helplessness'[15] in all the post-communist states of central and eastern Europe, enabling, they assert, the PDS and other successor parties to develop a role for themselves as agents within the party system that can incorporate the disparate feelings of discontent of (in this case) eastern Germans into one coherent voice. This dissatisfaction often has strongly anti-capitalist leanings, and the basis of the eastern German *Trotzidentität* is the demarcation that easterners make between themselves and westerners.

As a result, the dissatisfaction of many easterners with the effects of the transformation process, as well as continued uncertainty and mistrust of their new environment, has found expression in a vote for the PDS. The protest party approach illustrates many of the psychological beliefs of PDS supporters that supplement those of the bedrock of support that former GDR functionaries still provide. And it is indeed correct to presume that both ex-functionaries and the subjectively disadvantaged are 'protesting' – even if about different things: the former functionaries are protesting about their loss of pride and privilege; the subjectively disadvantaged, following the optimism of the unification years and the promises of 'flourishing landscapes'[16] and economic prosperity, about their failed hopes and ambitions. It is for this reason that the protest party approach contributes considerably to understanding how the PDS stabilised itself in eastern Germany throughout the mid 1990s.

Although many commentators still invoke the sociopsychological protest approach in explaining the electoral longevity of the PDS, it is not possible to view the PDS as a party of *pure* protest. As *Der Spiegel* observed in 1995, 'the widely stated clichés that stress that PDS voters are nostalgic SED beneficiaries, pure protest voters or opponents of German unity are only valid for a minority'[17] and, even though the PDS has, at times blatantly, attempted to play on these feelings in election campaigns,[18] the reasons for the party's continued survival are more complex than this approach alone can explain. Within its *electorate*, 'unification losers', in the form of those who have suffered losses of pride and privilege stemming from their lives in the GDR, clearly do not dominate.[19] Although the PDS fared disproportionately well amongst people with an advanced formal education (29 per cent of graduates in the eastern states in this category voted for the party in 1998), it also polled strongly in the less well-educated sectors of the electorate.[20] Pensioners remain slightly (19 per cent) *under-represented* in the PDS supporter profile, as do the self-employed (18 per cent – although this remains considerable higher than a left-wing, socialist party would normally expect), while workers (25 per cent), civil servants (25 per cent) and white collar workers (25 per cent) are all over-represented. In comparison to other parties (see table 2.2.) the PDS electorate remains heterogeneous and representative of eastern German society as a whole.[21]

Furthermore, feelings of dissatisfaction and discontentment with the political process are *not* confined to those who vote for the PDS (and/or the main right-wing parties in the eastern states, the NPD and the DVU): broad

Table 2.1. The results of the 1998 Federal Election per age category in eastern Germany (in per cent)

	CDU/CSU		SPD		Alliance 90/Greens		FDP		**PDS**		DVU/ NPD/REP	
	W	E	W	E	W	E	W	E	**W**	**E**	W	E
18–24	31	21	37	28	12	6	7	6	**2**	**22**	6	13
25–34	29	21	45	33	11	6	6	3	**2**	**22**	4	9
35–44	31	24	45	33	12	5	6	3	**1**	**22**	3	8
45–59	36	28	44	37	6	4	9	3	**1**	**23**	3	2
60+	47	34	39	38	3	2	7	3	**1**	**19**	2	2
Total	37	27.4	42.3	35.1	7.3	4.1	7	3.3	**1.2**	**21.6**	2.9	5

Source: Infratest Dimap, 1998.

Table 2.2. The results of the 1998 Federal Election according to education and occupation in Eastern Germany (in per cent)

	CDU/CSU		SPD		Alliance 90/Greens		FDP		**PDS**	
	W	E	W	E	W	E	W	E	**W**	**E**
Education:										
High	33	23	35	33	16	8	10	4	**2**	**29**
Middle	37	26	42	34	6	3	7	3	**1**	**20**
Low	39	34	48	38	3	2	4	3	**1**	**17**
Occupation:										
Worker	30	24	53	36	4	2	4	3	**1**	**19**
White- collar worker	31	25	46	35	10	6	7	3	**1**	**25**
Civil Servant	35	26	37	32	14	7	8	3	**1**	**25**
Self-employed	45	38	23	21	10	4	16	12	**2**	**18**
Out of work	23	19	49	37	11	4	6	2	**2**	**25**
Pensioner	46	34	41	39	2	2	7	3	**1**	**19**
In education	28	21	36	29	17	11	7	6	**4**	**22**

Source: Infratest Dimap, 1998, p. 57.

swathes of eastern German voters who choose to support the CDU and/or the SPD are also unhappy with the political and economic situation in eastern Germany.[22] Neugebauer and Stöss subsequently characterise a vote for the PDS as being something between a reaction to the ideological rhetoric of the GDR, and a mark of protest against the transformation from a socialist to a capitalist society.[23]

Yet, protest voters are generally viewed in political science as volatile swing voters and 'protest parties', by their nature, as transient phenomena that citizens only turn to in extraordinary conditions of political, economic or social dissatisfaction.[24] But in the case of the PDS one can see that evidence assembled since 1990 reveals voter alignment to be strong and sustained. In fact, the PDS has the most loyal supporters of any party in eastern Germany – a trait that would not normally be associated with protest parties.[25] Indeed, although the PDS played on its reputation as a protest party in the early and mid 1990s in particular, it is now clear that if easterners wish to protest electorally they tend to the parties of the far right – principally the German Peoples Union (DVU). The DVU even usurped one of the PDS's 1994 election slogans by claiming in the 1998 campaign that if easterners wanted to *Protest wählen* ('protest with your vote'), then they should vote for the DVU – precisely the role the PDS had claimed for itself in 1994. Hence, although the PDS profits from feelings of general dissatisfaction in the eastern states, characterising it as a 'protest party' is misguided.[26]

The PDS is, furthermore, regarded by many easterners as a largely normal party, rather than as a protest phenomenon and as a proponent of eastern German interests within regional and national political arenas. At the time of the 1998 Federal Election, for example, 67 per cent of easterners (but only 36 per cent of westerners) viewed the party as being 'democratic', while three-quarters did not object to the party being represented in the *Bundestag*.[27] It is, therefore, more accurate to consider the protest potential that the PDS mobilises in terms of an articulation of regional distinctiveness. Easterners object to the sidelining of their lives in the former GDR and the way that political, economic and cultural change has taken place *in their territory*. 'Protesters' view themselves as part of a clearly defined social and cultural grouping that exists within the eastern states, this is why an expressly territorial approach is valid when explaining the successes of the PDS.

The protest party approach does not, therefore, explain the successful mobilisation of votes by the PDS in eastern Germany *over a sustained period of time*. Protest tends to be short-term in nature, and, even at its most far-sighted, implies that when easterners become 'satisfied' with their economic and social positions within the FRG, the PDS will inevitably disappear from the party political landscape. In any case, there is little evidence to suggest that the eastern states are likely to catch up economically with the western states in the foreseeable future – and if at some point genuine equality *is* achieved, then the PDS may well have entrenched its position as an eastern German regional party sufficiently firmly to survive the healing of the gap in living standards between the eastern and western states.

The protest party approach also fails to illuminate the complex processes of identity creation that have taken place in eastern Germany. A successful analysis has to comprehend phenomena such as the support given to the PDS by many young people who never experienced life in the GDR (i.e. those in the 18–24 age group, see table 2.1.), the attractiveness of the party to people in all social strata within eastern Germany, and the fact that support has grown to be both loyal and well distributed – none of these characteristics of a party built on short-term protest, dissatisfaction and disillusionment.

The PDS as a modern, socialist reform party

A number of authors choose to view the PDS as a genuine socialist reform party, attempting to exert pressure on the SPD and the Greens from the political left. Many of the proponents of this approach appear to hold principles which the party itself espouses. The PDS is viewed as a renewed, democratic-socialist party that has grown out of the reforming wing of the SED. The emphasis shifts to the important long-term role that the PDS could or should play as the heir to the long-established Marxist-communist tradition in Germany. Commentators adopting this approach are often not afraid of calling for a structural realignment of the left, often involving the eventual dissolution of the PDS as it is today in favour of some other future constellation of left-wing political groupings. It is as a vigorous socialist party, possibly supplemented by an eco-liberal party, that the PDS would contribute to the 'ideological rearmament' of the German Left.[28] Fritz Vilmar encapsulates much of the analysis put forward by proponents of this approach when he notes:

> as an eastern German regional party … the PDS will stagnate in the respectable but futureless '20 per cent ghetto', ultimately remaining around the 5 per cent mark in all of Germany.

Vilmar contends that the rightwards shift of the SPD, as it distances itself from anti-capitalism and Keynesian economics, has generated sufficient space on the left of the political spectrum for a socialist/anti-capitalist all-German party to establish itself and as such 'the PDS has the chance to occupy the vacated position … (to the left of the SPD) … within the all-German political spectrum'.[29] Proponents of this approach, therefore, stress the need for a distinctive contribution from the PDS as a party to the left of the SPD and the Greens; only then could it exert substantial influence on the SPD, and, ultimately, on Germany as a whole.[30] Left-wing members of the PDS are also quick to warn against 'social-democratisation' of the party, fearing that if it were to move in this direction, it would not be being true to its socialist aims. While agreeing with these claims, the leadership of the PDS asserts that the SPD is moving so far to the right on issues such as the funding of the welfare state, social justice, peace and economic strategy that there is now a void to its left that the PDS has to fill. This means a broadening of the PDS's electoral base – and an acceptance of what many would contend were traditional socialist or social-democratic positions. This is certainly the position of a number of members on the right, who see a role for the PDS as a more broadly based left-wing party.[31]

Frank Unger has even called for the dissolution of both the PDS and the SPD in eastern Germany, in order to form a new political organisation that he proposes to call the Social Democratic Union (SDU). Those in the PDS who saw themselves as Communists would form a newer version of the KPD, while those on the right of the eastern SPD would (if they wished) form another centre party, or they would join the Alliance 90/Greens. The SDU would, he proposes, be a broad, eastern Germany *Volkspartei*, with its own *Fraktion* status within the Bundestag. This would enable socialism in Germany to be represented in a coherent and flexible manner. The SDU would enjoy a similar arrangement with the SPD to that the CDU currently does with the CSU.[32]

The leaders of the PDS have never gone as far as Unger proposes, and much prefer to cast the party as a democratic, reform-orientated, socialist party with an all-German future.[33] Further, the overwhelming majority of PDS members, as well as a considerable portion of its voters, remain committed to the ideal of a society beyond capitalism,[34] in a way that members of the SPD and the Greens do not. This having been said, the party programme of 1993 speaks rather circumspectly of socialism as an 'indispensable goal, a movement and a system of values' and a 'society in which the free development of the individual is the condition for the free development of all'.[35]

In practice the orientation of the PDS's programme remains vague and ill-defined, as an array of factions and undercurrents battle for the heart and soul of the party. Neugebauer and Stöss memorably characterised the struggles:

'revolutionaries stand in opposition to reformers, libertarians to dogmatists, fundamentalists to pragmatists and progressive forces against those with more conservative values';[36] the wide spread of ideological beliefs held ensures any characterisation of the party is consequently limited to that of a 'socialist' broad church of leftward opinion.[37]

Studies that analyse the PDS through the prism of socialist politics therefore highlight the ideological heterogeneity evident within the party. Proponents of this approach draw attention to the ideological distance between the reforming, pragmatic leadership and unreconstructed communists in the KPF and Marxist Forum. Their studies analyse what the PDS understands by the term 'socialism', what it has learnt from socialism in the GDR and what it must do if it is to create a coherent alternative to the capitalism it claims to despise.[38] This is especially important for the future of the PDS project as, despite the fact that the PDS has condemned Stalinism, it has yet to produce a coherent and systematic analysis of its own communist past. Only by accomplishing this can the party define and construct a definition of its current ideological identity.

It does, however, seem clear that an *expressly socialist party* must logically have only a limited function acting as a representative of regional interests. Proponents of this approach seem to avoid facing the reality of political competition in Germany today: the PDS is not a socialist party that happens to be particularly strong in one region of the country: rather, it is a regional party built on socialist principles. It has concentrated considerable efforts on expanding westwards, though with only marginal success.[39] The PDS-as-socialist-party approach is conspicuously unable to explain *why* the party has been so ineffective at spreading westwards. Proponents of this approach stress what the PDS *should* be; their analysis connects remarkably weakly with the reality of the PDS's present-day political position. A German socialist party would have to find much more resonance in western Germany than the PDS has managed to date before it could make this claim seriously. The regional appeal of the PDS certainly has socialist elements to it, but to get to the bottom of exactly what this appeal is, one must adopt an approach that takes into consideration the norms, values, culture and identity of eastern Germans.

The PDS has not been able to take on the mantle of the political left in western Germany because it has no roots there. In the western states the SPD effectively channels socialist sentiments into its political activities, whereas in the eastern states the PDS has been able to craft a role for itself as the unique representative of eastern German interests. In western Germany the PDS remains a party with few voters and even fewer members. This is best illustrated by a few simple facts: in 1994 the PDS had 975 *Basisorganisationen* (grass-roots groups) in Saxony Anhalt, 841 in Thuringia, 930 in Mecklenburg Western Pomerania, 1,619 in Saxony, 1,188 in Brandenburg and 953 in Berlin. In the west it had a combined total of 124 *Kreisverbände* and grass-roots groups across all ten states.[40] Judging by these statistics the PDS had almost as many organisational units in the Mecklenburg city of Rostock as it did in all of western Germany.[41]

The anti-System, extremist party approach

Through the early 1990s a considerable number of authors sought to analyse the PDS through the prism of a political-extremist approach, often comparing the PDS to parties such as the Republicans and the NPD. However, as time has passed, this approach has gradually lost its dominant position, even if a number of authors still continue to talk of the PDS as both extremist and anti-System. One of its most vocal proponents has been Patrick Moreau, who has produced a number of detailed studies on the position of the PDS within the constellation of German political parties.[42] He sees the PDS as a left-wing, anti-System, extremist party that both polarises and destabilises German party politics. Uwe Backes and Eckhard Jesse go further, claiming that the PDS's subversive influence poses a real challenge to the democratic actors within German politics today,[43] and the party has led to a *blockierte Demokratie* (blocked democracy) or to what has been called *polarisierter Pluralismus*[44] (polarised pluralism), in which the PDS threatens not only Germany's traditional coalition model of stable government, but also constitutional democracy as it has developed since 1945. The PDS is seen as having contributed to the 'polarisation' of the German party system by 'ideologising' political discourse and extending the political spectrum to include 'left-wing extremists'. The social and economic problems of transformation in eastern Germany have also fuelled debate on the rise of extreme right-wing sentiment, leading to the possibility of the CDU and SPD having to deal with parties on both their left and the right that reject the 'federal constitutional consensus'.[45]

The pragmatic left-wing nature of the PDS has led Jürgen Lang to refer to the PDS as an 'extremely opportunistic party' whose parliamentary orientation and commitment to representative democracy are purely functional.[46] Attempts to sideline elements like the KPF, the *AG Junge GenossInnen* (nominally the party's youth-wing) or the *Westlinken* (left-wing western Germans – whose discourse tends to be much more ideologically left-wing than that in the East) should, he says, be seen above all as tactical steps rather than as genuine evidence of democratisation within the party, as the PDS seeks tactical ways of achieving its anti-democratic aims.[47] Moreau, writing with Lang, concurs with this analysis:

> The political ideas of the PDS are tactical manoeuvres, whose aims stretch much further than their individual demands would have one believe ... [and] ... the PDS has developed an ideology that at first theoretically brings the existing system into question, in order, supported by pseudo-democratic mass acceptance with embellished, consciously diffuse aims, to eliminate it.[48]

Manfred Gerner agrees, claiming that the PDS merely pays lip-service (*Lippenbekenntnisse*) to democracy, and that the Marxist-Leninist tendencies of the party basis pose a clear and distinct extremist threat to the Federal Republic's democratic structure.[49] In particular, the factions on the left of the PDS cause commentators like Moreau, Lang and Gerner to further distinguish the party as 'extreme', as, in Moreau's words, the PDS has developed itself, particularly in western Germany, into an '*Anziehungspol*' (pole of attraction) for left-wing extremist elements[50].

Such authors argue that although the party has clearly developed and reorganised from its days as the SED, it has yet to genuinely reform. As Gerald Kleinfeld observes 'the result (is) a post-communist party, whose members largely continue to regard themselves as communists'.[51] Kleinfeld argues that the PDS has a classic communist party structure, and that these organisations are typical vehicles for orchestrating extra-parliamentary activity, as well as simultaneously undermining the social and political organs of society. He notes:

> Their goal is to exacerbate the conflict potential in society. The main point is not that the individuals who may be addressed by the groups represent a uniform party concept, but these individuals are contacted and mobilised for the PDS.[52]

The KPF (Communist Platform) is certainly the most well known of these groups, and in the mid 1990s its membership ranged somewhere between 1,000 (according to the PDS leadership)[53] and 4,500 (according to the KPF itself).[54] By 2001, Michael Chrappa and Dietmar Wittich claim, less than 1 per cent of the PDS membership was active in the KPF and Marxist Forum, while over 95 per cent had some contact with a PDS *Basisorganisation* – illustrating how few members directly associate themselves with these extremist elements.[55] Owing to the relatively small numbers involved, as was indicated in chapter one, it would not be particularly problematic to dispose of these extremist elements – the major obstacle to their expulsion remains the fact that the rank and file membership of the party would be fundamentally opposed to such a step.[56] In their work on the PDS, Moreau and Lang claim that 48 per cent of PDS supporters believe that communism will once again increase in salience, while 47 per cent of the PDS electorate hold up the idea of communism as a positive notion. They claim that 'PDS support still orientates itself towards the communist worldview and towards the hope of its realisation'.[57] Bortfeldt has also observed that 'a significant number of party members are in opposition to the (capitalist) system'[58] and, although they may not be members of the various extreme-left factions, the socialisation process within the GDR fosters considerable toleration of them within the party.

Orthodox members of the PDS's extreme left-wing groupings readily claim that the formation of the GDR was the first attempt on German soil to build a non-capitalist society. Sahra Wagenknecht and those around her on the Communist Platform even insist that the decline of socialism began with Nikita Khrushchev's condemnation of Stalin in 1956. Such statements are taken as being evidence of the shallow nature of the reform process undertaken within the party. If the groups around Wagenknecht superficially accept the pluralism within the PDS, and within German society as a whole, then, it is argued, this is for purely tactical reasons, and not out of the conviction that their is any genuine alternative to Marxism.[59] Proponents of this approach argue that the PDS has as its ultimate aim the gradual overcoming of constitutional democracy, followed by the imposition of a rather vague socialist order based on the ideals of Marx, Engels, Gramsci and Lenin.[60] Moreau has phrased it thus:

> The ideological foundation (of the PDS) is still built on classic traditions that also characterised both the SED regime and the international communist movement: Anti-capitalism, anti-imperialism, anti-Americanism and anti-liberalism unify in a political-economic project characterised by dirigist, statist and totalitarian tendencies.[61]

It is contended that the PDS should consequently be handled with caution. Yet it is noticeable that while the PDS is accused of ideological dogmatism, the parties of the centre-right have not been averse to using ideological weaponry in a clear attempt to de-legitimise the PDS in the eyes of the electorate.[62] The CDU/CSU frequently stresses what it beleives to be the extremist, unacceptable nature of the party. After the re-election, with the help of PDS votes, of the Social Democrat Reinhard Höppner as *Ministerpräsident* of Saxony-Anhalt in May 1998, CDU spokesman Otto Hauser claimed, for example, that 'it is roughly the same as if the National Socialists had, under another name, played a role in governing post-1945 Germany'.[63] Günter Beckstein, the Bavarian Home Affairs Spokesman, has observed that 'the PDS is an anti-constitutional party',[64] just as Theo Waigel has stated that the programme positions of the PDS illustrate that it is attempting to build a 'new' republic 'on political and economic structures inherited from the SED'.[65] In academic discussion, Eckhard Jesse has summarised the position of this school of thought in slightly less controversial, but no less unequivocal fashion by observing that:

> ... the PDS, through its origins in the SED, its programme, its ambivalent position on the use of force, its evasive approach to GDR history and its close links to anti-democratic action groups is, at its core, an extremist political party.[66]

This analysis is also supported by the Bavarian Office for the Protection of the Constitution, which continues to regard the PDS as an extremist party. According to their 1997 analysis of the party, the PDS ...

> ... belongs to the group of parties that can be defined as 'post-communist' or 'neo-communist'. These definitions are intended to show the PDS has not distanced itself from either communist ideology or practice. On the contrary, the PDS remains in its core traits very much the old party [the SED] ... [67]

The report further adds that:

> The PDS is a relic of the GDR and is politically responsible for the violent, and above all economic, problems in the eastern states ... the PDS remains 'neo-communist' as it has turned itself into a communist party along the lines of other western European communist parties, without reducing its communist, and therefore extremist, character.[68]

The reports of the Bavarian Office for the Protection of the Constitution illustrate that there remains a tendency to regard the PDS as an *Überbleibsel* (left-over) of the GDR. The fact that upwards of two million citizens vote for the party is not seen as sufficient reason for the questions that party asks, the criticisms it articulates, and the positions that it takes to be taken as seriously as those of other parties. Proponents of this approach prefer to dwell on the undoubted contradictions and problems that the party has in coming to terms with its own past and its left-wing ideological position, rather than what it says about (eastern) German politics and society *today*. The PDS itself, as one would expect, rejects notions that it is 'anti-System' or 'extremist' out of hand:

> To categorise the PDS as an extremist party is stupid, outrageous and completely ignores the development of the party. The party programme, it's statute and a range of party resolutions have established a clear break with Stalinism. The party has repeatedly declared that it respects the Basic Law ... and, furthermore, in the *Bundestag* the PDS has fought against attempts to undermine it.[69]

Helmut Holter, the PDS leader in Mecklenburg Western Pomerania, and a minister in the SPD–PDS coalition, has articulated this slightly differently, although in no less categorical fashion. Holter points out that the reform of any political system is not the same as seeking to overthrow it. As he observes:

> The PDS's support of the Basic Law and of the constitution of Mecklenburg Western Pomerania, and with it the acceptance of the legitimacy of the German state [*Staatswesen*] and of parliamentary democracy does not exclude discussion and constructive criticism of the deficits evident in contemporary democracy.[70]

Lothar Bisky is also adamant that the PDS is a 'part of the Federal Republic's society', although the party still clearly strives for a 'better society' and as such recognises and supports the idea that changes in Germany are only possible and desirable through the achievement of governmental majorities.[71] Despite the inability and/or unwillingness of the PDS's leadership to completely distance itself from its SED past, the PDS has moved irrevocably away from the structures that characterised the SED. As chapter one emphasised, inner-party democracy flourishes and the PDS remains the most '*Diskussionsfreudig*' (thriving in discussion) of all Germany's political parties. In this sense, the democratic changes and healthy debates that have come to characterise conferences since 1989 represent a distinct metamorphosis. The PDS *does* still need to continue re-defining its controversial past, but the numerous documents that the historical commission of the PDS produces illustrate that the party is making progress on this front. Claims by opponents that the PDS glorifies the GDR need clarification. The PDS is unwilling to dismiss the GDR as a footnote in history[72] and it is unwilling to accept that the attempt at building a socialist state was illegitimate.[73] Furthermore, the PDS (like many eastern Germans) is aggrieved at perceived attempts at 'sidelining' the lives and experiences of easterners before 1989[74].

The PDS is also prepared to admit that socialism in the GDR was fatally flawed. However, the PDS is adamant that the socialism that existed in central and eastern Europe was not fatally flawed *from the beginning*. In the view of the PDS, the collapse of socialism was necessary as it proved unable to react to the economic demands that competition with capitalism placed upon it. Furthermore, its deficiencies in terms of democracy and the inability of the leaders of the state-socialist countries to implement reforms necessary to counteract such deficiencies rendered it doomed to eventual failure.[75]

While it is clear that parts of the PDS membership are never likely to be able to come to terms with the failings of the SED and the GDR, the reforming leadership of the party has made considerable strides in this direction. The most notable example of this was an open letter by Gregor Gysi to the party in August 1996. In it he expressed his belief that most of the PDS membership were, in some form or other, party to 'real existing socialism', and were therefore a part of its failure. He stated that admitting this very fact was indeed painful, but there was no way of avoiding it. He claimed that the membership of the SED and the PDS had done too little to change the GDR for the better and that 'we' had defended undemocratic and anti-emancipatory practices for too long, even though these practices were not worth defending. Those people who still have not realised this, according to Gysi, clearly have not grasped the nature of the reform project on which the PDS is built.[76] The GDR's lack of democratic accountability, its dogmatic economic planning[77] and the huge contraventions of human and civil rights have all been condemned by the PDS.[78] The role of the SED in these crimes has also been admitted unambiguously.[79] While the PDS still has important questions to answer, it is clear, in light of its work on its programmes and practices, that it does not constitute a threat to the FRG's *democratic* consensus. The PDS is unambiguous, particularly in light of its experiences in the dictatorial GDR, on the need for societal change to be brought about through the democratic process. Anyone who wishes to oppose capitalism and the societal relationships that it fosters is welcome within the party, and although definitive statements of what the party hopes to achieve are lacking (particularly weak is its flimsy semi-definition of socialism), it has moved towards being a broad left-wing alternative to the SPD. It accepts the democratic 'rules of the game', and attempts to offer an alternative to the unjust capitalist system it perceives Germany to be caught in. Regardless as to the coherence of this alternative, the party has adapted to the system, and now adheres to the political rules like any other party.

Practical experience substantiates this. Following the PDS's much vaunted toleration of an SPD-Alliance 90/Greens coalition in Saxony Anhalt, as well its participation in a governing coalition in Mecklenburg Western Pomerania, it is clear that one must pay attention to the way the PDS has actually behaved in the real world of eastern German government. As Peter Bender commented in *Die Zeit*:

> The SPD and Greens have been tolerated by the PDS in Saxony Anhalt for four years – would this have been possible with a radical party? [Reinhard] Höppner's experience has been that when he has spoken with the CDU and the PDS, he could never rely on the support of the CDU, whereas he could with the PDS. The results were seen on election day [26 April 1998] – those people who wanted to vote 'radically' voted for the DVU.[80]

Proponents of the extremist approach have allowed their analysis to verge on ideological dogmatism, apparently having no wish to see the party as anything other than a disruptive political actor. Moreau, for instance, leaves little doubt as to what his opinion of the party is by calling his 1998 work a 'Profile of an Anti-Democratic Party': this goes against much of the evidence available on the internal dynamics of PDS political debate. The ideological opposition to socialism that such authors espouse means that they cannot bring themselves to accept that a socialist party can legitimately function within the FRG. They perceive the FRG, supported by the Basic Law, to be a state based on capitalist principles: something that the *Grundgesetz* is anything but clear about. Neu claims that a 'a change towards democratisation is not recognisable' and that the 'alleged change is of a tactical nature' – but even the most cursory glance at political activity within the PDS reveals that, if anything, the party suffers from too much ideological pluralism.[81] Criticism of the PDS as contributing to an ideological broadening of the political spectrum also appears hollow when viewed in the light of the party's clear acceptance of the Basic Law.

'Polarised pluralism' may make political life in the FRG more complicated for the CDU/CSU and SPD, but this is by no means a justification for ostracising the PDS. The party occupies a democratically legitimate political position in the German party spectrum and it garners votes on the basis of a democratic political platform – as such, Backes and Jesse's claims of 'blocked democracy' sound very like an exasperated recognition that the other parties are going to have to fight for votes with a fresh political opponent.

The overriding view amongst authors who adopt this approach is one of extreme scepticism and mistrust. They fall short of calling for the outright prohibition of the PDS, but they stress the importance of mobilising democratic forces against it. While legitimately pointing out the questionable commitment of the left-wing fringe to parliamentary procedures and to the social market economy, it is often apparent that too much attention is paid to factions like the KPF, the *AG Junge GenossInnen* or the Marxist Forum. The PDS may well still be under observation by the Bavarian Office for the Protection of the Constitution, but the party as a whole is not regarded as being extremist by the federal authorities. It seeks to change societal structures through policy initiatives, does not seek in any way to use violence and recognises and accepts both democracy in general and the democratic structures of the FRG in particular.[82] Proponents of this approach overlook the integrative role that the PDS plays in ensuring that left-wing ideologues are not cut off from the political system. The PDS therefore enables those eastern Germans who are never likely to come to terms with life in a capitalist society to find a place to vent their dissatisfactions. Its record at the micro-level of eastern German politics reveals that it is perfectly capable of competent political activity. Not only has the PDS been an efficient oppositional force, it has also indicated that it can be a constructive and dependable force *within* governmental structures. The unsavoury elements within the PDS are active contributors to the pluralist structure of PDS internal party democracy – but in no way do they dictate policy or PDS activity at the federal, regional or communal level. At the micro-political level, politics in the eastern states continues to function through personal interaction, and talk of PDS representatives wanting to overthrow the capitalist system fundamentally misunderstands both the nature of communal politics and the undeniable contribution that PDS politicians make at this level. One suspects that even if the party survives another twenty years, some of the proponents of this approach will continue to brand the candidates and constituents of the party as leftover SED stalwarts.[83] Furthermore, much to the chagrin of right-wing critics, there is nothing in the Federal Republic's constitution that expressly forbids the creation of a socialist economy. Therefore, it is distinctly dubious to claim that the anti-capitalism of the PDS is, in itself, anti-constitutional. Although the Unification Treaty of 1990 makes a specific point of emphasising that the economy of the FRG is a 'social-market' one, this is clearly meant to be an expression of the economic system as it was at the time. There is no clear and unambiguous passage that dictates that this has to remain so in the future.[84]

Hence, this approach paradoxically illustrates what the PDS is not: an extremist and anti-constitutional party. Rather, the party integrates disruptive left-wing elements into the political process, yet remains able to act within the constitutional limitations of the German political order. Viewing the PDS as the vehicle for left-wing extremist sentiment fundamentally misses the point that the PDS's *every-day political activities* are not in any way extremist. And this is manifestly obvious to the majority of electors in *both* the eastern and western states, who have long ceased to regard the PDS as an extremist political organisation.

The milieu party approach

Another popular approach taken when analysing the PDS has been to see it as the representative of a distinct milieu within eastern German society.[85] Jens Bastian has contended that the PDS is 'above all else a party of the milieu',[86] that remains specific to both its unique social environment and its culture. Richard Schröder elaborates further, describing the PDS as a 'milieu party with elements of a self-help group, kept together by a common feeling of protest',[87] while Hans-Georg Betz and Helga A Welsh stress the 'importance of the PDS as the main political representative of a specific socioeconomic and cultural milieu'.[88] After the 1999 elections Eckhard Jesse also observed that 'the PDS is principally a milieu party and its protest function is of secondary importance'.[89] Viewing the party as a representative of a distinct sociocultural milieu helps to illustrate that the party unites different groups, characterised by high levels of education, secularisation and urbanisation, and sharing similar cultural and political orientations.[90] These groups may be diverse, but they are united in their experience of having to come to terms with life in the FRG. Neugebauer has summarised the social milieu as one that is:

> ... defined by the comparable worlds in which the majority of its members live. They live largely in cities or towns, they are (or were) frequently white-collar workers, are (in comparison to members of other parties) in possession of higher levels of for-

mal education, are not religiously committed and belonged to the carrier-groups [*Trägergruppen*] of the SED at the different levels of party, state and societal system. This ensures that they largely represent the founders and the inheritors of the GDR system ... [91]

Throughout the 1990s the PDS was perceived as being unable to move away from the sociostructural base of the former *Dienstklasse* (ruling class)[92] of the GDR, with its roots firmly embedded in the SED, and in particular the *Aufbaugeneration*.[93] The milieu is seen as being relatively closed, as well as occupationally and geographically defined. These functionaries, in spite of their relatively rapid adaptation to life in the 'new' Germany, still feel (through joint experience) bonded together through loss of the pride and prestige that they had attained before 1989.[94] Heinrich Bortfeldt has emphasised how this logically meant that the PDS was initially viewed very much as an '*Auslaufmodell*', essentially a final resting place for those disaffected as a result of the abolition of the GDR and a temporary political home for the politically unsatisfied.[95] Bortfeldt argues that apart from the obvious 'external' factors, such as the general lack of acceptance of the party within the federal political system and the *Ausgrenzung* (exclusion) that accompanied this, 'internal' factors like a radically shrinking membership, the ageing of the party faithful and the lack of clear orientation would dictate that the milieu within which the party existed would soon shrink to the extent that the PDS would cease to be a relevant factor in national politics.[96] As with the protest party thesis, there is, therefore, an implicitly short-term nature to this approach. It is argued that those who feel particularly attached to the GDR will, by definition, become fewer and fewer over time and, as its supporter base shrinks, the PDS will die away. This conclusion was epitomised by Gordon Smith in 1992 when he observed that:

> Its federal-wide vote (2.4 per cent in 1990) as opposed to its share in East Germany alone (11.1 per cent) means that the PDS either must make significant advances in West Germany or somehow recover a following in East Germany. Neither eventuality is realistic.[97]

Until the PDS successfully returned to the Bundestag and performed above expectations in the *Land* elections of 1994, German political scientists held similar opinions. In the run-up to the 1994 federal election, for example, Manfred Gerner observed that 'it is doubtful that the PDS will find the method or the means to re-enter the *Bundestag*',[98] while two years earlier, in

1992, Heinrich Bortfeldt was even more conclusive:

> The PDS will not re-enter the *Bundestag* at the 1994 Federal Election. It has a national *Wählerpotential* (potential electorate) of around 1–2 per cent and is thus well on the way towards political *Bedeutungslosigkeit* [nothingness].[99]

This judgement has proven misguided. Analysts have slowly begun to discuss the methods, strategies and beliefs that underpin the party's apparent stabilisation within the German political system.[100] Contrary to initial projections, the contemporary milieu from which the PDS garners support has broadened and, to an extent, metamorphosed to include many who were never in the *Dienstklasse* of the GDR. This is something that proponents of the milieu party approach did not envisage and cannot adequately explain.

The skilful re-invention of the PDS as a party that represents eastern German interests stems from the changed nature of its appeal: as such the party has developed from being a 'milieu' party into a 'regional' party. A considerable proportion of the eastern German population have redefined their interests within the context of being members of an eastern German community. Patterns of electoral support in the eastern states since 1998 illustrate that the 'milieu' party is now an out-dated concept – the PDS is supported by a broad-base of eastern Germans. It has embedded itself in the social and political structures of all the eastern German *Länder* and is perceived by the electorate at large as an advocate of broad regional interests. The PDS has established itself as a result of a representation gap that eastern Germans widely perceive as resulting from the economic, cultural and institutional effects of the unification process.[101] This is something that the milieu approach tends to overlook, even if, implicitly, it points in this direction. The milieu is traditionally defined too narrowly, and it is limited to former servants of the state and the subjectively disaffected. Laurence H. McFalls is nearer the reality of the situation when he notes that the PDS:

> … represents a social process, namely the integration into the social order of the enlarged Federal Republic of Easterners who wish none the less to have the validity of their past recognised[102].

The original milieu (of those close to the aims and power structures of the GDR) within which the PDS existed in the early years is still in evidence, and is still very supportive of the PDS in terms of actively advocating the party's aims. The 'milieu' approach has, however, outlived its usefulness – the PDS's electoral base is now based on territorial affinity with eastern Germany. Eastern Germany may, at the societal level, still be in a process of transformation, as citizens continue to 'find their place' in the FRG, but at the economic and political levels eastern Germany is a space that will remain fundamentally different from the western region of Germany. The longer the perceptions of difference endure, the more likely it is that the societal cleavage will be sustained between eastern and western Germany, offering the possibility that the PDS will be able to anchor itself ever more firmly into the eastern German psyche and political system.

Eastern German Volkspartei?

In spite of the tendency to view the PDS as a transitory phenomenon, there has none the less been talk by some commentators, as well as in the popular press, of the PDS being an eastern German *Volkspartei* (people's party).[103] The concept of the *Volkspartei* was initially developed as an ideal type in the 1960s by Otto Kirchheimer.[104] A *Volkspartei* aims to maximise electoral potential over and above facilitating processes of social integration and articulating direct interests. In order to do this the ideological platforms of *Volksparteien* are held to be broader than other kinds of party as they attempt to transcend traditional economic, religious and other social divides in order to widen their electoral appeal and stress national interests.

The hypothesis that the PDS is an eastern German *Volkspartei* has been put forward periodically since the mid 1990s. Wayne C. Thompson argues that the PDS is indeed an eastern German *Volkspartei* 'in the sense that it integrates diverse groups of voters' to its cause,[105] and this proposition gained further credence following the 2001 Berlin election, when the PDS registered 47.6 per cent of the vote in the eastern parts of the city. The PDS's strong electoral performances in 1994, 1998, 1999 and 2001 were 'largely due to the party's ability to present itself as the only authentic advocate of East German interests' and 'to provide East Germans with a sense of identity'[106] – and it is this key political role that has enabled the PDS to stabilise itself in the legislatures of the eastern German state parliaments as well as the *Bundestag*. Through the 1990s the PDS illustrated that it remains a cross-class party, mobilising support from all sectors of eastern German society.

The political activities of the SPD and the CDU have inadvertently reinforced the PDS in its attempt to broaden its electoral base in the eastern states. The CDU, following the broken promises of the pre- and post-unification period, gradually lost much of its political credibility in the East, and by 1998 was viewed with scepticism and mistrust by large sections of the eastern German electorate. The SPD, after its initial failure to create an electoral base in eastern Germany in the early 1990s, took a number of years to gain political credibility, and even following the Federal Election victory of September 1998 the party soon plunged into electoral crisis in the East as a result of a number of heavy *Landtagswahl* defeats through the course of 1999. The inability of the 'national' parties to incorporate uniquely regional sentiments, beliefs and attitudes into their party platforms can provide broad-based regional parties with the opportunity to cement themselves into the political process as the articulators of regional difference (in whatever form this may take). The PDS has chiselled out a role for itself in eastern Germany doing precisely this – representing eastern Germans in regional and national political life.

The letter from Saxony

Claims that the PDS in an eastern German *Volkspartei* did, on one occasion, lead to calls from within the party for the PDS to concentrate on acting primarily as a representative of eastern interests within the national structure of a left-of-centre alliance. As a result of the consistent bedrock of eastern German support, Christine Ostrowski, a PDS member of the Bundestag from Saxony,[107] and Ronald Weckesser (the leader of the PDS on Dresden city council) presented, in a document that has become known as 'The Letter from Saxony', a strong argument for abandoning the party's strategy of attempting to grow into a 'national' rather than a 'regional' party, and for completely reassessing the PDS's raison d'être.

They claimed that what the PDS understands by the term socialism 'has to be defined by the experiences and beliefs of its millions of voters in the former GDR'.[108] They have called bluntly for the PDS to be an eastern German people's party, as all attempts to broaden the party's electoral base into western Germany have clearly failed 'as there is no place in the political landscape for a western version of the PDS … as the fact that the PDS results in the west lie below even the DKP's clearly illustrates'.[109] Ostrowski and Weckesser see the strength of the PDS in its representative function in the eastern states, and subsequently stress the PDS's successful representation of eastern German interests. They state that the CSU could be used as a strategic model for the PDS to seek to emulate, because, they maintain, as a leftist, regional party the PDS may be able to exert considerably more influence on the national (one presumes SPD-led) government.[110]

Despite the broad and often biting criticism that these comments drew from within the party,[111] it is clear that Ostrowski and Weckesser are offering a coherent approach that should be much more seriously examined.[112] Their calls for a re-evaluation of the political left in eastern Germany may be unpalatable for the PDS while they survive as a result of other influences, but the continued failure of the PDS's *Westausdehnung* indicates that sooner or later the party is going to have to admit that in the western states it remains a fish out of water. The PDS is successful in the East because of what it is – a regional advocate specific to the territory. Parties to the left of the SPD have never been able to build a firm footing in western Germany, and Ostrowski and Weckesser recognise the long-term reality – that the PDS is unlikely to buck this trend.

None the less, the sound base of PDS support that exists in eastern Germany cannot be regarded as solid enough to register the 20-plus per cent of the vote that is necessary to achieve consistent *Bundestag* representation, let alone true *Volkspartei* status. If the 5 per cent hurdle is to be transcended, then the PDS needs to increase its share of the vote in the eastern states to above 30 per cent. This explains the continued efforts of the reformist leadership to appeal to both younger voters (in contrast to the ageing membership), the middle classes (and particularly small businessmen) and to expand into the western part of the country. At the moment, and for the foreseeable future, the PDS needs to pursue every vote it can in order to clear the 5 per cent barrier. But long term, as election results in western Germany have repeatedly illustrated, the prospects of the PDS achieving anything more than minimal support outside its eastern base appear slim – if only because the vast majority of westerners still perceive it as an expressly eastern German political party.

The regional party approach

The discussion in this chapter has illustrated that scholars adopt a number of different approaches when attempting to pin down why the PDS has been successful in (eastern) Germany. Elements of all four approaches throw light on the reasons behind the party's success, but none has the capacity to see the PDS as anything other than a short- to medium-term phenomenon. All of the approaches underemphasise or neglect the importance of territory in explaining why the PDS has been so successful in eastern Germany, although this factor is clearly implicit in the protest and milieu approaches. These approaches do not, however, allow for the existence of a clear set of eastern German values, preferences and attitudes, as well as the existence of a party that has grown to give voice to them. Discussion of the PDS as an eastern *Volkspartei* highlights that, regardless of whether the PDS has actually achieved true *Volkspartei* status or not, the nature of PDS support is broad, heterogeneous and almost exclusively *regional* in nature. Hence this work introduces a new, original approach, enabling an analysis of the *regional* nature of the PDS's success to be undertaken without neglecting the valuable points that other authors have made.

During the 1990s it became clear that broader sections of the eastern German electorate were voting for the PDS in addition to those who were clearly protesting or who stemmed from the ideological 'milieu' that would traditionally support the party. Furthermore, in the 1998 Federal Election the PDS's support clearly began to level out across eastern Germany, and it could no longer plausibly be represented as a party that relied principally on the GDR stalwarts who predominate within the party membership (see tables 2.1. and 2.2.). The PDS lost, by a considerable margin, more of its support in the five eastern Berlin constituencies – the traditional *Hochburgen* (strongholds) of the PDS – than it did anywhere else.[113] Despite retaining the four seats (*Direktmandate*) that the it had won in 1994, the PDS still lost 5.7 per cent (of second votes) in Mitte-Prenzlauer Berg, 5.1 per cent in Hellersdorf-Marzahn, 5 per cent in Friedrichshain-Lichtenberg and 4.2 per cent in Hohenschönhausen-Pankow. In the fifth eastern Berlin seat, which Siegfried Scheffler won for the SPD, the PDS also lost 3.4 per cent.[114] Indeed, only in Köpenick-Treptow, with the high-profile candidature of Lothar Bisky, did the PDS manage to increase its proportion of *Erststimmen* (by 1.7 per cent).[115] Sigrid Koch-Baumgarten has subsequently observed that:

> the PDS is an expression of the 'east–west' conflict as a conflict of values, it is not the point of attraction for those critical of capitalism, but rather those critical of western culture and modernisation.[116]

The support base of the PDS is subsequently characterised more by its position towards the West than any zest for reform or overt anti-capitalism, although these two factors are unquestionably evident in its platform. This is a common trait amongst regional parties, as they articulate the sentiments of an 'in' group to act politically against the 'out' group. The PDS flourishes in an 'eastern German' community that needs political representation at the local, regional and national level. Only by invoking a regional approach can one adequately grasp the reasons why the PDS can voice regionally important issues in the all-German political process.

In order to compare the PDS with other regional parties, this work will introduce an analytical framework suitable for analysing regional party success – a typology of political regionalism and regional parties. This framework will enable the PDS to be seen, for the first time, in a cross-national context; it will help in the analysis of the cross-cutting cleavage between eastern and western Germany, as well as helping to interpret the methods and means used by the PDS to expound territorial difference. The strength and organisation of the 'western' parties has not prevented a regionally concentrated party from taking root, and making political capital from the economic, social, cultural and political deficits that eastern Germans have experienced since 1989. The typology will illustrate that by comparing other regional parties, and the methods and approaches that they employ, one can gain a much greater understanding of exactly how the PDS has mobilised regional political support so effectively in eastern Germany. The following chapter sets out to explain this framework in more detail.

Notes

1 The most detailed and sophisticated German-language study of the PDS's development remains Neugebauer and Stöss, 1996. For further analysis see in particular Barthel *et al.*, 1995; Segall *et al.*, 1999; and Sturm, 2000.
2 Probst, 2000.
3 Neugebauer, 1994, pp. 431–44.
4 Betz and Welsh, 1995, p. 98.
5 See Forschungsgruppe Wahlen, 1999c, p. 55. See the numerous election reports published by Forschungsgruppe Wahlen and Infratest Dimap for further evidence of this.
6 See for example, Schultze, 1995, p. 344.
7 Neugebauer and Stöss, 1996, p. 151. It is also misleading to contend that a majority of eastern Germans view themselves as unification losers: in 1998, 67 per cent of Easterners regarded themselves as being the exact opposite – the *winners* from the unification process. Infratest Dimap, 1998, p. 53.
8 Falter and Klein, 1994, p. 24.
9 Klein and Caballero, 1996, pp. 229–47.
10 Even in Berlin, where the PDS's considerable electoral successes are generally attributed to the high proportion of former SED *nomenklatura* resident in the eastern districts of the city, it is clear that the PDS's base of support is heterogeneous. For example, 18 per cent of 18–24 year olds in eastern Berlin voted for the PDS in the 1999 state elections, just as did 18 per cent of those aged 45–59. Nineteen per cent of PDS supporters were in full-time employment, while only 16 per cent were pensioners and 17 per cent were still in some form of education. See Forschungsgruppe Wahlen, 1999, pp. 28, 35.
11 See Gabriel and Niedermayer, 1997, p. 294. Sixty-seven per cent of the PDS membership

were, in 1999, over 60 years of age (see Segall *et al.*, 1999, p. 122), while 77 per cent of PDS members in the East were, in 2001, pensioners (Michale Chrappa and Dietmar Wittich, quoted in Tom Strohschneider: 'Befragung zum Thema: Der PDSler, das unbekannte Wesen?', in *Neues Deutschland*, 21 May 2001, p. 2.

12 Barthel *et al.*, 1995, p. 9.

13 Neu, 1994.

14 For a particularly lucid account of the political beliefs of the PDS membership see Probst, 1998b; or Probst, 2000.

15 Crawford and Lijphart, 1995, p. 180.

16 Helmut Kohl used the phrase 'blühende Landschaften' in an interview on *Tagesthemen* during the EU summit in Dublin on the 28 April 1990. His exact words were: 'when all the successful principles of the social-market economy become reality in the former GDR, then, in three or four years, we will have a flourishing landscape and we will all benefit from it'. See Haeger, 1998, p. 1.

17 *Der Spiegel*, 6 November 1995, p. 42.

18 During the 1994 Bundestag election campaign, for example, the PDS openly campaigned on the slogan 'Election Day is Protest Day'. See Thompson, 1996, p. 439.

19 Mushaben, 1997, p. 94.

20 More precisely (and only in eastern Germany), 16.6 per cent of Easterners without any qualifications voted for the PDS, while 19.9 per cent of those with *Mittlere Reife/Realschule* qualifications, 26.5 per cent of those with A Levels (*Abitur*) and 28.7 per cent with university degrees did so. See Infratest Dimap, 1998, p. 5.

21 Of particular note are the comparisons in the CDU electorate between the number of self-employed who support the party (38 per cent in eastern Germany) and the number of unemployed (19 per cent in eastern Germany). The number of those still in education (21 per cent in the eastern states) who voted for the CDU is also (from the point of view of the CDU) worryingly low. Despite its convincing victory in 1998, the SPD also displays considerable differences in sectoral support. This is shown in that only 21 per cent of civil servants supported the SPD in eastern Germany, while 39 per cent of pensioners gave their vote to the Social Democrats. Infratest Dimap, 1998, p. 57.

22 See Howard, 1995a, pp. 119–31.

23 Neugebauer and Stöss, 1996, p. 162.

24 The success of the right-wing DVU in the Saxony-Anhalt state election of 26 April 1998, when the party polled 12.9 per cent of the vote, despite having almost no party basis in the *Land*, would be a more typical example of a protest party attracting the votes of the socially dissatisfied, electorally volatile sections of the electorate. In the 1998 federal election, just 5 months after the DVU's triumph in Saxony Anhalt, the party did not manage to jump the 5 per cent hurdle in any state, and in the 1999 elections in the eastern states (in Brandenburg, Saxony, Thuringia and Berlin), the DVU was only able to poll enough votes to enable it to enter one eastern parliament (Brandenburg).

25 Falter and Klein, 1994, p. 24. Betz and Welsh, 1995, p. 92.

26 Sturm, 2000, p. 315.

27 Veen *et al.*, 1998, p. 43.

28 Minnerup, 1998, p. 214.

29 Fritz Vilmar in *Neues Deutschland*, 16/17 January 1999, p. 1.

30 The publication of the *Erfurter Erklärung* (Erfurt Declaration) is the only document that openly supports the creation of such a left-of-centre alliance. The declaration itself lament-

ed the state of German politics, and, even though it was critical of much of the opposition parties' policies and strategies, called for a change in the Kohl (as it was then) government. For further analysis see Hubble, 1998.

31 An example of an extension of the PDS's profile rightwards came in 1999 when Uwe Kitsch, a former SPD MdB in Bavaria, publicly renounced his SPD membership and joined the PDS.

32 See Unger, 1995, pp. 81–8.

33 Following the elections to the European Parliament in 1999, Dietmar Bartsch felt confident enough to proclaim that the PDS was a *sozialistische Volkspartei* (socialist people's party) in the eastern states. This gives recognition both to the PDS's strength in all sectors of the eastern German electorate and its ideological underpinnings as party that is in opposition to the capitalist structures of German society. See 'Wahlen entscheidend für die Zukunft der PDS', in *Schweriner Volkszeitung*, 15 July 1998, p. 1.

34 Lothar Bisky, the long-time *Vorsitzender* of the PDS, has defined the PDS as an 'out and out anti-capitalist party', stressing its willingness to change fundamentally the economic structures of German society. See 'Bisky kandidiert nicht noch einmal für den PDS-Vorsitz: Auf der Suche nach einer Alternative zum "angelsächsischen Kapitalismus"', in *Frankfurter Allgemeine Zeitung*, 8 April 2000, p. 2.

35 PDS, 1993, p. 11.

36 Neugebauer and Stöss, 1996, p. 114.

37 The PDS openly describes itself as an 'alliance of left-wing forces', stressing that its commitment to democratic socialism is not 'tied to any defined philosophical outlook, ideology or religion'. See PDS, 1993, p. 31.

38 See for example Benjamin (1996b). The 'mainstream' elements of the PDS remain highly critical of the state socialism that existed across central and eastern Europe before 1989. This can be seen by the large amount of literature available on PDS websites on *Geschichtsaufarbeitung* (http://www.pds-online.de/geschichte) and in more formal documents such as the Party Programme. In the 1993 Party Programme, for example, the PDS observes that 'many questions concerning our own history remain unanswered … (and) … the mistakes, shortcomings and crimes committed in the name of socialism have dismayed us and roused us to deep reassessments, so that we are critically examining our moral and political tradition in full consciousness of our own responsibility for the distortion of the socialist idea'. PDS, 1993, pp. 3–4.

39 In the second ballot in the 1998 Federal Election, the PDS received its highest share of the vote in the western *Länder* in Berlin/Kreuzberg/Schöneberg (4.4 per cent). It also registered between 3.5 per cent and 3 per cent in Bremen West, Hamburg Mitte, Berlin Neukölln and Berlin Tiergarten. See Infratest Dimap, 1998, p. 83.

40 Lang, Moreau and Neu, 1995, p. 37.

41 See Probst, 2000.

42 Moreau, 1992; 1996, pp. 54–61; 1998.

43 Backes and Jesse, 1993, p. 41.

44 Koch-Baumgarten, 1997, p. 873. See also Sartori, 1976.

45 Neu, 1999, p. 5.

46 Lang, 1995, p. 380.

47 Neu, 1997, pp. 20–24.

48 Moreau and Lang, 1996, p. 60.

49 Gerner, 1994, p. 242.

50 Moreau, 1998, p. 277.

51 Kleinfeld, 1995, p. 225.

52 Kleinfeld, 1995, p. 226.

53 'Sahra Wagenknecht, Chefin der kommunistischen Plattform: Von Goethe zu Hegel, von Hegel zu Marx, von Marx zu Lenin', in *Süddeutsche Zeitung*, 14 October 1994.

54 Lang, 1995, pp. 375–6.

55 Quoted in Tom Strohschneider: 'Befragung zum Thema: Der PDSler, das unbekannte Wesen?', in *Neues Deutschland*, 21 May 2001, p. 2.

56 Lang , 1995, pp. 369–80.

57 Moreau and Lang, 1996, p. 56.

58 Bortfeldt, 1994b, p. 1283. See also Spittman, 1994, p. 673.

59 Gerner, 1996, pp. 227–39.

60 Kleinfeld, 1995, pp. 226–30.

61 Moreau, 1998b, p. 286.

62 The most obvious (but by no means only) examples of this are the 1994 'red-sock' and 1998 'red-hands' campaigns by the CDU/CSU, openly playing on the controversial issue of past relations between social democrats and communists. Neither campaign had any *direct relevance* to contemporary political debate. The 1994 campaign was largely perceived to have been successful, although the 1998 campaign was noticeably dropped in the weeks preceding the federal election. This is as the eastern German electorate appeared to be tired of CDU/CSU references to such events, and their attempts to picture the PDS as a modern day extremist party.

63 Otto Hauser (CDU): 'PDS stimmt für Höppner – heftige Kritik aus Bonn', in *Leipziger Volkszeitung*, 27 May 1998, p. 1.

64 Günther Beckstein (CSU): 'Union fordert verstärkte Überwachung der PDS', in *Süddeutsche Zeitung*, 22 April 2000, p. 5.

65 Theo Waigel (CSU): 'Die geistigen Grundlagen der Christlich-Sozialen Union', in Hanns-Seidel Stiftung, 1995, p. 63.

66 Jesse, 1997, p. 99. See also Backes and Jesse (eds.), 1993, pp. 193–214. As far as this author is aware, nowhere is the PDS 'ambiguous' on the use of force. This applies in both the domestic and international arenas. At the international level the PDS is particularly 'unambiguous': as high-profile disagreements at party conferences illustrate, the PDS seeks a radical demilitarisation of international affairs. Debates on the Kosovo War in 1999 and the use of UN troops in international conflict at the Münster *Parteitag* (Conference) of April 2000 particularly illustrate this. See *PDS Disput/Pressedienst*, Nummer 4 (Disput) and Nummer 15/16 (Pressedienst), 2000.

67 Bayersiches Staatsministerium des Innern, 1997, p. 5.

68 Bayersiches Staatsministerium des Innern, 1997, p. 5.

69 Dietmar Bartsch: 'Wer macht eine extreme Politik?', in PDS *Pressedienst*, Number 20, 14 May 1998. See also http://www.pds-online/pressedienst/9820/24800.html

70 Holter, 1999, p. 2.

71 See 'Bisky kandidiert nicht noch einmal für den PDS-Vorsitz: Auf der Suche nach einer Alternative zum "angelsächsischen Kapitalismus"', in *Frankfurter Allgemeine Zeitung*, 8 April 2000, p. 2.

72 See Lothar Bisky's thoughtful speech held at the *Tränenpalast* in Berlin on the 7 October 1999. Lothar Bisky: '50 Jahre DDR – "Vorwärts und nicht vergessen?"' on http://www.pds-online.de/geschichte/9910/ddr50.htm

73 See line three of 'Das Programm der PDS: 2. Das Scheitern des sozialistischen Versuchs', on http://www.pds-online.de/dokumente/programm/punkt02.htm

74 See paragraph two of 'Das Programm der PDS: 2. Das Scheitern des sozialistischen Versuchs', on http://www.pds-online.de/dokumente/programm/punkt02.htm

75 See http://www.pds-online.de/dokumente/programm/punkt02.htm For a broader analysis of the PDS's interpretation of life in the GDR, the reasons for its failure and the SED's role in this see http://www.pds-online.de/geschichte.

76 See Gregor Gysi: 'Zur gegenwärtigen Diskussion in unserer Partei', *PDS Pressedienst*, Nummer 34, 1996, pp. 9-12.

77 See paragraph 5 on http://www.pds-online.de/dokumente/programm/punkt02.htm Furthermore, the PDS has also stated that the market is a necessary component of contemporary society. In one document, for example, it has claimed that 'we have to accept the market, but we don't want "*Markt pur*" (purely the market)'. See http://www.pds-online.de/geschichte/9808/weizsaecker-brief.htm

78 The PDS has explicitly stated this on a number of occasions, of which one of the most prominent came in a letter to ex-President of the FRG, Richard von Weizsäcker, in August 1998. See paragraph three on http://www.pds-online.de/geschichte/9808/weizsaecker-brief.htm

The process of *Geschichtsaufarbeitung* does, however, remain an uneven one within the PDS, hence differing groupings and platforms within the party often have different (and on occasion diametrically opposed) opinions on the same events. No issue highlights this more than the building of the Berlin Wall in August 1961. Unequivocal condemnations of the event can be found in statements made by a number of younger PDS members (including Halina Wawzyniak, then a member of the PDS Executive) in 'Geschichtsaufklärung versachlichen! Erklärung junger PDS-Mitglieder zum Politbüro-Prozess', in *PDS Pressedienst*, Nummer 36, 1997, p. 11, as well as in statements made by Petra Pau, leader of the PDS in Berlin and since 1998 MdB, and Carola Freundel, leader of the PDS in the Berlin city parliament in *PDS Pressedienst*, Volume 33, 1997, p. 43. A much less unequivocal analysis of the event can be found by referring to Hans Modrow: 'Zum Jahrestag des 13. August 1961. Persönliche Erklärung von Hans Modrow', in *PDS Pressedienst*, Nummer 35, 1997, p. 11.

79 'The traditional separation of powers was not adhered to and a democratic electoral system was not implemented … the right to criticise and to complain existed judicially, but in practice it was hardly ever realised.' See paragraph five on http://www.pds-online.de/dokumente/programm/punkt02.htm

80 Peter Bender: in *Die Zeit*, 14 May 1998.

81 Neu, 1999, p. 7.

82 Möller, 1998, p. 198.

83 Mushaben, 1997, p. 96.

84 Alber, Nübel and Schöllkopf, 1998, p. 622.

85 Bastian, 1995, and Betz and Welsh, 1995, pp. 92–111.

86 Bastian, 1995, p. 107.

87 Richard Schröder: *Frankfurter Allgemeine Zeitung*, see Kleinfeld, 1995, p. 242.

88 Betz and Welsh, 1995, p. 92.

89 Jesse, 2000, p. 76.

90 Hradil, 1995, p. 7. See also Vester, 1995, pp. 10–11.

91 Neugebauer, 1995, p. 51.

92 See Solga, 1995.

93 Koch-Baumgarten, 1997, p. 871.

94 Neugebauer and Stöss, 1996, pp. 162 and 285. Raschke, 1994, pp. 1453–64.

95 Bortfeldt, 1994b, p. 1283.

96 Neugebauer, 1996, p. 17.

97 Smith, 1992, p. 100.

98 Gerner, 1994, p. 59.

99 Bortfeldt, 1992, p. 295. See also Moreau, 1992, p. 459.

100 Krisch, 1998, p. 39.

101 Patton, 1998, p. 505.

102 McFalls, 1995, p. 59.

103 Michael Brie, in his thoughtful work of 1995, was the first to postulate that the PDS had developed into an eastern German *Volkspartei*; see Brie, 1995. See also McKay, 1996. For an example of politicians (of all political persuasions) describing the PDS as an eastern German *Volkspartei* see Johannes Leithäuser: 'Inhaltliche Auseinandersetzung mit falschen Parolen', in *Frankfurter Allgemeine Zeitung*, 21 October 1999, p. 2.

104 Kirchheimer, 1966, pp. 177–200.

105 Thompson, 1995, p. 446.

106 Betz and Welsh, 1995, p. 93.

107 Christine Ostrowski was a member of the *Bundestag* until December 1990, and once again from September 1998. Between 1990 and 1998 she was a member of the Saxony state parliament.

108 Ostrowski and Weckesser also observe that the failure of the westward expansion does not surprise them as those who associate themselves with the PDS in the western states are ideological left-wing radicals, and have nothing whatsoever in common with the successful communal politicians who are the face of the PDS in the eastern states. See Ostrowski and Weckesser, 1996, p. 5. See also http://www.christine-ostrowski.de/aktuelles.htm

109 Ostrowski and Weckesser, 1996, p. 5.

110 Ostrowski and Weckesser, 1996, p. 5.

111 Following the publication of the letter on 8 May, the pages of *Neues Deutschland* were full of commentaries, letters and contributions denouncing Ostrowski and Weckesser for attempting to undermine the PDS's proposed expansion westwards. PDS politicians were also quick to rubbish the letter (and its authors) in the most public of fashions. Heiko Hilker and Uwe Adamczyk, two MdLs from Saxony, claimed that Ostrowski instinctively sought media attention and as such would be overjoyed that she was in the political limelight. Claudia Gohde, a member of the PDS Executive with responsibilities for the western state organisations (*Landesverbände*), was struck by the arrogance of Ostrowski in claiming that western members of the PDS were simply left-wing ideologues, while Angela Marquardt claimed that she personally had much more in common with many western members of the PDS than she did with Ostrowski. For more evidence of criticism of the Letter see 'Auf ausgelatschten Wegen etablierter Parteien', in *Neues Deutschland*, 9 May 1996, p. 3.

112 *Neues Deutschland*, despite its staunch willingness to support the PDS's campaign to expand westwards, has also, on occasions, acknowledged that it is in eastern Germany that the PDS has the potential to make a genuine impact on German politics – therefore tacitly accepting the assumptions made by Ostrowksi and Weckesser. As *Neues Deutschland* observed on 9 January 1996, 'a new identity exists in the East ... characterised by a conscious opposi-

tion to the arrogance of western German politicians … and as a consequence the PDS is still yet to maximise its electoral potential in the eastern states'. See *Neues Deutschland*, 9 January 1996, p. 1.

113 The PDS gained votes in every one of the eastern states, except Berlin, where it lost 1.4 per cent and Mecklenburg Western Pomerania where its proportion of the vote (23.6 per cent) remained exactly the same as 1994. The gains ranged from 1 per cent in Brandenburg, to 4.1 per cent in Thuringia. See Infratest Dimap, 1998, p. 180.

114 Infratest Dimap, 1998, p. 64.

115 Infratest Dimap, 1998, p. 65.

116 Koch-Baumgarten, 1997, p. 872.

3

The PDS in the regional context: a framework for analysis

Regional parties are a disparate group of political actors; this is why no systematic framework of analysis has been created for studying them. This chapter will make a tentative attempt to redress this balance by developing a two-part typology to illustrate how regional parties mobilise specific territorial sentiments. The first part of the typology discusses two key structural variables that help create and sustain a regionally distinct political environment, or regional space. This part is applied in chapter four to explain the differences (in the spheres of economics, politics, culture, values and attitudes) between citizens of the eastern and western states. This fleshes out the notion of the eastern German identity of defiance. The second part of the typology highlights three characteristics that distinguish a regional party's activities within the political arena. They can be termed 'agency factors'. This part of the typology is applied in chapters five and six to illustrate how the PDS politically articulates this territorial difference.

The disparate nature of regional parties in the industrialised world dictates that a discussion of the factors that promote and support political regionalism is vital if the nature of regional parties' success is to be adequately understood. New, or renewed, cross-cutting and territorially sensitive divides may enable regional parties to establish themselves in a given party system, so breaking the dominance of 'national parties'.[1] The traditional parties' power of agenda-setting, their efficient organisations and their widely perceived representative functions can sometimes be overcome as new or alternative societal constellations form. This means that regional parties are highly heterogenous and very much a product of their place and time. The history of the region or nation therefore plays a determining role in dictating the precise form that regional parties take.[2]

In the case of Germany, the established parties have been unable to incorporate specific eastern German sentiment into their programmes and agendas. The process of identity creation in eastern Germany has been fuelled by the experience of life in the GDR before 1989 and the Federal Republic since. The contemporary eastern identity is, therefore, a reaction against the dominant culture of the FRG. The structural marginalisation of eastern German culture, values and interests exacerbated feelings of 'eastern Germanness'.[3] In brief, a space opened up in which a regionally concentrated party had a chance to establish itself.

Regional, national or both?

Before discussing specific regional parties, it is important to clarify and define the terminology employed here. This is a tricky task, as the term 'regional' remains something of an arbitrary concept. As Arthur Benz *et al.* note, regions are rarely tightly defined, and hence tend to suffer from being analysed and discussed in different ways by different authors.[4] Konrad Köstlin observes that producing a general definition of a region is in itself impossible, owing to their man-made nature and their ever-changing dynamics. Köstlin is adamant that the interaction of external (structural) factors with localised phenomena produce unique sets of human-inspired territorial circumstances – ensuring that regions remain impossible to generalise and, therefore, 'undefinable' in their make-up.[5] While Köstlin's argument has merit, the notion of a particular region can still take on a clear and coherent meaning over and above its own social, cultural, economic or political context. But one needs to be careful in interpreting exactly what this is supposed to mean. As structural phenomena, regions do not have identities, aspirations or interests. To gain content, the spatial attributes of a region must be associated with some politically relevant distinctions: in attitudes, identities, culture, levels of affluence and so on. Similarly, a basic and potentially divisive cleavage such as language does not, in itself, create political conflict – it does so only when language is associated with differential access to power, status or economic wealth. Hence, agents play a fundamental role in articulating and giving value to (territorial) structural difference.[6] Sylvia Pintarits has argued that there are indeed two reference points for regions: the first are economic/institutionalised/cultural characteristics that differentiate the region from the other. The second is the comparison with other regions that are clearly different, but formally take on the same role (i.e. they too are perceived or classified as regions).[7] Hence the characteristics that arise to differentiate a region from the whole, and are seen as taking on special territorial salience, are exaggerated/articulated by social actors.

For the purposes of this study a broad definition of the term region is employed. A region is a geographic entity within a nation-state. Regions may vary immensely in size and economic and social structure. They are human constructs, a result of the conceptual division of the world on the basis of a specific set of chosen criteria.[8] The selection and balance of criteria, of course, change with the geographical, social and historical setting. The definitive characteristics of regions are that they are geographically defined (on the grounds of historical precedent, judicial agreement or popular will) areas of territory *within* present-day nation states (although, once again, they may overlap national borders[9]) located between historical, cultural, linguistic or economic dividing lines. Moreover, many of the movements and parties that have been categorised as 'regional' often refer to themselves as 'national', defending long-held national traditions (be they cultural, historical, quasi-mythical or linguistic), with the aim of achieving separation, autonomy from, or simply greater recognition within, a more or less centralised state. Basque, Catalan, Quebecois, Scottish, Irish, Welsh, Breton and many other forms of national movement profess to protect and enhance the rights and culture of 'nations' of peoples who historically perceive themselves as being different from the 'foreign' state and elites who govern them from the centre. Whether they style themselves national or regional, these parties are active in a political space that is not congruent with the boundaries of the larger nation-state – and it is for this reason that they are included in this analysis of regional parties.

Classifying regional parties

If classifying regions is problematic, classifying regional parties is an even more complex task. Their heterogeneity ensures that they remain a diverse group and, electorally speaking, they were once famously derided as 'little more than an irritant'.[10] Lieven De Winter has, however, attempted to categorize regional parties with regard to the demands that they make on the state - and this approach does appear to be a helpful way of classifying regional parties' political will and ambition. Applying this classification, regional parties range from parties that lobby within the existing constitutional system for cultural recognition or economic resources, to parties that campaign for forms of regional autonomy, or even separatism and the creation of 'new' nation-states. De Winter regards the defining demand of a regional party's programme as a 'political reorganisation of the existing national power structure, for some kind of self-government'. He identifies 'protectionist regional parties' as representing a particular constituency (usually an ethnic or cultural community) that is of a unique character and, as such, claims to merit unique treatment. This often takes the form of cultural demands being met within the framework of the existing nation-state. 'Autonomist parties' are likely to accept power-sharing, provided that their particular region is seen to be given some form of 'special' status. The *Südtiroler Volkspartei* (SVP) is a prime example of this. To some extent, the *Convergencia Democratica de Catalunya* (CDC) and the *Partido Nacionalista Vasco* (PNV) in the Basque Country fulfil this criteria, because, although they do not exclude independence as an option, in practice they settle for autonomy. 'National-Federalist parties', meanwhile, seek a clear territorial re-organisation of the nation-state. A number of the Belgian parties, as well as the *Lega Nord*, *Sinn Fein* and *Herri Batasuna* are examples of this.[11]

Within this context, the PDS can be classified as a protectionist party, because it seeks to protect and enhance the interests of eastern Germans without demanding a reconfiguration of state structures. This having been said, the PDS has, on occasions, articulated demands for specific structures that would enhance the representation of eastern Germans – it calls for a new constitution, while stressing the importance of new forms of 'direct democracy'.[12] In more recent times, it has called for the new *Länder* to be given special constitutional rights to veto policies that are seen as being in contravention of the *Einheitsvertrag* (Unification Treaty).[13] Classifying the PDS in this way does not, however, reveal a great deal about the methods and means that it has adopted in achieving electoral success in eastern Germany. It is obviously articulating, forwarding, representing and/or defending interests and issues that are of particular relevance in the eastern states and it is for this reason that it fares so well in this region of Germany (see chapters 4, 5 and 6).

De Winter's attempt to classify regional parties is also unable to hide the fact that there is no agreement as to how many regional parties actually exist. Traditionally, regional parties have been defined as ethnonationalist parties that seek to defend the interests of a particular ethnic group. In 1991 Jan-Erik Lane, David McKay and Kenneth Newton talked of 44 such parties in western Europe;[14] Derek Urwin claims to have pinpointed 115 regionalist parties within 17 countries in the period since 1945.[15] Arend Lijphart contends that, while some countries have party systems where ethnic parties do not play significant roles in political life, *all* countries remain ethnically divided to some extent – hence the potential for ethnonational party success is always present.[16]

As these figures demonstrate, analysing regional parties, and the factors that spawn them, can become a conceptual minefield. The terms 'ethnoregional-ist', 'regionalist', 'ethnonationalist', 'nationalist' and 'regional' are all used to describe the phenomena of parties that do not compete in elections across all the territory of a nation-state and are particularly strong in one territory. Furthermore, many commentators tend to over-play the importance of some form of ethnicity in the success of regional parties. De Winter and Türsan explicitly describe regional parties as 'ethnoregionalist', stressing the ethnic fundamentals that underpin their success.[17] However, this terminology fits uneasily when applied to prominent parties like the *Lega Nord* in Northern Italy, a party that bases its political claims on a group solidarity that has little to do with ethnicity. This point is even conceded in the Italian case, Marco Tarchi pointing out that group identity is not necessarily 'ethnic':

> The claim of identity based on ethnicity and supported by folk-lorist forms of action (assemblies, demonstrations, graffiti written in dialect, costume parades) reduced them [the original Northern Leagues] to cultural epiphenomena and isolated them from the socioeconomic interests of the 'people', who in fact lacked the common ethnic or linguistic traits that these movements sought to represent.[18]

To avoid terminological pitfalls, the typology invoked here is split into two parts: section one discusses the problems of what differentiates a region from the whole and what prompts unique group identifications to show. This provides the foundations for section two, which deals with the nature and mobilising techniques and strategies of regional parties themselves. The whole typology will enable the social, political, economic and psychological differences between a region and the broader nation-state to be identified, as well as showing how regional parties are direct political representatives of these differences (see table 3.1).

Table 3.1. A typology of regionalism and the ways in which regional parties mobilise regional particularity

---

Structural and causal factors inherent in regionalism
- Cultural variables
- Socioeconomic variables

Agency factors in the mobilisation of regionalism
- Party leadership
- Party organisation
- Party policy

In reality, complex and unique combinations of these factors contribute to cleavage formation, and subsequently the development of regional movements that articulate territorial sentiment. It is not the aim of this study to explain why similar societal developments in one territory lead to particular party formation, while in other regions the 'national' parties are able to absorb such a challenge. The individuality of every case study makes this too large a task to undertake. Rather, this chapter aims to highlight the criteria that regional parties have to fill *if* they are going to be successful (it will not stipulate that the fulfilment of such criteria automatically means a regional party *will* receive popular support.)

Approaches to political regionalism

The study of political regionalism acquired a new lease of life in the world of political science after the 1960s. Arising from the pioneering work of Stein Rokkan and Seymour Martin Lipset, issues of territorial uniqueness, and the factors that lead to it developing and prospering, became mainstream topics. This is particularly true in terms of the concepts of centre and periphery, which, even if problems still surround their usage,[19] remain important tools for the study of territorial politics today.[20] The concepts of centre and periphery illuminate the ways in which the dominant cultural positions of centres influence and conflict with the subject culture that has tended to characterise peripheries – and hence how the relationship between the two can shape territorial identifications in nominally peripheral areas of a state.

The simplicity of the terms has led to 'centres' and 'peripheries' being applied to both territories and population groups in a given nation-state,[21] and analysts have often used quite different criteria in classifying territories and populations as either peripheral or central. It is clear that tighter definitions are necessary if the terms are to be usefully employed. The terms 'space' and 'distance' can be used to refer to two sets of relations: one physical, the other social and cultural. Stein Rokkan termed one a *geographical* space and the other a *membership* space. The membership boundary tends to be much more impervious than the geographical: you can cross the border into a territory as a tourist, trader or casual labourer, but you will find it much more difficult to be accepted as a member of the pre-eminent core group within the territory.[22] In areas where the interaction between the centre and the periphery is dominated by the core culture, and the interests of the core group predominate, it is clear that any peripheral identity will have very limited structural opportunities for reproduction. Yet a historically defined regional culture,[23] whether based on language (as is most common), religion or other unique cultural characteristics can still be cohesive enough to support peripheral identities.[24]

The development of the centre–periphery framework in the 1960s and 1970s led to issues such as social and cultural difference, income disparities and the unequal distribution of wealth being increasingly discussed in territorial terms.[25] Yet the concept of territory becomes politically significant as a result of the interpretation and values which a population ascribes to it – be they ethnic, historical or linguistic:[26] territory can, therefore, quickly become a concept charged with political meaning by people organising space for their own aims – a fact that the centre–periphery framework helps to highlight. In the 1960s frustrated political elites, realising the potency of politically charged ideas of territory, began increasingly to mobilise peripheral feelings of distinctiveness. The rise to prominence of regional movements throughout Europe in this period, based on the political articulation of regionally specific interests, is striking evidence of this. Furthermore, the centralising and modernising tendencies of modern-day capitalism have further increased the appeal of peripheral identities. Elite actors within (national or core) dominant cultures have encouraged *national* political integration, yet these processes also, paradoxically, contribute to an increasing awareness of regional consciousness, and a growth in the desire for identification and membership in a community more distinct and less impersonal than national society.[27]

It is within the context of the centre–periphery debate that a number of authors have developed theories of territorial mobilisation that explicitly stress the importance of centre building and central domination in provoking political regionalism. Structural dynamics have, often, been seen as being paramount in determining human behaviour within given regions.[28] These approaches stress that particular social, economic and/or political environments (or structures) combine to create peripheral uniqueness. This happens at a number of different levels, and can take the form of differential economic performance, cultural specificity (most often in the form of a separate language) or historical difference. At the political level, regionally based political parties act as agents of structural specificity, fostering and reflecting territorial consciousness and regional identification.[29]

Largely structural theories which cite uneven economic development across a given state,[30] internal colonialism[31] or ethnic competition[32] all claim, in their different ways, to account for regional mobilisation. For example, Tom Nairn produces, in explanation of the SNP's success in Scotland in the 1970s, a thorough economic explanation of the importance of international capitalism in dictating the differing political environments of regions in

Britain. He perceives Scotland's then-weaker economic base as leading to a general growth in the dissatisfaction with the 'British' parties, and a concomitant rise in nationalist sentiment.[33] Michael Hechter uses structural terminology in a different way, arguing that states like the United Kingdom (and, it can be argued, post-1989 Germany) have been built and 'integrated' by a process of domination by a central or core (ethnic) group. The centre dominates political, economic and cultural activity to the detriment of the periphery. Peripheral areas subsequently remain disadvantaged or exploited, and local cultures, while not disappearing, are subject to a systematic battering by that of the dominant group.[34] This has been well summarised by Peter Wagstaff when he notes that the 'centralisation of power, often perceived from the margins as internal colonialism, is the factor which provokes regional dissent and the desire for a distinctive voice.[35]

A different structural analysis can, however, be drawn from the competition between differing 'ethnic' groups in western Europe. Structural processes and constraints of modernisation dictate that ethnic groups are forced to compete for the same rewards and resources, as a result of the growing interconnectedness of what were once territorially and economically separate peoples. Put another way, the increasing integration of regional economies into the capitalist system has given rise to a resurgence in regional movements.[36]

While these approaches undoubtedly contribute to the understanding of the nature of political regionalism and the nature of centre–periphery politics, structures alone cannot *cause* predictable and specific political outcomes of regional party success. The proposition that a region and a people are in a peripheral position within a society does not inevitably lead to political regionalism and regional political parties becoming important actors. While regional parties do take advantage of structurally advantageous societal and economic conditions that are a product of a peripheral position, it is clear that structural factors only *assist in understanding* how regional parties are successful at the polls. As agents in the political process, the regional parties have to articulate the interests of potential voters and mobilise them in the political arena.[37] Hence, structures merely help to define the potential range of options and strategies available to actors; they can exacerbate specific territorial grievances or particularities, and as such increase the propensity for a regional party to develop. A specific regional environment provides a unique set of objective conditions in which different combinations of interests are defined within different cleavage structures.[38] Social and political action is therefore contextualised within the structural environments in which it takes place.

A party system that allows for the growth and stimulation of new and challenging voting habits is, of course, also necessary in allowing the expression and instrumentalisation of regional sentiment.[39] This process has two dimensions: firstly, 'traditional' parties are perceived as being unable to represent regional groupings. Secondly, regional identities must be strong enough to prompt political mobilisation behind a territorial cleavage. Other cross-cutting cleavages may dictate that even in areas where a considerable degree of regional consciousness is evident, it may not manifest itself in a particularist regional voice (as was the case in Scotland, for example, before the 1960s, when class and religious–ethnic interests were given priority over Scottish Nationalist drives).

Regional parties and the roots of party system development

Regional parties, as was noted earlier, are often seen as unique and different, and have not easily fitted into broad theories of European party system development.[40] Aside from the studies by Hoffman,[41] Levi and Hechter,[42] Rokkan and Urwin,[43] Newman[44] and, latterly, De Winter and Türsan,[45] the literature on regional parties is thin. Regional parties are seen as interesting little anomalies in the party systems of western European states. On the surface, regional parties do indeed appear to be heterogeneous, and it is clear that communist, socialist, social democratic, Christian democratic and far-right 'party families' have more in common across international frontiers. Most regional parties are small in size, and do not share a common train of economic thought or a common view of how society should be structured.[46] Their only commonality is their claim upon the state: they identify themselves with, and act (they claim) on behalf of, territories and groups that do not coincide with state boundaries.

Traditionally, interests, values and ideologies in European politics are seen as being linked in complex ways to produce a series of identifiable currents and trends that span the politics of the whole continent. Lipset and Rokkan conceptualised this in 1967, coming to see the party system as a dependent variable that had developed as a result of the fossilisation of cleavages that had long-held traditions within society.[47] They highlighted four main societal cleavages, stemming from one of the two great revolutions (the so-called national revolution and the industrial revolution): centre–periphery, state–church, land–industry and owner–worker. The final inclusion of all adults within the democratic process left little (or no) scope for new cleavages to be formed and/or mobilised upon, and so the parameters of party competition are perceived as remaining broadly as they were in the 1920s.[48] This does not mean that the same parties exist, but simply that the same cleavages are evident and they continue to shape the party system. In recent years there has been a mountain of scholarly works pointing out, however, that party systems are no longer as 'frozen' as Lipset and Rokkan once propounded.[49] The materialist/post-materialist divide across the industrialised world has added another dimension to the debate,[50] as well-educated, increasingly affluent citizens are perceived to be interested in, and politically mobilised around, 'new' cleavage-issues (the environment, peace) that find political representation in the emergence of Green parties.

Giovanni Sartori has, however, challenged the body of work that regards the party system as a dependent variable, and he characterises the party system as an independent variable, with the underlying tenet being that of party control.[51] This implies that societal changes do not necessarily set the parameters of a party system, and that changes only occur to the extent that parties lose their ability to set the agenda and subsequently lose their own influence on the system. In Sartori's words:

> A freezed (sic) party system is simply a party system that intervenes in the political process as an independent *system of channelment*, propelled and maintained by its own laws of momentum.[52]

Given institutional structures and electoral mechanisms provide clear constraints on, and incentives to, political parties, but it is leaders who choose which political space to occupy, which ideological orientation to pursue and what political strategy they wish to employ. Parties react to the environment around them, and the rise and fall of new parties indicates that parties are sometimes unable to react in such a way as to remain dominant over all political processes in a given state. Sartori's work would imply that the existence of regional parties results from the inability of the 'national' parties to represent the differing strands of societal opinion in a given region, or to set the agenda for political discussion, as the evolutionary processes that generally lead to party system adaptation cannot deal with the unique challenge of articulating distinct territorial sentiment.

In eastern Germany, radical societal transformation has influenced the factors underlying political mobilisation, as (western) parties fail to grasp the specific nature both of the transformation process and the legacy of forty years of state socialism. If party systems mould themselves to societies over the course of time, then Sartori's arguments remain strong, and offer a logical explanation for the stabilisation of the PDS as an articulator of eastern German interests. The West German party system was placed on to an immature democracy that had contributed neither to the system's development nor its efficacy – and as such has found it difficult to adjust to a 'foreign' political way of life.

Wide-ranging and thorough (as well as often being complex) though such analysis is, literature on party system change still fails to offer explicit reasons for the existence and proliferation of specifically regional movements. That they are there, and are embedded in the cleavage structures of certain societies, is not disputed, but generally the reasons adduced for this and for their expansion are not clear-cut. Derek Urwin contends that the majority tend to be products of the 'national' revolution that created, redefined and stabilised state structures across Europe. Parties like the *Südtiroler Volkspartei* in Italy, and the *Slesvig Parti* in Denmark[53] are excellent examples of this. They fit into the party system as articulators of clearly defined ethnic groups that ended up on the 'wrong' side of national boundaries in the period of nineteenth-century state-building. It is also clear that the extended suffrage facilitated the organisation of parties for the protection of minority and territorial interests.

This is, however, about as systematic as most analysis of regional parties across the western world tends to get. This is principally because no thorough method has been developed for analysing the factors that underpin the existence of regional parties. In order to be politically successful regional parties have to wrest agenda-setting powers from the major parties and, given the advantages that the national parties possess, this can be a difficult task. Secondly, they have to be able to politically exploit latent territorial identification (which has often arisen from structurally unique factors), stressing how they, and they alone, represent the interests of the regional population. The territorial cleavage has to be pronounced enough to prompt voters to cast their votes on these grounds, in the belief that the regional party is acting in their best interests. The typology presented below is a tentative effort to conceptualise this into an analytical framework.

A typology of structural and causal factors inherent in political regionalism

The creation of unique spaces where regional parties can flourish is dependent on the interaction of two broad phenomena: cultural and socioeconomic variables. Because of differences in historical background, constitutional constraints and/or economic imperatives, regional spaces can take very different forms. However, the distinctiveness of a territory ensures that political competition functions in a different way to the larger nation-state of which the territory is a part. In political terms, national parties are not able to encapsulate regional specificities into their programmes and platforms – and, as a result, territorially specific parties can rise to prominence as advocates of regional interests.

Cultural variables

Cultural variables frequently play an important role in explaining the existence of distinct regional spaces. Even where regions possess negligible institutional frameworks through which to exert influence in the wider nation-state, the medium of culture and ethnic difference may ensure that distinct forms of territorial identification remain evident within society. Territorial identities may well be strengthened and sharpened as a consequence of economic difference, but generally identities are *based* within a cultural context. Cultural identities stem from that fact that people are naturally tied to their territory by the characteristics and distinctive processes of socialisation that they inevitably undergo. More precisely, they identify with their kin, with their language, and with other cultural–ethnic traditions that differentiate them from other citizens of the larger nation-state. Many of the territorial identifications that are prevalent across Europe and the democratic world therefore exist within the context of (ethno-) cultural difference.

However, both ethnicity and culture remain highly contested concepts, and so must be applied with great care to real-world politics.[54] Suffice it here to say that ethnic identities are grounded in the belief that a group has its roots in a common ancestry, and that notions of community are based both on birth and a shared native culture.[55] As was mentioned earlier, a number of authors have described ethnicity as the structural variable upon which *all* regional parties mobilise support;[56] indeed it is true that ethnic claims lie at the root of much political regionalism, and regional party success. This stems from the fact that ethnicity is a powerful motor of identity creation.

Culture, while often used interchangeably with ethnicity, is understood here to mean a pattern of experiences, opinions, evaluations, knowledge and attitudes that exist in connection with a distinct social system. 'Indigenous' or 'unique' cultures can and do develop, or exist, more or less independently from other cultural systems within a given society (in the case of a nation-state). When discussing the nature of *territorial* identification, the notions of ethnicity and culture, defined as they are here, can and do frequently overlap, and while authors may argue about the exact nature of the identification that they are discussing, one thing does normally remain clear: the identification, be it ethnically or culturally based, is almost always *territorial* in its nature. The identity relates to a history, a set of events, people, practices, traditions, myths and legends that are related to a distinct piece of territory.[57] This territorial identification differentiates the region from the larger nation-state of which it is a part.

The territorial-political expression of ethnocultural difference in the form of ethnonationalism is widespread across Europe. Historical identities have been crystallised over long periods of time, and some continue to sit uneasily within the present institutional structures within which they find themselves.[58] This is most apparent in the southern and eastern corners of the continent, but ethnic tensions are also visible in western European states. Many 'ethnonationalist' regional parties are also in evidence, seeking national liberation from a (perceived) illegitimate and unjust central authority. They use the territorial cleavage within a state to further ethnonationalist aims,[59] focusing on intrinsic rights to justice and self-determination for a (persecuted) ethnic community. Or, as Anthony Smith phrases it, ethnically based parties seek 'the restoration of a degraded community to its rightful status and dignity' and through the aim of a separate political existence the 'goal of the restoration and the social embodiment of that dignity'.[60]

Perhaps surprisingly, the use of the term 'ethnic' found little resonance in the academic world, and tended to be widely ignored,[61] until the 1970s, whereafter it was often claimed that ethnicity was over-used as an explanatory tool.[61] But transcending academic discussions as to the applicability of the concept, ethnic consciousness has proved a powerful force in, firstly, fostering group identities, and, secondly, mobilising groups of people to protect or enhance their ethnic integrity or uniqueness. Forms of mobilisation vary: militant ethnonationalism[62] is evident in a number of states, ranging from the terrorist tactics of the Provisional Irish Republican Army (and its political wing Sinn Fein) in its attempt to achieve the incorporation of Northern Ireland into the Republic of Ireland, to *Herri Batasuna* (HB) and its frequently alleged representation of similarly brutal ETA activists dedicated to constructing a separate Basque state outside the central authority of Spain and France.

The Basque case is an excellent example of the complex political nature of ethnic identification (and regional party support). A perception of oneself as a member of a specific ethnic group by no means ensures uniformity of political will. Davydd Greenwood highlights five different Basque political orientations: these orientations variously support political autonomy within a federated state or as a semi-autonomous province; outright separatism for all of the seven traditional Basque regions in the form of a 'Basque Nation-State'; a withering of European states and the emergence of a Europe of ethnic groups; agnosticism and cynicism towards any form of political settlement, no doubt as a consequence of centuries of adverse political experience; and, finally, a group of Basques who, at the time of writing, were more or less favourable to the existing regime.[63] These widely differing ideologies and political strategies spread much more widely than a mere appreciation of one's Basque identity, and hence it should be no surprise that there are a number of Basque nationalist parties. As Pauliina Raento observes, the relative unity of Basque nationalists no longer exists, instead they have been divided into mutually antagonistic groups.[64] In theory, these groups all share the original nationalist ideal of an independent, territorially unified Basque-speaking state, based on a clear structural divide between Basques and 'others'. The reality is, however, that the Basques are bitterly divided over what 'national self-determination' should mean, how this should be achieved and who can legitimately decide this. 'One-province' populist parties have even emerged within the Basque Country.[65] The *Partido Nacionalista Vasco/Eusko Alderdi Jeltalea* (PNV/EAJ) remains the strongest force in the region, drawing in conservative and Catholic Basques, alongside the smaller *Eusko Alkartsauna* (EA). Tensions between the EA and PNV have, however, created problems in regional government, as decisions adopted by a PNV leader have not always coincided with those of an EA President of the Basque government.[66] None the less, both parties support the Spanish state, and accept the general goal of autonomy as a means of satisfying their ambitions for Basque self-determination. In alliance with the all-Spanish PSOE (socialists) they have been able to form governmental alliances in the Basque autonomous region.[67] HB was only established in 1979 and has tended to appeal to disaffected youth, and in particular to the urban unemployed.[68] It is part of the Basque National Liberation Front (MNLV - as is the terrorist organisation ETA) and sees its principle as that of liberating the Basque homeland from Spanish control.

Ethnonationalism, of course, does not necessarily seek separation from the centre, and some nationalist movements (often the more successful ones) prefer to seek a 'better deal' for their region and their people. The Catalan *Convergéncia i Unió* (CiU), an electoral coalition that successfully embraces Christian Democracy, liberalism and socialism, is a case in point here. Since the legalisation of political parties in Spain in 1975, the CiU has dominated Catalan politics, consistently seeking more autonomy for Catalonia within the centralist Spanish state, emphasising the importance of a flourishing Catalonian language and cultural development within broad Spanish structures. As one author puts it, the CiU 'seeks the maximum power for Catalonia with the minimum trauma for the rest of Spain'.[69]

Ethnonationalist political parties specifically use culture as a mobilising tool. Certain values are represented by many members of a group, they provide similar emotional linkages and arouse similar active tendencies. With this in mind, members of this group have the experience of sharing ideas, sentiments and desires.[70] A number of regional parties have grown out of cultures that long pre-date the modern state, as is the case in both the Basque Country and Catalonia where both cultures are bound by traditions and languages that divide them from their Castilian neighbours. They have struggled for centuries to retain their ethnic identities in the face of modernisation and state-enforced assimilation – something that reached a peak during the Franco dictatorship.[71] External pressure to alter or suppress peripheral uniqueness in fact often served the purpose of crystallising this cultural core, and strenuous efforts were made to defend these core principles. Evidence of this can also be found in Scotland where the development of a Scottish consciousness had much to do with the attitudes and behaviour of the English. Distinctive national institutions like the education system and the system of law have helped Scottish identity to remain prevalent, as Scots of all walks of life learn to appreciate ingrained and institutionalised cultural difference within the United Kingdom.

Culture can, and does, act as symbolically integrative (through the use and acceptance of myths, symbols etc.) and as a basis for solidaristic political mobilisation against a collectively perceived threat or degradation. Clive Hedges has stressed the 'crucial cultural underpinnings' of nationalist ideology in places like Wales and Northern Ireland[72] and it is clear that many of the founding fathers of fledgling nationalist movements were primarily cultural nationalists[73] who perceived their national culture as being threatened by state centralisation. As the power and prestige of an independent new state offered the best opportunity to defend a threatened peripheral culture and value system, cultural nationalists saw the necessity of aligning themselves with political nationalists in order to challenge the central state – hence many regenerative cultural programmes were formed in political terms. In Catalonia, for example, only by forming alliances with the economically hegemonic business classes could cultural nationalists gain adequate financial support, and as a result cultural arguments were framed in such a way as not to threaten the vested interests of economic elites. The cultural movement of the *Renaixença* (dating from the 1840s to the 1870s) proved the ideal basis for nationalism to become more widespread, as the lost freedom of Catalonia and the renewed concept of ethnic identity prospered under the guidance of a cultural revival.

An indigenous regional/national language is often an extremely important cultural variable; a language spoken only by residents of a particular territory will be a very obvious identity marker, naturally creating 'in' and 'out' groups. However, the experiences of the Basque Country and Wales,[74] where less than fifty per cent of the population speaks the distinctive language of the region, illustrate that it is not essential to be a speaker of Basque or Welsh to be clear and decisive in ones self-appreciation as a citizen of that region/nation. None the less it is obvious that the existence of a unique language does act as an identity marker for a large number of people within these territories. Indeed, multiple regression analysis (taking into account the size of a region, population, sectoral unemployment, regional GDP, the degree of autonomy etc.), applied to the study of a number of regions in the EU by Derek Hearl, Ian Budge and Bernard Peterson has shown that only the presence of widely spoken language and, to a much lesser extent, the degree of overall unemployment and industrial employment are significant determinants of what they describe as ethnoregional voting.[75] This implies that support for regional-nationalist movements appears to be based more on cultural than material grounds – and consequently that socioeconomic structural models of voting behaviour do not explain regional political mobilisation.

However, when discussing the creation of regional spaces it would be misleading to place too much stress on language at the expense of other elements of cultural uniqueness. Collective memory, a unique history, or a simple sense of belonging are also common motivators of calls for the defence of cultural difference and the creation of territorial identifications – and it is for these reasons, for example, that non-Welsh-speaking citizens of Wales identify strongly with their nation.[76] Basques,[77] Catalans,[78] Flemings,[79] Scots[80] and South Tyroleans[81] (to name but a few) see themselves principally as citizens of the region/nation where they live rather than of the larger nation-state of which their nations/regions are a part. This contrasts strongly with the state-level identity of, for example, Northern Italians,[82] most Walloons[83] and Swedes in Finland,[84] emphasising how processes of identity creation take differing forms in differing spatial environments.[85]

Regional symbols and characteristics often play key roles in (re)defining cultural movements and territorial identities, and they contribute to their successful passage through generations. These symbols may vary widely in form, and only have genuine meaning to select groups within society. They may be historical events that are remembered and celebrated, flags or symbols that have taken on unique meanings, or parades, processions or marches that have grown to be carriers of distinct regional identities within the broader regional space. Group customs, traditions and institutions sustain special routines and foster feelings of distinctiveness, serving as a means of excluding those not perceived of as being within the 'in' community. It is here that nationalism and regionalism clearly overlap, as symbolic places, boundaries and frontiers often have a key place within the context of both *national* and *regional* self-appreciation.

Examples of the importance of tokens of national and regional identity are numerous, as they are at the core of psychological attachment to particular territories and peoples. While it is clear that all *nations* within nation-states[86] are built around national myths, it is also the case that *regions* are susceptible to myth-making – the process is intrinsic in formulation of communities and 'we' identities. Northern Irish politics, for example, is littered with references to past events and, particularly in recent years, the issue of where Northern Ireland's fraternal orders – The Orange Order, The Apprentice Boys of Derry and the Royal Black Institution - are allowed to march has come to be of great symbolic importance to all communities. Although only a small number of marches are regarded as contentious,[87] the symbolic importance of these occasions ensures that they are now high-profile political exercises. The yearly scenes of confrontation at the Drumcree church illustrate how the symbolic marking of historical events by marching through the streets of Northern Ireland has come to be seen as a touchstone for the strength of the Protestant faith in Northern Ireland.

Not all regional symbols and characteristics are so intrinsically divisive as the marches in Northern Ireland. The antics of secessionists in Northern Italy are treated with mild amusement by most other Italians, as 'Padanians' continue to mobilise around the Padanian flag[88] and even around a (self-proclaimed) Padanian state. There have been clear attempts to foster an identity in the Northern provinces of Italy by 'creating' the instruments of statehood – although this has met with mixed success. While the sense of identity of Northern Italians in Padania is strong in that it is clear and distinct in its disdain for southern Italians, there is little positive identification with the *state* of Padania.[89] Furthermore, although the North/South cleavage in Italian politics is plain and obviously important, any attempt to create a Padanian state or symbols of 'Padanianism' are looked upon by Northerners and Southerners alike with distinct coolness.

Regional symbols are particularly important for the continuation of territorial identities in times of repression, as they often provide the only legal (or if illegal, largely undetectable or non-extinguishable) method of preserving regional cultures and the relationship between a territory and its population. Symbols act as a glue that holds together societies that are undergoing processes of forced assimilation with a dominant culture. Both the historic nations of the Basque Country and Catalonia fall into this category; the repression that the Francoist regime placed upon them was in many ways counter-productive, as it lent symbols of nationalist culture (and particularly language) far greater importance than they would have otherwise acquired.

This illustrates that cultural variables have to *cross-cut* other societal cleavages if they are to promote political mobilisation. The mere existence of distinct cultural phenomena and of unique territorial identifications based around them is not necessarily sufficient to spawn a regional party defending or promoting territorial uniqueness. Although an identity may exist and be widely held, it must be politically salient if it is going to be the basis for political mobilisation. It must be seen as more important than other traditionally strong identifiers such as social class and religious denomination. The agents who seek to give voice to territorial identity must also have opportunity structures (in terms of resources and organisation) that allow them to be heard within the political process. Successful regional parties are those that have become most adept at fulfilling this role.

Socioeconomic variables

Socioeconomic variables are another set of key structural factors that help to create regional spaces. This is particularly true when the economic 'system' is seen to be failing the citizens of a particular region. This can be in a radical and abrupt way, as happened in Italy at the beginning of the 1990s, or it can be rather more subtle and slow moving, as was the case in Scotland in the 1960s, 1970s and 1980s. Furthermore, if changes in the socioeconomic base correspond, even only roughly, to the parameters of a coherent set of cultural values, then the effects of these changes may be amplified considerably – as a regional identification becomes apparent in a number of different spheres within society. It is for this reason that the most successful regional parties are those that exist in regional spaces where culturally unique societal traits are linked and interwoven with socioeconomic difference.

Regional parties have often not been slow to make political capital out of the claim that the national government has mismanaged a region's economic assets – whether it be that the region is economically underdeveloped (Scotland) or economically more advanced (western Canada, northern Italy).[90] The key variable, however, remains the same: citizens grow uneasy and dissatisfied in the region within which they live, as the 'system' does not respond to their needs and demands, and/or economic outputs fail to meet their expectations – prompting new or renewed territorial cleavage to come into existence and/or rise in political salience.

Regional identifications and territorial cleavages have often been most prominent in Europe's more affluent areas (Flanders, Brussels, Bavaria, Northern Italy, South Tyrol, Catalonia and the Basque Country). The affluence of these regions relative to their nation-states has prompted citizens to tend to regard themselves (often correctly) as net contributors to the nation's wealth, and as such to be sceptical or critical of the central administration's redistributive economic policies. They perceive the fruits of their diligence as being wasted on the less hard-working, even parasitic, citizens of other regions – hence a sense of popular discontent arises within a particular territory. The case of Northern Italy and the *Lega Nord* is perhaps the most celebrated modern example of this. The *Lega* has established itself as an articulator of popular protest, directed principally at the inefficiencies, inadequacies and plain corruption of the Italian state.[91] The formation of a self-contained polity in northern Italy long predates the existence of the *Lega*, as it also outdates the unification of Italy in the late nineteenth century. The community that the *Lega* represents has long displayed social and economic characteristics different from those of their southern Italian compatriots. The existence of a civic community,[92] coupled with dissatisfaction at the redistributive economic policies of the central Italian state, prompted the *Lega* to actively manufacture a group identity and a feeling of community in northern Italy for its own political ends. The group identification had long been apparent, but it needed a political actor to mobilise it around a clear set of policy preferences. The LN has succeeded in politicising a regionalist cleavage which cross-cuts the left–right division formed by the two 'poles' that have come to dominate the nascent Italian party system. Such developments illustrate that goals of increased self-governance and/or autonomy are rational not just in cultural terms, but also in economic terms, as groups of people come to view territorial reorganisation and representation as being beneficial to their economic and social well-being.[93]

Regions that suffer detrimental side-effects from socioeconomic change can also develop strong regional consciousness. More often that not, this has been linked with an expressly cultural understanding of one's own identity (i.e. in Wales and Scotland), but it is also clear that the weaker economic position of, say, Scotland vis-à-vis England (in particular when linked to the discovery of North Sea oil) prompted a much-increased sense of regional injustice. This once again illustrates that regional consciousness is most likely to thrive in territories where cultural uniqueness and material difference combine to reinforce each other.

Rapid socioeconomic *change* can indeed be a catalyst for political regionalism to develop. However, only rarely since political parties established themselves in the fabric of western polities have such processes been rapid and sustained enough to engender radically different constellations of political parties. Lipset and Rokkan's 'freezing hypothesis' illustrated how the influence of the two revolutions led to a crystallisation of support in many western European polities around the four major social cleavages. Although social change has consistently been taking place,[94] it has rarely been rapid enough, or drastic enough, to prevent the major parties from adapting to the new political environment. For social change to prompt the political rise of a regional space, the effects have to be explicitly regional in their nature – and they have to challenge the way of life and/or economic well-being of the community in a radical and new way. This has occurred, though not frequently, in the past, and the globalisation of economic activity implies an increased propensity for it in the future.

An important contributory factor in spawning the 'new nationalism' in Catalonia, for example, was the wave of inward migration that occurred during the 1960s. Although Catalonian nationalism has traditionally been both more moderate and cultural than many other forms of ethnic nationalism, the changes Catalonian society underwent in the 1960s crystallised Catalonian self-perceptions in their struggle to preserve their own identity as well as their cultural heritage. The parties that came into being in 1975 had little trouble mobilising Catalans along this renewed territorial divide. The process of economic modernisation in the middle of the nineteenth century in the Basque Country also prompted regional consciousness to be sharpened as a result of demographic changes. The Basque people became 'proletarianised'[95] and young Basques found themselves being displaced from the countryside to the cities. Immigrants also flooded the country from Castile (already seen as the principal oppressor in many Basque eyes), providing clear competition for Basques in search of work and a new role within Basque society. The issue of language was quickly relegated to a side-issue – the Basques were now speaking the same language (Castillian Spanish) as the immigrants against whom they were competing – and the question of social background rose in importance. Basque nationalism underwent a renaissance, and was the clear beneficiary of this change in societal structure, as the issue of immigration saw Basque nationalist leaders (and principally Sabino Arana y Goiri) abandon cultural nationalism in many of their political statements.

In the UK, the existence of clear economic disparity helped the SNP to radically improve its position within the British party system in the 1960s and 1970s. Although the SNP was created as long ago as the late 1920s, it was only able to make genuine electoral process as the British state proved unable to deliver economic prosperity to Scotland. Nationalist claims in Scotland consequently tend to be based on distinctly practical arguments about institutions, accountability and (economic) policies rather than on ethnicity and cultural distinctiveness. The party system in Scotland, although superficially unchanged, can no longer legitimately claim to give Scots a regular chance of being on the 'winning side' – hence the failure of the system to accommodate Scots' economic and political interests has strongly contributed to a rise in the support for the SNP. Class and partisan dealignment, though initially slow, has certainly gone furthest in Britain's peripheral regions, as is emphasised by the failure of the Conservatives to win any seats in either Wales or Scotland in the 1997 election and just one seat in Scotland in 2001.

Other forms of material disparity include the embourgeoisement of western society which has also led to the weakening of traditional social cleavages. As workers have attained greater material wealth, and as general increases in prosperity have been achieved, some traditional socially mobilising variables have decreased in importance, leaving the field open for other factors to emerge as key determinants of the vote. As De Winter has observed:

> Ethnoregionalist parties were more successful in introducing the new cultural and regional sources of identity because their offer referred to dormant or lower-order identities. These are the product of pre-modern cleavages: the opposition of local and regional cultures against the introduction of a homogeneous national culture by the centre, which is associated with a larger movement towards homogenisation (in economic, financial, judicial, military, diplomatic terms) linked to the emergence of the nation-state.[96]

Regional parties do not, as a rule, tend to profit from radical political or economic change, unless the effects are territory-specific, or the regional party happens to be in a particular advantageous starting position. For example, the *Lega Nord's* criticisms of the Italian state as a nest of cronyism and corruption were given credence by the gift (in political terms) of the concurrent launch of judicial investigations into exactly the same allegations.

Cultural and socioeconomic factors therefore tend to combine to engender territorial difference. Regional spaces exist on the basis of structural factors that facilitate the creation of territorial cleavages which cross-cut other cleavages within the larger nation-state. It is the cross-cutting nature of this cleavage that lends the region/nation its unique status. Citizens of the regional space recognise the boundary of their core territory, even if this is only implicit (as is the case in Northern Italy) and non-institutional. A clear set of cultural variables tend to be evident, distinguishing the regional space from the larger nation-state, often leading to the creation and reproduction of a unique territorial identity. This sense of 'uniqueness' becomes amplified if it is reinforced by clearly definable socioeconomic differences - in terms of either advantageous or disadvantageous economic positions vis-à-vis the larger state. It is these regions where regional identities are strongest and regional spaces most pronounced.

Agency factors in the mobilisation of regionalism

Having seen how structural variables contribute to the creation of regional spaces, we turn to the role of agents in making sense of these variables within the political process. Regionally acting agents within the political process exhibit a number of characteristics that differentiate them from the 'national' parties and enable them to exploit the regional uniqueness characterised by the cultural and socioeconomic variables discussed above.

Party Leadership

Groups of regional elites have to translate the concept of difference into understandable language in order for the citizens of a region to become aware of their 'differentness'. A conscious or sub-conscious regional identity will not prove strong enough to provoke political expression at the regional level if the elites within the region do not make the case for treating it as a salient electoral issue. The manifestation of a territorial cleavage within a nation-state's society has to be made to be the key mobilisational variable in the battle for votes, otherwise regional issues will remain just one set of arguments amongst many. Elites need to create a regional or nationalist reinterpretation of a past history, of an economic situation, or of some other form of territorially salient issue, before presenting it to the populace in an accessible way.[97] It can be, of course, that regional elites try to do this but fail as a result of a lack of enthusiasm from the region's indigenous group. But unless there is a political elite acting on regional uniqueness, the symbols, sentiments and characteristics discussed above are highly unlikely to shape voting behaviour.

Although it is by no means essential for one prominent individual to fulfil this role, it is noticeable that personalities like Sabino Arana y Goiri in the Basque County, and, more recently, Umberto Bossi in Italy, have had a profound influence on their regional movements. Charismatic and multifunctional leadership (in that one person takes on many of the most important functions within a regional party) frequently occurs in the nascent period of nationalist/regionalist party development – something that is most visible in Catalonia, where Jordi Pujol still remains a dominant figure in the CDC.[98] Frans van der Elst, one of the founding fathers of the *Volksunie* in Flanders, also dominated his party for over twenty years, while Plaid Cymru changed profoundly under the 36-year tutelage (1945–1981) of Gwynfor Evans.[99]

Robert Harmel and Lars Svasand have defined the initial stages of party development as requiring a leader who can successfully combine and apply creative, communicative and charismatic skills. Regional parties demand these characteristics in particular because of their general need to generate a broad ideological appeal. The characteristics that Harmel and Svasand identify enable the leader and the party to shape and communicate the party's message effectively, and a large number of regional parties have been the beneficiaries of such a form of leadership.[100] Yet, as and when parties develop and stabilise, the nature and style of leadership often changes.[101] As the first, charismatic, leaders vacate their positions the regional movement has to remain organisationally strong, strategically focused and united (factionalism must be avoided), ensuring that the party does not lose sight of its goals and avoids a descent into internal conflicts of direction and ideological outlook. This is what Harmel and Svasand describe as the second stage of leadership. The third stage is one of gaining credibility and reliability, particularly in terms of coalition formation and, where applicable, governmental performance. It is not inconceivable for leaders to see their parties through all three of these phases. De Winter, for example, claims that the founders of *Rassemblement Walloon*, the *Front Democratique des Francophones*, *Plaid Cymru*, the *Lega Nord* and the *Convergéncia i Unió* in Catalonia were all still in leadership positions as their respective parties reached the stage of *Regierungsfähigkeit* (the ability to govern).[102]

While all parties need effective elites, they are of particular importance for regional parties. The regional party elite has to convince the public at large that they have a cultural or territorial identity worth politically expressing over and above other societal identities. Arana is probably the most successful example of this: he even managed to invent many of the key components of mythical Basque nationhood (the nascent nation's name, flag and national anthem). It is imperative that elites demonstrate to the wider electorate why, and how, the centre is 'discriminating' against the region in question by offering regionally specific answers to the questions that they themselves very often force on to the political agenda. Leaders embody the very nature of the project by being charismatic, visible and intellectually sharp.

Party organisation

To better mobilise regional uniqueness, regional parties tend to display flexible, decentralised organisational structures. Following on from this, decentralised party structures tend to facilitate the prioritisation of *policy* over *office holding*.[103] Kaare Strom argues that the more that decision-making within a party is decentralised, the greater will be its prioritisation of the defence of policy positions, rather than pragmatic attempts to achieve governmental participation. Structures designed to give the grass-roots membership a sizeable say in deciding a party's policy will be likely to constrain its elite's scope for adopting electorally optimal policies (and thus maximising their chances of achieving office). They are also likely to attract more activists to the party in the first place.

Regional parties have displayed a marked tendency to have decentralised organisations even if this is still under the tutelage of one charismatic and respected leader. Regional parties see the necessity of increasing their 'embeddedness' within their region, and as such place greater value on a motivated and enthusiastic membership than do non-regional parties. Hence, they tend to be stronger at traditional campaigning (i.e. door-to-door canvassing, manning information stands and so forth) and their membership tends to have more opportunities to take part in party activities and to fulfil representative functions. In the Basque Country, for example, the PNV has explicitly stated that all of the decisions that are taken within the party are to be made with the principle of subsidiarity in mind.[104]

Party structures, therefore, tend to be horizontally organised, as they attempt to maximise political gain by involving as many members in positions of responsibility as possible. Such an open and flexible party organisation, with the increased possibility of formal political participation on all levels of the hierarchy, also produces a high level of political commitment. It has become a trait of regional party activity that activists are highly energetic, motivated and visible (if often inexperienced).[105] Hence regional parties often give the impression of being nearer to the citizen than other parties, relying on an active and enthusiastic membership to push a uniquely regional policy line.

Regional parties often embed themselves into the regional culture by being active in other societal groupings. In regions, for example, where the indigenous language is perceived as being under threat, regional parties will seek to infiltrate and support pressure groups that defend it. Where regional identities are strong, regional parties will seek to 'spread their net' over a wide variety of regionally specific organisations, so as to contribute to the broad civic and cultural life of the region. This is particularly true where parties have a large number of cultural nationalists, but it is also evident in areas where 'political nationalism' remains dominant. If regional identification exists, regional party activists realise that they will be the only ones actively articulating this in the political arena – and a network of aligned groups within society ensures that the articulation of this message is clear, widely heard and inclusive.

Party policy

Although all political parties have policies and strategies, it is noticeable that regional parties frequently stress the importance of a coherent and relatively narrow set of 'core' territorially specific policies. In contrast to other major parties, who tend to mobilise along nationally important societal cleavages, regional parties clearly take advantage of cleavages that either *divide* or *differentiate* the region from the national whole. This can be done in many different ways; the key territorially-specific pillars of a regional party's programme often generate the electoral and activist base on which the party is built.

'Core policies' are therefore very important to regional parties. The *Front Democratique des Francophones* (FDF) is perhaps the best example of this, as it has been politically successful on the basis of one particular core idea – the defence of the interests of the Francophone residents of Brussels. The FDF was formed in 1963 with this sole purpose in mind. It enjoyed a meteoric rise in popularity in the late 1960s, when it rose to be the strongest party in Brussels. Since the mid-1980s, however, it has attracted less popular support (although its voter base does remain stable) – generally around the 11–12 per cent mark. Although the FDF's voters are spread over many ideological and religious groupings, ensuring that its support remains noticeably heterogeneous, it holds together because of the bond of its one common goal.[106]

Other regional parties also display a core group of regionally specific policies that distinguish them from other (national) political parties. They can be based on the claims of cultural nationalists or they can be socioeconomic in nature, as in the case of the LN, or of course an amalgam of both of these. The programmatic direction of regional parties is, however, inherently place-specific in nature, even if, as a result of governmental participation, they are also forced into holding positions on 'national' areas of policy (as happened in Belgium). The *Volksunie* and RW also, if from a somewhat wider political platform than the FDF, articulate key policy concerns on the subject of language recognition (for the *Volksunie*) and the defence of cultural rights in a linguistically divided state.

Concluding remarks

This chapter has seen the creation of a typology consisting of two parts, suitable for conceptualising the structural determinants of political regionalism and the agency variables behind the mobilisation of this in the political arena. Furthermore, it has placed the typology within the context of other ideas on political regionalism, as well as connecting to debates on the reasons for, and position of, regional parties within broader questions of party system formation and change. The first part of the typology conceptualises what is meant by the term regional space and illustrates how cultural and socioeconomic variables come together to create cross-cutting territorial cleavages within a larger nation-state. Chapter four applies the typology to the eastern German case to explain the cultural and socioeconomic differences between eastern and western Germany.

The second part of the typology illustrates the manner and means that regional parties employ to mobilise territorial uniqueness. The forms of party leadership, organisation and policy that characterise regional parties enable them to give voice to the regional uniqueness picked out in the first part of the typology. Regional parties act as agents in the political process, making specific use of the territorial cleavages that structural variables help to create with a given society.

The development and consolidation of parties representing regional interests is characterised by a multitude of differing, overlapping and often original factors. Regional parties have successfully moulded these into a strategy emphasising territorial differences between region and centre. The party has to construct a form of group identity, or regional identification, in order to create a niche for itself within the political life of that region. It has to use the historical, social, economic, political and cultural tools at its disposal to articulate regionally salient issues that derive from a territorial cleavage in political competition. However, no matter what guise a territorial cleavage takes, a regional 'feeling of togetherness' and an identification with a group and/or region is of paramount importance if regional parties are to be electorally successful.

The second part of the typology is employed in chapters five and six. At the level of both rhetoric and policy, the PDS has been successful as a result of its articulation of unique eastern German sentiment. The typology reveals that the PDS is in a unique position: its political strengths are in the areas where eastern German preferences and attitudes differ from those of western Germans. In terms of party organisation and political rhetoric the PDS is also able to exploit unique advantages (its decentralised party structures, high membership, links to the GDR and so forth), and thrive where other, western, parties are at an immediate disadvantage. Chapters five and six therefore illustrate that, like other regional parties, the PDS uses regionally specific political factors to its advantage. However, before this can be done, we must analyse and characterise eastern German uniqueness; so the next chapter concentrates on illustrating how and why eastern Germany and eastern Germans differ from western Germany and western Germans.

Notes

1 Bartolini and Mair, 1990, p. 57.
2 Urwin, 1985, p. 167.
3 Hogwood, 2000, p. 65.
4 Benz, Crow and Holtmann, 1998, p. 15.
5 Köstlin, 1979, pp. 25–38.
6 Elkins and Simeon, 1980, pp. xi.
7 Pintaris, 1996, p. 29.
8 Knight, 1982, pp. 514–31.
9 An example of this is to be found in the Basque country, where Sabino Arana y Goiri, the founding father of Basque nationalism, synthesised the geographical extension of the Basque land as 'Zazpiak-bat' (seven into one). By this he was indicating that the four provinces on the Spanish side and the three 'départements' in France should be united in the formation of a free Basque homeland. See Conversi, 1997, p. 53.
10 Urwin, 1983, p. 250.
11 De Winter, 1998, pp. 204–5.
12 PDS, 1993, p. 13.
13 PDS, 1998, p. 8.
14 Lane, McKay and Newton, 1991, pp. 125–32.
15 Urwin, 1983, p. 228.
16 Lijphart, 1990, p. 491. While Lijphart may be taking this argument farther than necessary, it is clear that modern-day nation-states are not normally home to homogeneous ethnic groups. For this reason plural societies tend to have minority groups within their national borders. Within Europe, perhaps only Portugal and Iceland can be regarded as anything like exceptions to this rule. See Knight, 1985, p. 249.
17 De Winter and Türsan, 1998.
18 Tarchi, 1998, p. 144.
19 The centre–periphery paradigm may have enjoyed popularity in the last thirty years, but it has not been without its critics. It has been rejected on the grounds that it is relatively simple in its nature and it has only weak explanatory value: centres and peripheries can be perceived as being everywhere, and centres are more than likely to have some sort of periphery attached to them, just as peripheries can often have some form of centre. However, such criticisms tend to be based on an over-expression of geography, to the exclusion of other supplementary ways of conceptualising centre–periphery relations.

What may, in fact, be important are distances in economic, cultural, social, ethnic, political or psychological, rather than geographic, terms. For a fuller discussion of this and other criticisms of the centre–periphery model see Meny and Wright, 1985, pp. 1–9.

20 Flora, Kuhnle and Urwin, 1999, p. 109.

21 It is important to make the distinction between territorial centre–periphery distinctions and those that are based on ethnic–cultural contrasts. One can, for example, talk of an imported proletariat as a 'sociocultural' periphery even though it is resident in a central area. Regardless of whether the terms are used in connection with territories or people, it is important that the geographical content remains visible in some form, otherwise the dichotomy becomes indistinguishable from other societal conflicts.

22 Flora, Kuhnle and Urwin, 1999, p. 104.

23 For a detailed discussion of the meaning of 'regional political cultures', see Simeon and Elkins, 1980, pp. 31–76.

24 Urwin, 1985, p. 162.

25 Meny, 1987, p. 3.

26 Gottman, 1975, p. 29.

27 Meny, 1987, p. 5.

28 This is not meant to imply that proponents of such approaches would necessarily describe themselves as 'structuralists'. On the contrary, it is simply an ontological point on the positions which they implicitly take up within the structure–agency debate – in other words their tendency to privilege structures over agents. See Hay, 1995, p. 193.

29 Agnew, 1981, pp. 275–89.

30 Nairn, 1981. George Hoffman has encapsulated the commonly held perception in this approach by observing that 'modernisation and industrialisation in many multinational societies has an uneven impact on a country's regions and has contributed to regional consciousness'. See Hoffman, 1977.

31 For further analysis see Hechter:, 1975; Hechter, 1985.

32 Ragin, 1979.

33 Nairn, 1981.

34 Hechter, 1975.

35 Wagstaff, 1994, p. 12.

36 Meny, 1987, p. 5.

37 Hay, 1995, p. 189.

38 For a detailed discussion on the nature and types of cleavages with western democracies see Lane and Erikson, 1999, pp. 37–75.

39 Duverger, 1964.

40 Müller-Rommel, 1998, pp. 17–27.

41 Hoffman, 1977.

42 Levi and Hechter, 1985.

43 Rokkan and Urwin, 1983.

44 Newman, 1994.

45 De Winter and Türsan, 1998.

46 Urwin, 1982, p. 426.

47 Lipset and Rokkan, 1967.

48 Bartolini and Mair, 1990, p. 57.

49 See for instance, Dalton, Flanagan and Beck, 1984. For evidence of empirical support of this position see Rose and Urwin, 1975.

50 See in particular Inglehart, 1977.

51 Sartori, 1968; Sartori, 1969; Sartori, 1976.

52 Sartori, 1968, p. 21.

53 Urwin, 1982 p. 429. Urwin does concede that not *all* regional parties result from this period of a state's history. The particular examples that he uses for this are the *Front Démocratique des Francophones* and the *Rassemblement Wallon* in Belgium.

54 Hall and Gieben, 1992.

55 Staab, 1998, p. 127. The term ethnicity is derived from *Ethnos*, the Greek word for 'nation', and is seen as characterising common descent. Objective blood relationships do not necessarily have to exist, rather it is a subjective belief in a common line of descent which helps to define an 'ethnic identity'. It is for this reason, that, in the words of Max Weber, ethnic group identity is unique in that it is a presumed identity. See Weber, 1968, p. 389.

56 See for example Urwin, 1982, p. 428.

57 The Welsh Eisteddfodau, for example, are unlikely ever to take place in the English border towns of Chester, Shrewsbury or Hereford, just as the Scottish Highland Games will not normally be seen in the cities of Carlisle, Newcastle or Durham. They remain cultural events that are intrinsically tied to their territory of origin.

58 The status of Corsica within the French political system, the Northern Irish question within the UK and the Basque problem within Spain are all representative of the uneasy place of historically defined communities within contemporary nation-states.

59 Knight, 1982, pp. 514–31.

60 Smith, 1979, p. 22.

61 Connor, 1973.

62 The term 'Ethnonationalism' originally dates back to writings by Walker Connor in 1973. By this he means 'internal discord predicated upon ethnic divergence' and calls for self-determination by an ethnic group. For more analysis of this concept see Connor, 1973, p. 2; Conner, 1977; Connor, 1994.

63 Greenwood, 1988, pp. 85–6.

64 Raento, 1997, p. 191.

65 Raento uses the examples of the christian-conservative *Union del Pueblo Navarro* (UPN) and its splinter group the *Convergencia de Demócratas Navarros* (CDN) in Navarra, as well as the *Unidad Alavesa* (UA) in Alava. Raento, 1997, p. 192.

66 Colomé and Lòpez-Nieto, 1998, p. 243.

67 Ross, 1996.

68 Keating, 1988, p. 230.

69 Ehrlich, 1997, p. 213.

70 Znaniecki, 1963, p. 85.

71 For an excellent discussion on the origins and development of politics and culture in both the Basque Country and Catalonia, see Conversi, 1997.

72 Hedges, 1988, p. 102.

73 Cultural nationalists had/have no or little interest in achieving an ethnically or culturally homogeneous nation-state. Their interests lay much more in preserving their right to speak a language, to celebrate festivals etc. Political nationalists, on the other hand, saw value in breaking with the centre completely, and creating a nation-state within which such cultural expression could freely find voice. Their political goals were voiced in relation to the centre, and principally in their wish to have nothing to do with it.

74 It is only relatively recently that English has risen to be the main mode of communication of Wales. Philip Jenkins claims that Welsh remained the customary means of communication throughout the nineteenth century; as late as 1890 roughly 60 per cent of Welsh citizens spoke the traditional language. In earlier periods (i.e. the sixteenth and seventeenth centuries) the figure is likely to have been around 90 per cent. See Jenkins, 1992.

75 Hearl, Budge and Peterson, 1996, pp. 179–80.

76 Ragin, 1979, pp. 619–34; Rawkins, 1985.

77 There are numerous works on the history and development of Basque identity and Basque nationalism. See for example Payne, 1975; Clark, 1979; Ross, 1996; Raento, 1997, pp. 191–204; Conversi, 1997.

78 See Ross, 1996; Conversi, 1997.

79 See De Winter, 1998; De Winter and Dumont, 1999.

80 For a particularly good analysis of national sentiment in Scotland and the SNP's place in this, see Agnew, 1985; see also Brown *et al.*, 1998.

81 For an excellent account of the development and current position of the *Südtiroler Volkspartei* see Holzer and Schwegler, 1998.

82 Ruzza and Schmidtke, 1993; Giordano, 1999.

83 Buelens and Van Dyck, 1998.

84 Urwin, 1983.

85 De Winter 1998, p. 216.

86 While this book does not aim to dissect the mobilising forces behind specifically national movements, it is clear that many regional parties refer to themselves as nationalists, and as such the two concepts clearly overlap. The creation of regional and national identities are therefore closely entwined in many sets of circumstances. The external contexts of these identities distinguishes whether they are seen as national (e.g. Wales, Catalonia, Scotland) or regional (Northern Italy, South Tyrol and so on).

87 They are 'contentious' as the route that they take leads the Protestant marchers through predominantly Catholic areas. March organisers claim that the routes are 'traditional' and were originally mapped out when Protestants were in the majority in these areas. Catholics, meanwhile, stress that changing social demographics mean that some of the areas through which Protestants want to march are now overwhelmingly Catholic, and as such the marches take on a triumphalist tone, as they often commemorate historic Protestant victories over Catholics. Subsequently Catholics have often organised counter-demonstrations and have vociferously campaigned for certain marches to be re-routed.

88 The League's symbol became the warrior Alberto da Giussano juxtaposed onto a profile of Lombardia. It is a historical-mythological reference to the oath of Pontida and to the Battle of Legano where the towns of Padania rallied together to defeat the emperor Frederick Barbarossa. See http://www.leganord.org/eng/brief.htm

89 Giordano, 1999.

90 This can find actual articulation in a number of different ways. The SNP and the Reform Party of Canada have stressed the 'centre's' waste of oil reserves, for example, while the Northern League has enthusiastically bemoaned the South's waste of northern taxes. See Patton, 1998, p. 510.

91 Daniels, 1999, p. 77.

92 Putnam, 1993.

93 De Winter, 1998, p. 216.

94 An example of this is the steady change of balance between people living and working in

rural environments, and those living in urbanised areas. Over the course of the twentieth century this change has been unrelenting, but it has not been rapid enough to throw major parties out of sync. In the words of Sartori, the party system has acted as a system of channelment, adapting to changing political circumstances.

95 Conversi, 1997, p. 48.
96 De Winter, 1998, p. 218.
97 Williams, 1981, p. 395.
98 Ross, 1996, p. 498.
99 De Winter, 1998, p. 222.
100 Harmel and Svasand, 1993, p. 74.
101 De Winter, 1998, p. 223.
102 De Winter, 1998, p. 223.
103 Strom, 1990.
104 Ugarte and Pérez-Nievas, 1998, p. 98.
105 Patton, 1998, p. 511.
106 Buelens and Van Dyck, 1998, p. 56.

4

The creation of a regional space and the process of identity creation in eastern Germany

Defining the term 'eastern German identity' is not a straightforward task. The terminology that is invoked can often be complex, even, on occasion, contradictory. Some commentators talk of '*solidarität*' (solidarity), or more specifically of an '*Ostidentität*' (eastern identity) or '*ostdeutschen Wir-Bewußtsein*' (eastern German consciousness), while others prefer terms like '*Trotzidentität*' (identity of defiance), '*Abgrenzungsidentität*' (an identity of demarcation), '*Ost-Trotz*' (eastern contrariness), '*Ostbewußtsein*' (eastern consciousness), '*neues ostdeutsche Selbstbewußtsein*' (new eastern German consciousness), '*Ost Lebensgefühl*' (eastern feeling for life) or simply '*Ostalgie*' (eastern nostalgia) or '*Nostalgie*' (nostalgia). While all of these terms have their merits, it is clear that authors often use a particular term to highlight specific elements of the process of identity creation in which they are interested. This makes the task of pinning down precisely what eastern German identity is exceptionally difficult. Furthermore, as Rolf Rießig has pointed out, an appreciation by an eastern German that he or she is from the eastern states is by no means tantamount to saying that the concept of an eastern German identity is monolithic. As he puts it:

> When measured against the Federal Republic as a whole, the East is a specific social and communication area. In this sense it is a relative entity. This is, however, the only common denominator that binds the East together. It is different to the West.[1]

Socialisation and situation

The 'we' feeling in eastern Germany stems from the collective experience, and the socialisation effects, of having lived under the SED dictatorship in the years up to 1989. This is coupled with the situational particularities of living through the transformation from state socialism to capitalism after that date. The eastern German 'identity of defiance' therefore needs to be placed in the context of life *before* 1989, as well as of life *after* unification. As Carsten Zelle has observed, 'it is not only socialisation … (in the GDR)… that has influenced value structures post-1989, but also the present … (economic, political and social) … situation'.[2] Taken together, these two processes have contributed to the creation of a specific regional space, a specific regional culture and a specific regional identity that differentiates eastern Germans from Westerners. As Lothar Fritze eloquently puts it:

> An eastern German identity has arisen out of a combination of typical characteristics from life in the GDR, similar difficulties under new societal circumstances and similarities in interests that have arisen from the dissipation of the euphoria that originally surrounded unification. This identity … is … seen functionally, a protective wall against dreaded social and moral de-classification, as well as a medium of articulation for common eastern German interests.[3]

The processes of socialisation in, for example, the villages of rural Western Pomerania were (and still are) very different to those of citizens in industrial Saxony. The level of education that a citizen receives will also play a role in shaping values, just as different generations may have considerably different beliefs, values and attitudes on account of their life experiences. This is particularly true when one remembers that an 80-year-old eastern German pensioner will have experienced the social, political and economic uncertainty of the inter-war years, twelve years of Nazi dictatorship and the Second World War, the life and death of the GDR and the transformation processes that followed unification in 1989. Eastern Germans do not, therefore, have a uniform set of opinions, values and attitudes.[4]

Carsten Zelle has illustrated this by demonstrating that certain groups within eastern Germany are affected by the two processes of 'socialisation' and 'situation' in different ways. Former servants of the GDR regime, as one would perhaps expect, have much stronger socialist tendencies than other eastern Germans, and as such tend ideologically much more towards the PDS.

This link is further strengthened if they have been exposed to unemployment after 1989. However, eastern Germans who had little contact with the disgraced GDR regime, and particularly those who have also been lucky enough to retain their jobs throughout this period, generally remain more 'liberal' in their *Weltanschauung*.[5] Kai Arzheimer and Markus Klein, meanwhile, have illustrated that younger eastern and western Germans (between the ages of 18 and 24) have very similar attitudes, orientations and belief structures. This is particularly true of those who have been well educated, indicating the importance of formal education in installing liberal democratic values.[6] Arzheimer and Klein also observe that older eastern German citizens, who had considerable life-experiences in the GDR (and perhaps beforehand), tend to be much more reticent in their support for democratic institutions, political parties and the liberal democratic order.

Although it is undoubtedly true that eastern Germans are affected by the processes of socialisation and transformation in differing degrees, it is just as clear that the two processes have combined to become a motor of identity-creation as they affect, in some way, the vast majority of all Easterners. Zelle himself states that more eastern Germans than western Germans remain in favour of 'socialism' – and a broad cross-section of the eastern population regardless of economic positions has both more favourable leanings towards socialism and also expects the state to be more active in everyday economic life. This is a direct result of the processes through which Easterners, from all social strata, and of all political persuasions, have lived.

Historical memory and lived experience ensure that every eastern German possesses his or her own GDR within themselves, and this helps to shape and characterise their contemporary perceptions of both their past and their present position within society. For Easterners, the GDR remains the object against which the present reality in the FRG is compared. This remains true for the former industrial worker, the former dissident, the former party functionary and the former Stasi informer. Furthermore, the social integration of Easterners and Westerners since 1989 has not been the process of slow and continuous 'coming together' that most people expected in 1989: instead it has been characterised by what Stephen Kalberg calls 'tension, disjuncture, discontinuity, conflict, contempt, dislocation and discontent'.[7] Western Germans, whether they realised it or not, were unwilling to accept that their understanding of how political, economic and social life in a 'united Germany' was to be conducted should substantially change. They remain(ed) sure of their identity, and saw no need to question any of the underlying tenets of it. For western Germans there tended to remain only Germans – and Germans have the traits and characteristics that they ascribe to themselves as western Germans.[8] It was for eastern Germans to learn how to become like western Germans, not for citizens of both German states to reassess their positions and come together in one new nation-state. Easterners were therefore not expected to continue to display differing cultural and psychological orientations to Westerners.[9] For this reason the rise and stabilisation of an eastern German identity of defiance is often seen as either a continuation of a socialist heritage, nostalgia for the certainties of an expansive welfare state or a conscious rejection of western German norms and values.[10] Misunderstandings and misconceptions of this sort have provided the basis for the invigoration of collective consciousness in the eastern states.

Provocative and stimulating though such analysis is, it is clear that debates around the issue of 'eastern German identity' have tended to take place within a vacuum as far as other works on identity-creation in other regions are concerned. The eastern German case is, for largely understandable reasons, seen as unique and not susceptible to the same kind of studies as other distinctive regional identities. The analytical framework introduced here offers a way of redressing this balance.

Cultural variables

If we choose to define culture as the sum total of ways of living accumulated by a group of human beings, customs, activities and attitudes that are widely understood and transmitted from one generation to another, then elements of a distinctive culture are evident in eastern Germany.[11] As Dietrich Mühlberg puts it, 'it goes without saying that cultural differences irritate ... (the relationship) ... between eastern and western Germans, even if ... (Easterners and Westerners) ... are linguistically and ethnically united'.[12] Before elaborating on what these differences are, it is important to place them within the context of the processes of socialisation that lives in the FRG and GDR offered. When the effects of these processes are interwoven with the lived experience of social, economic, political and psychological transformation in the 1990s, it is clear that the foundations of a unique eastern German social, political and cultural community have been laid.

A set of subjective orientations developed within the GDR in response to the constraints of life there, shaped and re-shaped by conditions under the SED dictatorship. A similar process occurred in the FRG, only this time the norms, values and attitudes of westerners were moulded by a very different political, social and economic system. In the eastern German case, McFalls has described such a process as 'a creative historic, social and psychological response to the structures of real existing Socialism'.[13] However, it is clear that these 'responses' were crafted specifically for life in an authoritarian dictatorship, not a free-market, liberal society. Put in a radically simplified way, the structures (the institutions) that exist in (eastern) Germany today are not a good fit with agents (eastern German orientations vis-à-vis these institutions).[14]

'East German consciousness' in its pre-1989 form had, however, little to do with the concept of the 'socialist national consciousness' that the SED attempted to create, principally because the SED's attempts at manufacturing an East German identity were based on the fusion of two incompatible concepts: class consciousness and national consciousness.[15] But a distinctive 'East German identity' *did* begin to take shape even if it did not necessarily correspond to the official 'socialist national consciousness' that the SED continued to invoke.[16]

After 1989, cultural lag prevented Easterners from embracing new societal norms rapidly, as the adoption of new systems of governance will not automatically cause rapid cultural adaptation to these norms – culture needs time to 'catch up'. The collective post-1989 consciousness that has developed in eastern Germany is an adaptation strategy in the face of the problems and conflicts that unification has helped to crystallise.[17] The collective experience of having to come to terms with new societal contours under capitalism quickly fostered solidarity with neighbours who were experiencing similar difficulties.[18] The euphoria that greeted unification was quickly replaced by disillusionment, as the capitalist FRG proved unable to meet all the demands that the Easterners put on it. These disappointments ranged from high-rates of unemployment and the consequent loss of personal esteem, to the degrading of personal existences in the GDR. Furthermore, in 1990 it appeared that Easterners tended to take the Unification Treaty at its word. Despite the widespread wish for a rapid abolition of the GDR, many Easterners still perceived unification as a coming-together of two states as equal partners in search of a joint future. Easterners soon realised that this was far removed from the truth. Very little from the GDR was seen by western Germans as worth retaining, and East Germany was effectively joining the FRG in much the same way that the Saarland had done in 1957.[19]

Easterners have frequently been described as 'immigrants in their own land'[20] – a reference to psychological orientation rather than physical position. In December 1990 87 per cent of Easterners were of this opinion: by May 1997 this figure had dropped only marginally to around 80 per cent. The West German state expanded to become the all-German state – yet even though the population of *Germany* increased by a fifth overnight, the structures of the new state did not adapt themselves to the demands, wishes and wants of Germany's new citizens. Hence dissatisfaction with the 'ready-made state' quickly ensued.[21] The psychological de-classification of eastern Germans has indeed affected *all* Easterners as it has hit (simultaneously) the upper, middle and lower echelons of eastern society.[22] The upper echelons of GDR society (academia, the military, those who worked for, or were close to, the SED power–centres, the bureaucracy) were almost immediately deprived of the positions they possessed in the GDR, as the state that they had served for many years imploded. Although frequently able to re-build their lives in an economic sense, they remained permanently deprived of the power and privilege that they once possessed in the GDR. In the middle classes (or what can best be understood as middle classes), the industrial and agricultural base of the GDR was crushed by the demands of global competition. Companies that might have been able to restructure, modernise and remain competitive with western firms were also closed down.[23] *FacharbeiterInnen* (craftsmen) and the technically able were, therefore, deprived of their jobs and forced to seek work in industrial sectors where they often had neither the relevant competencies nor experience. At the lowest levels of GDR society the effects of rapid de-industrialisation were obvious as companies were forced to lay off nearly three million people in the course of just over twelve months[24] - throwing out of productive employment, above all, women, those with lower (or no) qualifications, foreigners and the less socially mobile. That many Easterners have since found employment is not the point. Their lives were fundamentally changed overnight and many of the old securities were taken away. Rainer Geißler has conceptualised this by stressing that social mobility in the eastern states has been at best horizontal, but often vertical – and vertically downwards, as the *Absteiger* ('those on their way downwards') have descended from positions of power and influence to lower-ranking positions within German society.[25] Although these processes affected eastern Germans in different ways, it is clear that the vast majority of Easterners experienced a change in their social status in some shape or form.[26]

The complex interaction of pre- and post-1989 combined experiences have seen a significant proportion of Easterners develop a different set of attitudes to those prevailing in the west, ranging across areas such as foreign policy, health and welfare, the role of the state, evaluations of Germany's social and political system, appreciation of German democracy and attitudes to the GDR and its treatment in contemporary discourse. This was so pronounced that the ISDA and Emnid public opinion research organisations explicitly concluded, in 1994, that 'one cannot speak of a levelling out of attitudes across eastern and western Germany', as Easterners' preferences remained very different to those of Westerners.[27] On a number of key issues (although not all) eastern Germans consistently display quantifiably different value preferences than western Germans, and it is as a result of these that a cultural eastern identity exists. The PDS, as chapters five and six illustrate, is uniquely strong in articulating exactly these differences in the political process, therefore filling the 'representation gap'.

The past as the present

The management of memory in the FRG, and particularly in the eastern states, has been one of the most contentious issues in post-unification Germany.[28] The debate has often been tinged with bitterness and recrimination, and Easterners have found themselves having to defend their pre-1989 existences in a way that many never expected they would have to at the time of unification. Easterners have also openly reflected on the characteristics in their past that differentiate them from Westerners, in an attempt to re-legitimise their own lived experiences.

Communicative memory in eastern Germany remains informal, non-structured and inclusive, occurring and re-occurring through the everyday interaction of eastern German citizens. It is an interchange of direct memory of the recent past through the prism of the collective.[29] Cultural memory, the type which much younger eastern Germans are likely to possess, is much less spontaneous than communicative memory, and relies on *perceptions* of the past rather than *experience*. Hence eastern Germans of all ages carry inside their heads vivid pictures and assumptions about all aspects of the GDR, though these 'GDRs of the mind' differ, firstly, from reality, secondly, from the perceptions of other Easterners and thirdly, and most importantly, from Westerners' – a consequence of the last having no or very few linkages to the GDR. One should not consider memories of the GDR as an accurate reflection or photographic image of the past as it really was, but rather as a *re-construction*. Memory is, by its very essence, a creative process,[30] deliberately selective and often refracted and changed by the prism of an individual's attitude to current reality – hence the GDR that Easterners carry and apply in their comparisons of past with present will be unique to them, rather than a universally accepted historical truth. The uniqueness of memory therefore divides Easterners from their western counterparts as it forms a fundamental part of their self-appreciation.

As a result of the lack of an eastern German ethnicity, citizens of the eastern *Länder* do not have an ethnic or national identity to call into their consciousness as a foundation to their feelings as 'outsiders' in the Federal Republic. This has led to a conscious distancing of western Germans, who are perceived as holding attitudes and norms that are at odds with those of eastern Germans. Easterners remain strongly averse to what they perceive as western Germans dictating to them about, firstly, their past and, secondly, how they should lead their lives in the present. In 1995, for example, 97 per cent of Eastern Germans were of the opinion that only those who had lived in the GDR had the right to *mitreden* (voice an opinion) on the subject of what it was like.[31] Easterners are also much more likely to view the GDR in positive terms than western Germans (see table 4.1.). In 1994 only 9 per cent of western Germans thought that the GDR had more good sides than bad, whereas 35 per cent of eastern Germans did so. Even fewer western Germans thought that this was the case in 1998 (6 per cent), while 17 per cent more Easterners thought this to be true (36 per cent). It is also clear that over a third of all eastern Germans still remained of the opinion that the GDR had more positive sides than negative ones. When one also considers that many more Easterners (36 per cent in both 1994 and 1998) thought the good and bad sides roughly matched each other (of westerners, only 18 per cent thought this in 1994, 16 per cent did so in 1998), it can be seen that roughly two-thirds (71 per cent in 1994 and 72 per cent in 1998) of all eastern Germans were not prepared to condemn the GDR as having more bad than good sides. These figures highlight just how the issue of the GDR splits contemporary German society. The extremely defensive mentality of eastern Germans stems from the (perceived) dominance of western German actors within the institutions of the enlarged FRG and Westerners' prominent positions in all decision-making arenas. The institutionalised processes of 'work-

Table 4.1. Attitudes to the GDR in eastern and western Germany in 1994 and 1998 (as per cent).

'GDR had more good than bad sides'

	1994		1998	
	West	East	West	East
Disagree Completely	43	12	50	9
Tend to Disagree	24	15	21	16
Both good and bad sides	18	36	16	36
Tend to Agree	6	22	5	25
Agree Completely	3	13	1	11
Middle Value	2.33	3.21	2.22	3.29

Source: DFG-Projekt 'Politische Einstellungen, politische Partizipation und Wählerverhalten im vereinigten Deutschland 1994 und 1998', in Neller, 2000, p.580.

ing through' the history of the GDR have been very much 'top-down' and dominated by western Germans, and as such Easterners have felt distanced from these processes. Furthermore, the perceived lack of any questioning of the drawbacks and mistakes of West Germany or the present FRG have given the impression that Easterners need to question all aspects of their lives, while Westerners do not.

The *Abwertung* (downgrading) of life in the GDR has prompted Easterners to attack many of the norms that are taken for granted by western Germans. They react to the sidelining of their previous existences in the GDR by bemoaning deficiencies in the western German political, economic and social system and by granting certain institutions and processes from the GDR a much higher status of approval than they ever had before 1989. The GDR's paternalistic welfare state, job security and the lack of unemployment are all highly regarded in retrospect (no matter how inefficient or ineffective they were). The anti-militarist, anti-fascist rhetoric of the SED also appears to have been upgraded into suspicion of NATO and the organisations of the international capitalist system. In response to their perceptions of their political, economic and social inferiority within a united Germany, eastern Germans have regained their solidarity and their identification with, if not pride in, the GDR.

The methods by which unification was achieved and implemented have ensured that western Germans set the parameters for the everyday lives of eastern Germans. This has prompted a *Trotzreaktion* (counter-reaction) in eastern Germany, with over 70 per cent of Easterners believing that Westerners are no longer needed to control and direct the eastern transition process.[32] When the predominance of Westerners in positions of power is coupled with their demographic dominance in the unified state, it appears that a self-perpetuating process has been set in motion, where western Germans dominate political debate throughout Germany. Hence, eastern Germans are keen to blame their current disadvantageous economic situation (lower wage levels and higher unemployment relative to the west) on the method and mode of economic transformation – and implicitly on the western German actors who directed it. Rarely is eastern Germany's economic plight diagnosed principally to be a result of the moribund East German economy that had to be transformed in 1989. Opposition to what is widely perceived as the equivalent of an occupying regime (namely the 'new masters' from western Germany) is therefore common and often intense, just as is the discourse of blaming the '*Wessies*',[33] and such sentiments have risen to form a key part of the eastern German *Trotzidentität*.

Germany and its relationship with the outside world

Attitudinal differences between eastern and western Germans were perhaps most starkly revealed in mid 1999 on the issue of the Kosovo War, when Easterners and Westerners viewed the participation of German soldiers in an international crisis in very different ways.[34] Opinions on the emotive issue of Kosovo may well have been highly charged, but the development of regional differences in opinion on the subject of, for example, NATO and the deployment of German troops in out-of-area activities illustrate that the legacy of the Cold War may be more evident than many analysts initially believed was the case. For example, in 1993, 59 per cent of western Germans favoured *Bundeswehr* participation in internationally controlled missions. Only 35 per cent of eastern Germans did so.[35] By 1996, these figures had dropped to 32 per cent and 19 per cent respectively .[36]

The participation of *Bundeswehr* troops in UN peacekeeping missions has been persistently viewed in much more sceptical terms. The propensity of Germans in the new *Länder* to offer less support to an active *Bundeswehr* is further highlighted if one takes specific policy scenarios into consideration. The debate concerning the placement of NATO and German soldiers in Bosnia was such an issue (see table 4.2).

This would indicate that Easterners tend to possess more negative attitudes and value judgements towards the institutions of the international security framework and particular to Germany's role within it. The increased emphasis on 'peace' and the non-participation of German forces in interna-

Table 4.2. The stationing of *Bundeswehr* troops in Bosnia: 'Do you believe that it is correct that German troops are taking part in the NATO force in Bosnia, or should German troops not be involved?' (September 1995).

	Total	Western Germany	Eastern Germany
I agree that German troops should take part	45	50	25
I think that German troops should not be involved	43	38	64
Undecided	12	12	11
Total	100	100	100

Source: Noelle-Neumann & Köcher, 1997, p.1147

tional military activity have their roots in a general disillusionment with the 'western world' as a result of the harsh introduction to it that many eastern Germans have received, and years of SED rhetoric against the 'aggressive' West.

Eastern German symbols and characteristics

Cultural identification with the GDR has also been demonstrated in other less explicit ways than those touched upon above. Hence, despite the death of the GDR, symbols and characteristics from the pre-*Wende* period have come to form an important part of the eastern German cultural landscape. They take a number of different and varied forms (ranging from novels such as *Am kürzeren Ende der Sonnenalle* or *Helden wie wir*, to eastern German products, and even internet sites dedicated to eastern Germany and the GDR[37]) and are often seen as relatively uncontroversial ways of expressing nostalgic feelings towards a citizen's own past.[38]

Such symbols are also evident in many areas of every-day life. The arguments concerning the trivial (or so one would have thought) issue of the *Ampelmännchen* (the little men who are on the red and green lights at pedestrian crossings) in the mid 1990s came to epitomise the lingering cultural clashes that were evident in reunified Germany.[39] Eastern Germans saw such issues as ideal prisms through which to reject the imposed uniformity that the western German system of bureaucracy and order was often perceived as placing them under. The Trabant, to use another example, is no longer a car that is widely despised. Of the 3.2 million that were produced in Zwickau over the course of 30 years, 1.5 million were, in the mid 1990s, believed to still be on the roads across central and eastern Europe.[40] Once perceived as being destined for rapid extinction, the Trabant has spawned fan clubs and societies all over eastern Germany which celebrate the continued existence of what was once the butt of many western German jokes.[41] Eastern goods in general are sold in numbers that few would have predicted in 1989. Duckenfield and Calhoun do not shrink from describing the renaissance of eastern German products and icons as further contributing to 'the creation of an eastern German cultural identity'.[42] They see the buying and selling of East German icons as an attempt to create and express an independent eastern identity without the need to form costly political organisations and groupings, or submit to existing institutional formulas.[43] Eastern Germans have refrained from exploiting the new institutional structures that have been imported from the West, or the channels of collective action that a nascent civil society offers them, when wishing to articulate dissatisfaction with particular policy choices imposed upon them. Eastern Germans continue to search for, shape and re-shape the norms and values that differentiate them from western Germans, and one sees the peculiar phenomenon of the market acting as an arena in which this regional particularity is expressed.

This stems from the vast differences in the consumer worlds of the FRG and the GDR pre-1989. Having initially shunned eastern products in late 1989 and early 1990 in order to 'Test the West', eastern Germans quickly saw value in reversing this trend as and when they perceived the West as not being all that they had expected. Conrad Lay hints at the fundamentals behind such a phenomenon by observing that:

> The line that divided Germany for forty years was a division into two differing goods worlds. This was not just emphasised in two politically divergent ideologies, but rather in the lowly spheres of everyday life: in food and drink, in Jeans and TV sets, in coffee, refrigerators and gherkins, so in many of the things that cultural historians describe as 'material culture'.[44]

Long before the East was opened up to the West in 1989 and 1990 it was clear that eastern Germans knew and recognised western products, if only through the much-publicised '*Päckchen von drüben*' ('packets from (relatives) over there') and from infrequent visits. The extent of this is naturally somewhat difficult to quantify, but it is estimated, for example, that between 10 and 15 per cent of all the coffee that was drunk in the GDR stemmed from the FRG, illustrating how focused on West German products East Germans could be.[45]

With the fall of the Berlin Wall, Easterners wanted the long-sought-after opportunity to forget their own imitations and alternatives to the genuine western articles. Freedom became something tangible that could be eaten, tasted, smelt, put on, bought and owned. Even goods such as bread, milk and fresh produce were bought from western German producers, and the sales of eastern German goods plummeted. Western German produce was seen as epitomising the Easterners' wishes to forget their own dreary goods and lifestyles, and to start to live as Westerners were doing. These conceptions of western material hegemony did not, however, last long. In concrete terms, this is evident in the wide variety of 'eastern goods' that have since made a comeback. Psychologically, Easterners were totally unprepared for Westerners to be so dismissive of anything that had its roots in eastern Germany – including, of course, almost all products that had been made there. The ambivalence of western Germans towards eastern products came to be seen as an indictment of the hard work, often in trying circumstances, that East Germans had invested in building their lives pre-1989. Hence the idea of 'Test the West' came to an end almost as quickly as it had commenced, and in 1990 eastern Germans started to return to buying their own *Ostprodukte*.

The proportion of eastern Germans preferring to buy goods that are locally produced increased from 67 per cent in 1991 to 82 per cent in 1993.[46] In 1995 a mere 53 per cent of respondents said that they would buy products on the basis of quality and price, whereas 45 per cent said that wherever possible they bought eastern products. Only 2 per cent preferred western German products to eastern German ones.[47] The range of *Ostprodukte* and eastern brand names that have come back onto eastern German shelves is subsequently wide and diffuse – Florena cream, Spee and Fit washing liquids,[48] Rotkäppchen champagne,[49] Spreewald gherkins, Foron refrigerators, Club Cola, Bautzener mustard, Burger crispbread, Nordhäuser Korn (schnapps), f6 cigarettes and Radeberger beer to name but a handful – and the strategies with which many of them are marketed play on the concept of eastern German togetherness and the combined feelings of identity that many Easterners continue to feel for one another. ('Der Osten hat gewählt: Kathi' ('The East has voted: Kathi') is one of the advertising slogans used by eastern Germany's leading producer of *Backmischungen*, explicitly referring to the product's territorial and historical anchorage. Karo cigarettes declared an 'Attack on the taste of unity' in 1991, as they attempted to win back market share from their western German rivals.[50] One of Club Cola's slogans is yet more explicit: 'Club Cola – unser Cola', referring expressly to its past heritage, before continuing 'Von einigen belächelt, ist sie doch nicht tot zu kriegen: Club Cola aus Berlin' ('Belittled by some, but it will not be wiped out: Club Cola from Berlin').[51] This echoes sentiments felt by many eastern Germans – defend yourselves and do not be scared to fight back in the face of western German dominance.

Philip Morris, the biggest producer of cigarettes in the world, employs different strategic approaches in eastern and western Germany. Marlboro is the market leader in the West, while f6 is the most popular cigarette in the eastern *Länder*. As the Philip Morris Press Office in Munich has been quoted as saying:

> F6 stands for the good, and the trusted, from days gone by and helps to express eastern German identity confidently. F6 does not stand for misunderstood conservatism, but rather a piece of eastern German cultural history that is represented through the smoking of this cigarette, something that in the last few years has become a meaningful part of identity formation for the cit-

izens of the new *Länder*. The open and demonstrative identification with one's own taste as the expression of a newly developed eastern German consciousness therefore finds expression in the smoking habits of the citizens of eastern Germany.[52]

Despite the fact that the quality and the methods of production have changed considerably, and that f6 is owned by a world-wide company that has no roots in the eastern states, the powerful emotional message is clear. The cigarette is 'one of ours', and we are pleased about it. The marketing strategy for such products is always similar – the brand name is retained, even if the outward appearance is modernised, while the quality is improved to western standards. Therefore both continuity and tradition are retained, while simultaneously expressing the new *Lebensgefühl* (mindset) of the post-1989 era.[53]

The coffee market is perhaps the most extreme example of Easterners expressing their own territorial preferences. Before 1989 a large amount of coffee consumed in the GDR stemmed from West Germany, yet by the end of 1998 Röstfein GmbH expected that *Rondo!* coffee, the most popular of the GDR brands, would sell over 6,000 tonnes (making it the third most popular brand available in the eastern states).[54] This provides further evidence that the days of western supremacy purely on the grounds of heritage are long over. When questions of subjective quality and taste arise, eastern German products are very much at the forefront of eastern German minds. This does limit the type of regional product to everyday goods and some slightly less common luxuries – but the eastern German realises that his or her choices in the new shopping centres are decisions with clear subjective undertones, and although eastern products have strong historical significance, they are also vehicles for actual opinions.

It has become clear that eastern Germans do not wish to obliterate the GDR totally from their minds. Their present-day picture of it may not match the reality of what it was; none the less, for many it was 'home' for forty years, and as such many eastern Germans have no or little wish to see it completely written out of history. The symbols and characteristics mentioned briefly above are clear examples of how this historical memory is still relevant in identity creation and articulation today.

Socioeconomic variables

The second variable in the typology created in chapter three concerned the importance of socioeconomic factors in helping to foster a territorially specific form of identification and a regional space. It is to the nature of these socioeconomic variables that I now turn.

Economic disparity between eastern and western Germany

Economic dislocation in the East has left the new *Länder* in a weak and, even in the long-term, economically disadvantageous position. This economic difference has contributed to the process of identity formation in the East in that it has left many citizens deeply unsatisfied with the economic *system* within which they live, as it is the economic system that is seen as not responding to the wants and needs of citizens of the eastern states. This alternative development has its roots primarily in the ineffectiveness of the GDR's planned economy, as well as in the secondary strategies of economic transformation adopted in the post-1989 period.

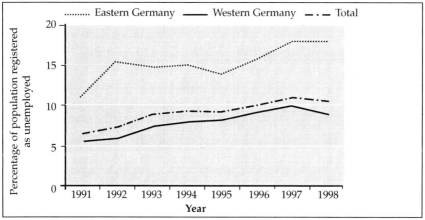

Figure 4.1. Unemployment in Eastern and Western Germany (in per cent). Source: Institute für Arbeitsmarkt- und Berufsforschung der Bundesanstalt für Arbeit (IAB), Kurzbericht, Nr.1/26 Februar 1999, p.11.

Figure 4.1 highlights one of the key basic differences between the economy in eastern and western Germany: the rate of unemployment. Following the collapse of most of the labour-intensive industries that existed in the GDR, the eastern states are afflicted with pockets of severe structural unemployment. The majority of Easterners have, at the very least, been forced to change jobs since reunification, while most have had to suffer periods of unemployment. Given that unemployment did not exist in the GDR, the social and psychological effects of this are amplified greatly as Easterners find themselves unable to enjoy the respect that being in employment is perceived as offering. The promise of economic prosperity is, despite relative increases

Table 4.3. Net income per month in Germany (in per cent)

	Germany		Western Germany		Eastern Germany	
	Per house-hold	Main earner	Per house-hold	Main earner	Per house-hold	Main earner
Under 1,000 DM	1	2	1	2	2	3
1,000 - 1,249	2	3	2	2	3	7
1,250 - 1,499	3	5	2	3	5	12
1,500 - 1,749	3	7	3	5	5	13
1,750 - 1,999	5	9	5	8	6	16
2,000 - 2,499	11	18	10	17	14	24
2,500 - 2,999	12	17	11	18	14	12
3,000 - 3,499	13	13	13	15	16	7
3,500 - 3,999	10	8	10	10	10	3
4,000 - 4,999	15	8	15	9	13	2
5,000 - 5,999	11	5	12	5	7	1
6,000DM +	14	5	16	6	5	—

Source: Noelle-Newmann and Köcher, 1997, p.12

in individual prosperity, widely seen as having been broken, as western Germany continues to enjoy economic affluence that is far greater than that in the East. Table 4.3 illustrates this in terms of net income per month.

The fact that levels of prosperity in eastern Germany are much higher than they were pre-1989 is irrelevant: eastern Germans continue, as they have done throughout the period since unification in 1990, to measure their economic (as well as social and political) position in comparison to *Westerners* and not citizens of the other former state-socialist countries. And it is this direct comparison that leads so many Easterners to be dissatisfied with their economic position within the FRG. Table 4.3. and figure 4.2 illustrate this more precisely.

Dissatisfaction with the outputs of the social market economy has therefore led Easterners to be much more critical of the economic system. This has been conceptualised internally by Easterners in more positive interpretations of socialism and the role of the state, as these notions nominally offer the prospect of greater material security and lower unemployment.

Egalitarianism, socialism and the role of the state

A strong undercurrent of the eastern German cultural identity touched upon above surrounds egalitarianism. Easterners are perceived both as looking back with 'rose-tinted glasses' to the GDR and 'upgrading' a state-socialist system that is now perceived in a better light than it ever was while it existed.[55] The 'upgrading' of certain GDR institutions *should not*, however, be

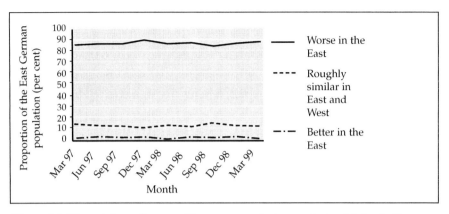

Figure 4.2. The opinions of eastern Germans towards the standards of living in Germany. Source: Emnid: Umfrage und Analyse, Heft 3/4, 1999, p.7.

taken as a form of collective amnesia towards the negative aspects of the SED dictatorship, rather it is a self-interested preference for the social welfare system and security that the GDR (in hindsight) offered.[56] It is for this reason that Easterners tend to aspire towards more social equality and support greater government expenditure on 'social' issues.[57]

Citizens of the western *Länder*, meanwhile, tend to show a heavy predominance towards the values of 'freedom' or 'individualism'. Between 71 per cent and 80 per cent of the population of western Germany said, in 1995, that the concepts of freedom, freedom of speech, *Rechtsstaat* and democracy were very important to them. However, the *Sozialstaat*, social justice and a lessening of the income differentials were regarded by a mere 40 per cent of the western population as being of great importance. The picture in the eastern *Länder* was somewhat different. Between 57 per cent and 61 per cent believed that ideas associated with 'freedom' were very important, while 62–67 per cent regarded the second grouping as being of great importance.[58] The preference for egalitarian ideals has also been reflected in assessments of the concept of 'socialism'. In December 1992 only 22 per cent of Easterners were in favour of socialism in principle, while 49 per cent were against it. By September 1994 the gap had narrowed considerably (33 per cent versus 40 per cent), and by May/June 1998 *more* 'Ossies' favoured socialism than opposed it (41 percent versus 36 percent).[59] In the words of Peter Bender, Easterners remain 'unknowing socialists,[60] as GDR socialisation leads Easterners to demand more from the state than western Germans, to value the egalitarian welfare system of the GDR and to see the virtues of full employment. Despite experiencing real-existing socialism in the GDR,

Easterners have considerably greater appreciation for the ideal of socialism than their western counterparts, and they also associate many more positive facets of life with it. By 1998 as much as 26 per cent of the eastern German population even regarded communism as a positive concept.[61]

A direct comparison between the opinions of eastern and western Germans at the time of the 1994 and 1998 Federal Elections shows that considerable disparities exist in their evaluations of socialism. In 1994 only 21 per cent of Westerners had any sort of positive attitude towards socialism, whereas 58 per cent of Easterners did so. In 1998 these figures had hardly changed, with 22 per cent of Westerners and 59 per cent of Easterners regarding socialism in a positive way.[62]

If one explicitly asks the question within the context of the failed socialist experiment in the GDR, then the differences remain just as apparent. They also remain surprisingly consistent over time, illustrating that their is a clear and distinct ideological divide between Westerners and Easterners over this issue (see figure 4.4). Although Easterners are aware of the (perceived) shortcomings of the contemporary German institutional and political framework, a particular factor is seen as crucial in regard to the fostering of the majority of tensions between Easterners and Westerners: the over-riding dominance of capitalist economic structures.[63] Consequently, Easterners continue to hold attitudes that are socialist in nature – even if Easterners themselves are not necessarily aware of this.[64]

A considerable number of Easterners appear highly sceptical of the ability of the market to solve society's problems. Not only would a majority of

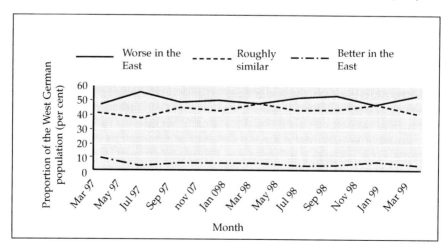

Figure 4.3. The Opinions of western Germans towards the standards of living in Germany (Source: Emnid: Umfrage und Analyse, Heft 3/4, 1999, p.7.)

Table 4.4. 'What could be the correct way forward for Germany? That the state takes a more active role in shaping the economy, or that the individual shows more initiative and initiative is better supported?' (September 1998, in per cent)

Population	Total	Western Germany	Eastern Germany
That the state takes a more active role in the economy	21	15	42
That more personal initiative (*Eigeninitiative*) is supported	64	70	39
Undecided	15	15	19

Source: Segall *et al.*, 1999, p.42.

Table 4.5. 'What is better, companies belonging to the state or companies being privately owned?' (September 1998, in per cent)

Population	Total	Western Germany	Eastern Germany
Companies belonging to the state	13	8	32
Companies being in private ownership	68	76	38
Undecided	19	16	30

Source: Segall *et al.*, 1999, p.43.

Easterners rather see a more active state, but one-third also prefer to see companies being owned by the state: in order, one presumes, to stop their owners from making exaggerated profits (see tables 4.4. and 4.5). This is not replicated at all in western Germany, where only 8 per cent of Westerners prefer to see companies in public ownership. Three-quarters of Westerners prefer firms to be privately owned, compared to 38 per cent of Easterners. The eastern German preference for increased state activity, socialism in general and their feeling that they, as Easterners, are in a position of institutionalised inferiority has lead many Easterners to become particularly critical of what they see as the apathy of the central government in Bonn/Berlin. This is in spite of clear attempts to alleviate economic dislocation in the East through tools such as the *Arbeitsbeschaffungsmaßnahmen* (ABM – Job Creation Schemes), the *Solidaritäts-zuschlag* (solidarity supplement), *Länderfinanzausgleich* (financial equalisation mechanism between *Länder*) and the huge financial investments that have been made in eastern German infrastructure and the eastern German business environment. Easterners still clearly believe that, as a peripheral group away from

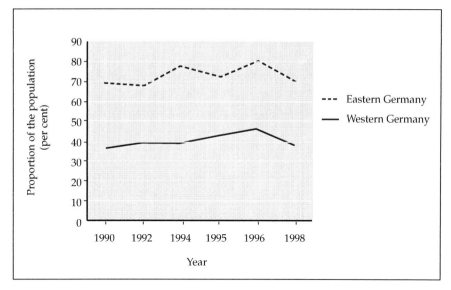

Figure 4.4. Is Socialism a good idea that has been improperly carried out in the past (per cent)? (Source: ALLBUS 1991–1994 and 1998, KSPW-Studien 1995 and 1996.) See Neller, 2000, p. 579.

the 'centre' of western Germany, they suffer because central government is not doing enough to improve standards of living in the East or close wage differentials with the West. Figures 4.3 and 4.4 illustrate this explicitly.

Easterners therefore possess attitudes and orientations that remain largely socialist in nature and egalitarian in their expectation. While freedom is widely accepted as a positive ideal, Easterners stress the need to achieve a greater parity of living standards in the FRG – principally because they see themselves as being the group who would benefit from such parity. The experience of seeing the SED dominate economic, political and social life in the GDR has not dissuaded the majority of Easterners from the view that the state needs to take an active role in shaping the economic environment. This is in clear opposition to the dominant beliefs of western Germans, who have grown up in, and got used to, a state playing a restricted (if still clearly defined) role in economic and social affairs.

Institutional transfer and the uneasy acceptance of democratic structures

Lived experience has led Easterners to distance themselves from the institutions of the Federal Republic. This has become a clear tenet of the eastern

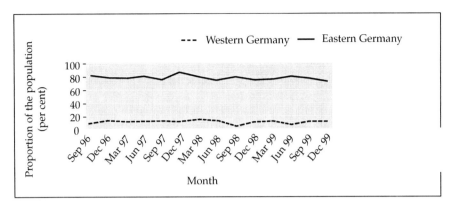

Figure 4.5. In its attempt to achieve equality of living standards in Eastern and Western Germany is Bonn doing too little? Percentage answering yes. (Source: Emnid: Umfrage und Analyse, Heft 3/4, 1999, p.9.)

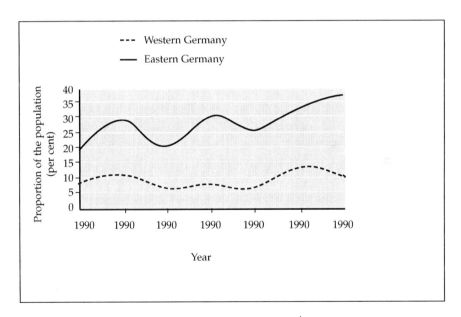

Figure 4.6. Q: is the democratic order that we have in Germany the best way of organising a state ("Staatsform"), or is there another that is better? A: There are others that are better (in per cent). (Source: Noelle-Neumann & Köcher, 1997, p.657.)

German identity of defiance. Institutions and formal organisations of collective action need both to be formally embedded and supported within the broader sociocultural environment – if they are not then there remains the inherent risk of the institutions at best functioning poorly and at worst failing and collapsing (or being replaced) altogether. Political cultures do not change quickly to adapt to new institutional settings. Hence Westerners have, after an initial period of transition, come to view the institutional landscape of the FRG positively, as they grew up with, and got used to, the system over many years. Easterners remain unconvinced about western German democracy, even if they remain supporters of democracy as a system of governance.[65] Western German democracy is not seen to respond and reflect the views and interests of eastern Germans: it is perceived as functioning on a western German agenda. Institutions clearly need to 'grow out' of a given society, and the direct placement of institutions needs to be anchored in traditions, routines, attitudes, expectations and experiences that are not automatically created with the institutions themselves.[66] Numerous public opinion surveys have further confirmed the assumption that eastern Germans have less confidence in Germany's institutions of governance than do Westerners. Such distancing from the institutions of the FRG also has much to do with the expectations that Easterners had when the GDR acceded to the FRG, and the subsequent disappointments when these expectations were not met. The cynicism that many Easterners felt before 1989 has been re-established in their consciousness, and as such Easterners remain sceptical about the ability of the FRG's institutional structures to fulfil their needs. Hans-Joachim Maaz has exhibited the most extreme elements of this by observing that 'instead of Honecker we now have Kohl, rather than the SED we now have the 'Treuhand'.[67] Although perhaps a little excessive, Maaz encapsulates the disillusionment and distance that many Easterners feel towards their new state. The quality of a democracy hinges not only upon citizens' sense of being represented, but also their perception that political elites govern effectively.[68] Only when both of these prerequisites are met will the institutional patchwork of a state be widely supported.

The transfer 'en masse' of the West German institutional system on to the territory of the GDR was the quickest and easiest of the differing processes of transformation to complete. As a result of being able to watch West German television,[69] or occasional visits to West Germany, or perhaps of having relatives in the Federal Republic, many East Germans were surprisingly familiar (even if only at a superficial level) with the societal system and much of what went on in the FRG. Hence, it came as no surprise that they appeared to embrace the newly expanded institutions remarkably quickly. Politically at least, East Germany was effectively annexed by West Germany.[70]

Therefore, like most parts of West German life and culture, the Federal Republic's political parties, pressure groups, trade unions, employers' associations etc. all extended their structures eastwards. Indigenous political development was largely strangled, as western actors and methods dictated the entire process. Contrary to popular belief, as early as 1990 East Germans displayed a reluctance to view the political and institutional framework of the FRG as being perfect. Only 13.2 per cent of Easterners were of the opinion that West German political and societal structures should be transferred en masse to the eastern states, while 82 per cent thought that sections of the West German institutional structure were *Verbesserungsbedürftig* (in need of improvement).[71] In 1992, 65 per cent of Easterners thought that Germany still needed a new constitution, while in 1993 this figure had risen to 72.9 per cent. A mere 3.4 per cent of Easterners thought in 1993 that the *Grundgesetz* in its present form was a sufficient document for Germany in the 1990s.[72] Numerous public opinion surveys have confirmed the assumption that eastern Germans have less confidence than western Germans in democracy as a whole (see table 4.6).[73]

Table 4.6. Q: 'Is the democratic order that we have in Germany the best way of organising a state ("*Staatsform*"), or is there another that is better?' A: Democracy in Germany is the best 'Staatsform' (in per cent)

	Western Germany	Eastern Germany
1990	81	41
1991	77	34
1992	78	41
1993	75	32
1994	79	35
1995	70	28
1997	69	23

Source: Noelle-Neumann & Köcher, 1997, p.657.

The experience of Western Germans with democracy is much more positive. Westerners tend to associate it with both freedom and material prosperity. Easterners *do not* see the western German democratic order, imposed as it was from outside, as being the optimum mode of governance. They do not tend towards rejections of democratic systems *per se*, as the experience of a highly non-democratic form of rule remains too close at hand. They are, however, clear in their belief that the German model of governance needs an overhaul. Culturally distinct suspicions of political elites tend Easterners towards more direct forms of democracy, just as Easterners are eager to achieve more 'economic democracy' (in the sense of increased representation of the working classes at the workplace).

There are also clear differences when the issue of the *Gesellschaftsordnung* (the social order) is analysed. Eastern Germans remain persistently less-satisfied with the social order within the FRG, as table 4.7 illustrates. In 1993 only 4.9 per cent of eastern Germans were 'very proud' of Germany's democratic institutions, as against 18.5 per cent of westerners. Meanwhile, 32.6 per cent of easterners were either 'not at all proud' or 'mostly' not proud of such institutions. Only 14.9 per cent of westerners fell into these two categories.[74] These figures reveal that eastern Germans are neither as appreciative of the political system as they were when East Germany vanished, nor when taken in comparison to western Germans. The dissatisfaction with the political model of government in Germany today acts as an identity creator, in as much as sentiment in the East follows a broad, underlying, less positive attitude towards the political system than is the case in western Germany. This does not imply that the current institutional system needs, from an eastern German point of view, to be overthrown – rather that new, specifically eastern German concerns have to be suitably addressed in order for wider acceptance to follow. Politically articulating dissatisfaction with the transformation process has been difficult for all of the parties that stem from West Germany. Eastern Germans often seem to be passive observers of a polity and economy that they perceive to be following an agenda dominated by western Germany. This agenda stems from the numerical superiority of western

Table 4.7. Do you agree with the following statement? 'I am convinced that our society is heading towards crisis. The political process is not going to solve these problems. We will only be able to do that if our political system fundamentally changes.'

	Agree	Disagree	Undecided/Do not know
Population	43	33	24
Western Germany			
1986	16	61	23
1988	25	48	27
1995	30	50	20
1997	39	36	25
Eastern Germany			
1995	41	36	23
1997	59	18	23

Source: Noelle-Neumann & Köcher, 1997, p.652.

Germans just as much as their prominence in many positions of influence. Western political parties are often, therefore, seen as being part of the problem. Trust in the political parties in the eastern states is particularly low: the work of Fuchs and co-workers shows that, on a scale of −5 to +5, parties recorded a score of −1.26 in 1993, rising marginally to −0.5 in 1995. In the western staes, however, levels of trust are much higher (-0.52 in 1993, rising to +0.07 in 1995).[75] Data published by Emnid also reveals that not only do Easterners have lower levels of trust in institutions and organisations in the Federal Republic (table 4.8.), but those Easterners who express such sentiments most clearly are more likely to vote for the PDS. PDS supporters distrust *all* German institutions to a greater extent than the supporters of other parties (with the sole exception of trade unions: PDS members' trust marginally exceeds that of CDU and FDP members). Chapters 5 and 6 illustrate how the PDS reflects such sentiments in its political work.

Electoral behaviour in eastern Germany: the stabilisation of a regional party system

How are such regional differentiations reflected in the nature of the German party system? Empirical research into the electoral behaviour of the Easterners whose opinions and attitudes differ from Westerners reveals that the PDS has indeed come to take up a very particular representative function in eastern Germany. The PDS is not, by any means, the only visible difference

Table 4.8. Party preferences and trust in institutions: percentage of party supporters expressing trust in the given institution (September 1999)

	CDU	SPD	FDP	B'90	**PDS**
Bundestag	53.8	47.8	31.9	59.3	**28.4**
Police	85.5	80.5	62.5	76.5	**56.8**
Parties	24.4	26.7	15.5	15.1	**10.5**
Trade unions	49.5	63.7	46.7	56.6	**51.8**
Constitutional Court	84.2	72.9	84	82.6	**58.8**
Federal Govt	40.5	41.5	22.1	45.5	**18.0**
Justice system	76.7	63.8	63.2	67.1	**38.8**
Army	86.3	72.6	61.2	58.8	**46.9**
Verfassungsschutz*	71.5	63.7	55.9	65.7	**16.6**
Companies	56.5	48.0	64.1	44.9	**17.8**

Note: * Office for the Protection of the Constitution

Source: Emnid: *Umfrage und Analyse*, 11/12, 1999, appendix.

between the eastern and western German party systems. The presence of the DVU in two eastern legislatures and the virtual non-existence of the FDP and B90/Greens has ensured that three 'relevant' (in the Sartorian sense) parties are evident in the six eastern legislatures.[76] This is in stark contrast to the ten western legislatures, where the PDS has not managed to achieve representation in any *Land* parliament, and the FDP and Greens (and occasionally the Republicans and DVU) consistently fight to achieve more than 5 per cent of the popular vote. The existence of two different 'regional party systems' has therefore ensured that the nature of party competition and party interaction is very different in eastern and western Germany.[77]

The reasons for such a differentiation lie in the inability of the western parties to incorporate the characteristically eastern German attitudinal and value positions into their political platforms. Yet many authors who posited social-psychological models of electoral behaviour around the time of the *Wende* hypothesised that, as the two Germanies came together, the western parties were likely to exploit what was expected to be virgin electoral territory in the eastern states and so come to dominate political activity there.[78] Even though Easterners had had no direct experiences of the western system of political interest articulation, and eastern German society was not likely to present the mosaic of cleavages that shaped western German political and electoral competition, the western parties were clearly convinced that they could cultivate such unfamiliar terrain to their advantage.[79] If they had succeeded in doing this, the West German party system would have simply expanded and become the 'German party system'.

Following the *Volkskammer* elections of March 1990, and certainly after the Federal Election of December 1990, it did appear that the initial predictions that the western parties would be able to successfully move eastwards were largely proving to be correct. At these elections eastern Germans gave the impression that they had quickly and easily aligned themselves to the contours of the West German party system. Although Alliance 90 and the PDS survived the expansion of the western party organisations, their presence did not have any significant effect on the nature of the party system that developed. A combination of 'quasi-party identification'[80] with the western parties, fostered both by limited exposure to the western political system before 1989 and the effective profiling of the former *Blockflöten* (the CDU and the predecessors of the FDP) in 1990, had assisted Easterners in coming to terms with the western political system and in making sense of their new environment.[81]

Initial elections, therefore, indicated that the western parties had indeed been able to channel the interests of the former citizens of the GDR into their political platforms. The prospect of economic affluence, representative democracy and individual freedom was widely perceived as being sufficient to anchor the western parties in eastern German civil society. However, the western parties were unable to continue setting the agenda and articulating the concerns of eastern Germans in the fashion that these initial developments had led most analysts to predict. Easterners soon came to resent the dominance of these foreign bodies in their political landscape, particularly as it became clear that the socioeconomic features that had developed over years in the West had not been 'mechanically transferred' to the East.[82] Popular disillusionment with the political process (or *Politikverdrossenheit*) subsequently became a widespread phenomenon across the eastern states.

Russell Dalton argued as late as 1996 that Easterners remained in a state of pre-alignment rather than one of genuine alignment.[83] Electoral volatility remained (and remains) higher than in the West (see below), as Easterners appear more prepared to vote for the party which they perceive to best represent their interests at a given time.[84] Detlev Pollack and Gert Pickel claim that in 1998 only 56 per cent of eastern Germans saw themselves as 'psychologically attached' to a party, whereas 72 per cent of Westerners did so.[85] Jürgen Falter, Harald Schoen and Claudio Caballero forward slightly different figures, but never the less make the same point when they claim that in 1998 37.8 per cent of eastern Germans had no party identification whatsoever (compared to 26 per cent in western Germany). Their survey analysis also highlights that not only do fewer Easterners have strong or very strong party identifications (24 per cent versus 32.4 per cent in western Germany), but that the length of time that citizens possess such orientations is much shorter in the eastern states than it is in the West. Given that citizens of the GDR had no (or little) direct contact with the western German political parties before 1989 and that party identifications take significant time to develop, this should in itself not be too surprising, but the fact that only 24.4 per cent of Easterners (compared to 55.9 per cent of Westerners) possess sustainable party identification over 'many years' indicates considerable psychological differences are still very much in evidence.[86]

Over the course of the federal and state elections of the 1990s Easterners therefore developed sustained patterns of electoral volatility. This is illustrated by the fact that in 1998 31 per cent of Easterners (compared to 21 per cent of Westerners) voted for a different party than they had done in the previous Federal Election (in 1994).[87] Despite these tendencies, PDS supporters are more likely than other parties' supporters to be constant, and to remain so over a longer period of time. Over the course of the 1990s support for both the CDU and the SPD rose and declined in alarming (for the parties concerned) fashion. The CDU, in particular, suffered heavy losses in eastern

Germany in the late 1990s, with a mere 58 per cent of those who voted for it in 1994 chosing to do so again in 1998.[88] At the 1998 Federal Election the CDU vote was down 15.3 per cent in Saxony, 12.1 per cent in Thuringia, 11.5 per cent in Saxony Anhalt, 9.3 per cent in Mecklenburg Western Pomerania, 7.7 per cent in Berlin and 7.3 per cent in Brandenburg.[89] Even the SPD, despite its considerable gains in eastern Germany in 1998, actually polled fewer votes in Brandenburg than it did in the 1994 Federal Election.[90] The PDS, meanwhile, has maintained a solid bedrock of support over this entire period. In eastern Germany at the end of 1990, 35 per cent of PDS voters defined themselves as 'committed party voters', while only 15 per cent of CDU and 11 per cent of SPD voters regarded themselves as such. The Alliance 90/Greens (30 per cent) and the Republicans (27 per cent) had more committed supporters than the two main *Volksparteien*.[91] By 1993, 62 per cent of PDS supporters regarded themselves as having a strong party identification, while only 36 per cent of CDU voters and 24 per cent of SPD voters saw themselves so.[92] At the 1998 Federal Election the number of PDS supporters with a strong and durable party identification remained largely unchanged (61.7 per cent) – ensuring that the PDS remained, by a considerable distance, the party with the most loyal support in the eastern states.[93] The 1998 election also illustrated that the PDS is able to attract voters from *all* other parties, not just the ideologically adjacent SPD (from whom the PDS garnered an extra 80,000 votes) and the Alliance 90/Greens (who saw 40,000 voters leave them for the PDS in 1998[94]): the *90,000 CDU voters* who shifted to the PDS between 1994 and 1998 are striking testimony to this.[95]

Despite the large increase in the SPD's proportion of the vote at the 1998 Federal Election, the PDS still *retained* a higher percentage of voters than the SPD did. Eighty-two per cent of those who voted for the PDS in 1994 did so again in 1998, while only 80 per cent of SPD supporters remained loyal – a fact that, when the impressive expansion of SPD support is taken into account, highlights just how steadfast the PDS's voter base remains. As Infratest Dimap observed after the state elections of 1999, the PDS, in stark contrast to both the SPD and the CDU, has a large, committed and enthusiastic group of supporters, making it a strong and resilient political opponent in the eastern states.

> The PDS is not only ideologically anchored in eastern German society, it is also sociologically and organisationally rooted there. The relationships of (eastern) voters to the western German parties are rather more unstable, and traditional loyalty to a particular party plays a less important role in dictating voter support.[96]

The PDS is not seen as part of the western-German-dominated political system – and so has been able to mobilise support as a part of eastern German society. 'Virulent' disappointment with 'western Germany, with the Federal Government and with Bonn politics' enables the PDS to politically articulate the dissatisfaction with parts of the transformation process, just as the PDS can concurrently defend life pre-1989.[97] These were not issues when the western parties competed in the original elections after unification in 1990. The new and different electoral market that the processes of socialisation and transformation have brought about is ripe for exploitation by a home-grown party that can mobilise such territorial uniqueness. Whereas in previous years disenchanted voters chose to abstain from the electoral process, the 1998 elections illustrated an increased willingness to actively engage in politics. While turnout at the 1998 election remained marginally lower in the East (80.1 per cent) than in the West (82.8 per cent), this represented a 7.5 per cent increase on the 1994 figure.[98] And the PDS was able to benefit from this, as 44 per cent of its voter increase between 1994 and 1998 came as a result of a successful mobilisation of previous non-voters.[99]

A third of Easterners changed party preference between 1994 and 1998, while only 69 per cent of citizens actually voted in both elections.[100] Voters only build up party alignments over time, as they perceive a party to be consistently representing their interests. This is usually the case as cleavages stabilise within societies, and as parties mobilise alongside them. Those societal cleavages in eastern Germany that are familiar to western eyes (for example, socioeconomic, religious or ethnic) are still very shallow, and seen to be far less significant than the territorial one between East and West – a perception from which only a specifically eastern German party can benefit. The political environment in eastern Germany is characterised by a markedly high degree of secularisation. While over 60 per cent of western Germans regard themselves as being a member of one of the Christian denominations, less than 30 per cent do so in the eastern states. This has (had) key repercussions for the CDU in particular, as it has traditionally relied on a religious (and especially Catholic) base of support.[101] While it is true to say that those Easterners with religious beliefs still tend in large numbers towards the CDU, it is clear that this does not lend the CDU the structural advantage that it has traditionally benefited from in the western states. Conversely, the atheist heritage of the PDS has prevented it from garnering the support of Christians all across Germany, and at the 1998 Federal Election only 1 per cent of Catholics and 2 per cent of Protestants voted for the party. However, 16 per cent of Germans with no religious denomination gave their second vote to the PDS in 1998.[102]

Reinventing eastern German self-understanding

In summary, the differences in attitudes and perceptions that are evident between eastern and western Germans have prompted Easterners to distinguish themselves *consciously as Easterners*, and have helped to grant the divide between eastern and western Germany an unanticipated political salience. Within the context of socialisation in the GDR and the experiences gained in post-1989 Germany, cultural variables have come to play an important role in shaping the eastern German identity of defiance. This has affected a number of key areas: Easterners have, for example, quantifiably different attitudes to the past, and particularly to life in the GDR and to 'what it was really like'; they remain sensitive to what they perceive as judgmental attitudes by Westerners, and are disappointed by the apparent willingness of western Germans to erase the GDR from memory. This leads them to retrospectively upgrade a number of aspects of life in the GDR that they previously did not perceive as being of particular importance.

In cultural terms, the most 'proactive' rejection of western German norms can perhaps be seen in the rejuvenation of unique eastern German symbols and characteristics. These range from the defence and preservation of small and relatively unimportant icons from GDR times such as the *Ampelmännchen* or the Trabant car, to explicit attempts to support, through the prism of the market, uniquely eastern-German products in the all-German market place. The rejuvenation of brands once explicit to the GDR has subsequently been surprisingly widespread and successful. Socioeconomic differences between the eastern and western states are also important contributory factors in the stabilisation of an eastern German identity of defiance. Even the most cursory glance at the economic statistics reveals that eastern Germans are, in comparison with western Germans, more likely to be unemployed, more likely to earn less and endure a lower standard of living. However, it is not just the bare facts of the economic situation that act as a motor of identity-creation: more important still is the widespread perception of economic inefficiency and uncompetitiveness that Easterners regard as existing in the eastern states. Even those Easterners who consider themselves as having profited from unification, and the transition to a market economy, still to tend to view their general situation as being much more negative than it actually is. Furthermore, this imbalance appears likely to continue into the foreseeable future, as the eastern German economy and eastern standards of living remain behind those in the West. The importance of this economic cleavage is magnified because eastern Germans entered the FRG with the explicit expectation of 'living like Westerners' – and, although the majority of eastern Germans are wealthier than they were in 1989, they have not achieved economic parity with western Germans. When this is combined with the widespread social dissatisfaction caused by the perceived *Abwertung* (downgrading) of pre-1989 eastern German life, it is clear that latent potential exists for a different set of political interests to be articulated.

Differential economic performance has prompted Easterners to support policies that offer greater egalitarianism within Germany today. The value of individual freedom remains important, but there is an increasing perception that more emphasis needs to be placed on equality. Such support for egalitarian ideals has contributed to an increased appreciation of the concept of socialism in the eastern states. Citizens are broadly supportive of a more increased role for the state in orchestrating and controlling economic activity. All of these characteristics stem from a complex combination of socialist values and the uncertain transformation process. Chapters five and six outline how the PDS has created a role for itself as the articulator of these differences within the political arena.

Notes

1 Rolf Rießig: 'Der Osten will nicht verachtet werden', in *Die Tageszeitung*, 23/24 May 1998.
2 Zelle, 1998b, p.34. For a more detailed review of these positions see Neller, 2000, pp.575–6. See also Grix, 2000b, pp.109–24.
3 Fritze, 1997, p.107.
4 See Neller, 2000, pp. 571–602.
5 Zelle, 1999, pp. 12–14.
6 See Arzheimer & Klein, 2000, p. 396.
7 Kalberg, 1999, p. 35.
8 Mühlberg, 2000, p. 54.
9 Mühlberg, 2000, p. 47.
10 Probst, 1998, p. 4.
11 It is, of course, unclear what political culture actually is. This is not a debate that this work needs to go into, so for greater analysis of the definitional problems when discussing political culture see Kaase, 1983, pp. 144–71. For a discussion of the concept in the context of German unification see Mühlberg, 2001, pp. 30–38.
12 Mühlberg, 2001, p. 30.
13 McFalls, 1995, p. 140.
14 Pollack, 1999, p. 82; see also Almond & Verba, 1963.
15 McKay, 1998, p. 23.
16 Schweigler, 1975, p. 74.
17 Welsh, Pickel & Rosenberg, 1997, p. 135.
18 Walz & Brunner, 1997, p. 13.

19 Meier, Reblin & Weckesser, 1995, p. 19.

20 The existence of such feelings has been widely documented in both the academic world and the popular press. For a particularly lucid discussion of the issue see Walz & Brunner, 1997, pp. 6–20.

21 Rose & Haerpfer, 1997, pp. 100–121.

22 Vester, 1995, p. 30.

23 Prior to the currency union of July 1990, the *Bundesbank* estimated that between 50 and 70 per cent of eastern German firms could 'survive' the transition to a social market economy. In the event, barely 25 per cent did. This is no doubt due to the optimistic expectations that West Germans had of the East German economy, which was in a much worse condition than the East German figures had led western observers to believe. See 'One Year of German Monetary, Economic and Social Union', *Deutsche Bundesbank* (Frankfurt: Deutsche Bundesbank Monthly Report, July 1991), pp. 18–30 quoted in Padgett, 1992.

24 In October 1990 9.2 million Easterners were in employment, whereas by December 1991 this figure had plummeted to 6.2 million. See 'The Eagles Embrace', in *The Economist*, 30 September 1995, p. 22.

25 This, once again, is not a reflection of *material* circumstances within eastern Germany, but rather subjective self-understandings. It goes without saying that citizens who are unemployed, are on job-training schemes or have taken early retirement (*Vorrüheständler*) have experienced reductions in their standing within society. In 1996, however, Geißler claimed that 83 per cent of all Easterners had experienced a *Niveauwechsel* ('a change in their position within society') that involved them taking a drop in social status. See Geißler, 1996, p. 245.

26 Vester, 1995, p. 30.

27 Ferchland *et al.*, 1995, p. 35.

28 Jan Assman has chosen to stress two distinct ways in which memory is transmitted between societal groups and between generations. 'Communicative Memory' is a shared memory of the recent past. This is obtained through the social interaction of citizens who actively remember the events. 'Cultural Memory', according to Assman, is a formally constructed version of past events – which intrinsically leaves itself open to manipulation by groups within society (for example intellectuals, the media, politicians and so forth); see Assman, 1999. For further analysis of this in the West German context see Gay, 2000.

29 Gay, 2000, p. 8.

30 Gay, 2000, p 12.

31 'Stolz aufs eigene Leben', in *Der Spiegel*: Nummer 27, 1995, p. 49.

32 'Ein neues Selbstbewußtsein im Osten', in *Wochenpost*, 2 October 1996, p. 4.

33 Offe, 1996, p. 180.

34 Differences of opinion between Easterners and Westerners on the issue of the Kosovo War persisted throughout the entire conflict. For detailed opinion poll evidence of this see 'Kritik am Krieg wächst': *Schweriner Volkszeitung*, 31 March 1999; 'PDS: Mehrheit gegen die NATO Angriffe' Emnid survey in the *Frankfurter Allgemeine Zeitung*, 3 May 1999, p. 2; 'Umfrage: Deutsche halten Koalition trotz des Kosovokrieges für stabil', in *Die Welt*, 8 May 1999, p. 4.

35 Ferchland *et al.*, 1995, p. 5.

36 Ferchland *et al.*, 1995, p. 5.

37 Many such sites now exist, but two of the most popular are http://www.ddr-alltagskul-
    tur.de and http://www.ossiverband.de
38 Neller, 2000, p. 571.
39 Duckenfield & Calhoun, 1997, pp. 54–69. For information on the (ongoing) campaign to
    save the Ampelmännchen see http://interactive.de/ampel.html
40 John Dornberg: 'Five Years After Reunification – Easterners Discover Themselves', in
    German Life, December 1995/January 1996 on http://www.germanlife.com/
    Archives/1995/9512_01.html
41 In February 1998 there were still 378,000 Trabants registered in Germany. Of these,
    140, 000 (37 per cent of all Trabants) were in Saxony. This may be because Zwickau,
    where Trabants were produced, is situated in this state. The Trabant does, however, clear-
    ly have fans elsewhere – even North Rhine Westphalia has a registered 4,300 Trabants
    within its borders. See *Berliner Morgenpost*, 23 February 1998. Furthermore, many clubs
    and societies have sprung up in support of the Trabant. According to one (by no means
    all-inclusive) source, 123 such societies exist. See http://www.trabinet.de.
42 Duckenfield & Calhoun, 1997, p. 54.
43 Duckenfield & Calhoun, 1997, p. 55.
44 Conrad Lay: 'Der Siegeszug der Ostprodukte – Zur Mentalitäts– und Produktgeschichte
    der deutschen Vereinigung'. On http://www.oeko-net.de/kommune/kommune1-
    97/tlay197.html
45 'Jacobs Krönung', in particular, took on the status of being the most loved coffee import-
    ed from the West, carrying with it implicitly positive political propaganda.
    http://www.oeko-net.de/ kommune/kommune1-97/tlay197.html
46 'Wehre dich täglich': *Der Spiegel*, Nummer 52, 1993, pp. 46–49.
47 'Stolz auf's eigene Leben': *Der Spiegel*, Nummer 27, 1995, p. 42.
48 Spee and Fit remain the market leaders in the eastern German cleaning substances mar-
    ket. See Ahbe, 1999, p. 89.
49 2.9 million bottles of Rotkäppchen Sekt were sold in 1991. This figure rose to 5.7m in
    1992, to 10m in 1993 and to 17m in 1994. See 'Stolz auf's eigene Leben', *Der Spiegel*:
    Number 27, 1995, p. 59.
50 See Gries, 1994, p. 1049.
51 Lay, 1997, p. 3.
52 Quoted in Lay, 1997, p. 4.
53 Lay, 1997, p. 5.
54 Röstfein GmbH had reckoned that in 1997 they were likely to sell between 100 and 200
    tonnes of *Rondo!* The company were forced to rapidly expand as a result of this renais-
    sance, and in 1997 Röstfein doubled their number of employees from 40 to over 90. See
    'Röstfein Kaffee feiert 90 jähriges Jubiläum': *Röstfein Gmbh*, Pressematerial, 1998, quoted
    in Ahbe, 1999, p. 91.
55 For a particularly thorough analysis of this phenomenon see Welsh, Pickel & Rosenberg,
    1997, pp. 103–36.
56 Mahr & Nagle, 1995, p. 294.
57 Zelle, 1998b, p. 34.
58 Zelle, 1998b, p. 25.
59 Segall *et al.*, 1999, p. 43.
60 Bender, 1992, p. 28.
61 Segall *et al.*, 1999, p. 46.

62 DFG-Projekt 'Politische Einstellungen, politische Partizipation und Wählerverhalten im vereinigten Deutschland 1994 und 1998', in Neller, 2000, p. 580.

63 Kalberg, 1999, p. 39.

64 Koch, 1997b, p. 97.

65 Pollack & Pickel, 1998, p. 17.

66 Pollack, 1997, p. 3.

67 Maaz, 1991, p. 28.

68 Kitschelt *et al.*, 1999, p. 345.

69 The picture that West German television offered East Germans, despite giving them insights into the material prosperity on offer in the Federal Republic and to the state's institutional structures, was later revealed to be inadequate in preparing them for 'die realexistierende Bundesrepublik'. The positive image of material wealth and democratic freedoms was in stark contrast to the economic insecurity and sense of helplessness that eastern Germans found themselves experiencing after 1989. See Gehring & Winkler, 1997, p. 480.

70 Within the West German *Grundgesetz* (Basic Law) two possible mechanisms existed for uniting the two states. Article 146 left the way open for the drawing up of a new constitution, with possibly a new assembly and probably a referendum to pass the document into law. This article was created in the very event of a reunification becoming possible, and gave the impression of two equal partners coming together in one state. However, Article 23 enabled states or territories to 'accede' to the Federal Republic, and this was the route the Saarland took into the Federal Republic in 1957. This method was, effectively, a legal and constitutional annexation, and was the option Helmut Kohl and his coalition partners, many argue to serve their political purposes, used to unify the two countries.

71 See Meier, Reblin & Weckesser, 1995, p. 6 for further analysis and details.

72 When questioned, 22.3 per cent of Easterners were of the opinion that a modified and updated Basic Law was necessary, and that if this took place then the need for a new constitution would be alleviated. Meier, Reblin & Weckesse, 1995, p. 19.

73 For a thorough discussion of this issue see Fuchs, Roller & Weßels, 1997, pp. 3–12.

74 Blank, 1997, p. 43.

75 Surveys 'Einstellungen zu aktuellen Fragen der Innenpolitik' (IPOS), 1991–1993 and 1995. In Fuchs *et al.*, 1997, p. 9.

76 Berlin is the only notable exception to this. The Greens are not politically influential in the eastern part of the city, but their strong presence in western Berlin has ensured that they continue to achieve parliamentary representation in the *Berliner Abgeordnetenhaus*.

77 Hough & Grix, 2001, pp. 159–68.

78 Bürklin & Klein, 1998, p. 168.

79 It is clear that two cleavages have been of particular importance in the Federal Republic: religion and class. See Weßels, 2000, p. 132.

80 Bluck & Kreikenbom, 1991, pp. 495–502.

81 Dieter Roth disputed the existence of 'quasi-party identifications' in the March 1990 *Volkskammer* elections, describing the electoral behaviour of Easterners as 'issue voting in almost its purest form'. However, after the 1990 election the existence of superficial party alignments was widely accepted. See Roth, 1990, pp. 369–93.

82 Weins, 1999, p. 50.

83 Dalton, 1996, p. 44.

84 The proportion of the vote that each of the three main parties receives is also much more variable in the eastern states than in the west. Examples from Mecklenburg Western Pomerania highlight this. In the *Landkreis* of Demmin, the CDU polled 51.7 per cent in the last communal elections, while it only registered 14.6 per cent in Schwerin II. The SPD registered 12.3 per cent in Rügen II, but 48.8 per cent in Wismar. The PDS is also susceptible to this phenomenon, although not to the same extent as the CDU and SPD. For example, whereas the PDS polled 36.4 per cent in Schwerin II, it only managed 16.3 per cent in Mecklenburg-Strelitz. See Dieter Wenz: 'Ein Land für Wählergemeinschaften', in *Frankfurter Allgemeine Zeitung* 12 June 1999, p. 16. For a detailed breakdown of the election results in Mecklenburg Western Pomerania see http://www.mvnet.de/inmv/stala/wahl/kommunalwahlen.htm

85 Pollack & Pickel, 2000, p. 124.

86 Falter, Schoen & Caballero, 2000, p. 247.

87 Weins, 1999, p. 51.

88 Weins, 1999, p. 51.

89 Infratest Dimap, 1998, p. 13.

90 The SPD polled 1.5 per cent less in the Federal Election of 1998 than it did in 1994. Infratest Dimap, 1998, pp. 12–13.

91 von Beyme, 1993, p. 106.

92 Neu, 1994, p. 1.

93 Neller & Gabriel, 2000, pp. 553–5.

94 Infratest Dimap, 1998, p. 36 and p. 42.

95 If just the eastern states are considered, the PDS actually gained 130,000 votes from the CDU. Infratest Dimap, 1998, pp. 36–7. The PDS was able to perform similarly well in eastern German state elections. In Saxony in 1999, for example, the PDS persuaded 48,000 of those who had not cast their vote at all in 1994 to support the party, as well as 42,000 former SPD voters, 21,000 former CDU voters and 13,000 voters from the Alliance 90/Greens. See Porsch (PDS): 'Unsere Zukunft liegt nicht in der Gegenwart anderer Parteien, sondern in einer Partei als Netzwerk demokratischer Bewegung', speech at the sixth *Landesparteitag* of the PDS in Saxony, in *PDS Pressedienst*, Nummer 2, 14 January 2000. See also http://www.pds-online.de/pressedienst/0002/09.htm

96 Infratest Dimap, 1998, p. 11.

97 Infratest Dimap, 1998, p. 11.

98 Infratest Dimap, 1998, p. 21.

99 Of the 430,000 people who voted for the PDS in 1998 but had not done so in 1994, 190,000 came to the party after not having voted at all in 1994. The right-wing parties, having started from a very low starting base, also mobilised considerable numbers of non-voters, as, unsurprisingly, did the SPD, who took advantage of the widespread feelings that governmental change was necessary. See Infratest Dimap, 1998, p. 36.

100 Infratest Dimap, 1998, p. 38.

101 At the 1998 Federal Election the CDU polled 47 per cent of the Catholic vote and 33 per cent of the Protestant vote across Germany. Of those with no affiliation, 21 per cent voted for the CDU. Figures from *Forschungsgruppe Wahlen e. V.* on http://www.aicgs.org/wahlen/elect98.htm

102 See Forschungsgruppe Wahlen e. V.: http://www.aicgs.org/wahlen/elect98.htm.

5

The PDS: mobilising easternness

Given that the social, political and economic differences between eastern and western Germany have taken on such contemporary significance in the country as a whole, it should not be surprising that a regional party has established itself as an articulator of eastern German difference. But, of course, the fact that it is the PDS, the party that grew out of the dictatorial SED, that has come to fill this niche generates not just surprise, but often disgust and derision. The following two chapters aim to show exactly how the PDS has managed, despite such a negative starting position, to mould itself into this role. The leaders of the PDS have skilfully re-shaped the party, making it much more attractive to citizens from all echelons of eastern German society. Despite its ageing membership, the PDS remains in an organisationally advantageous position vis-à-vis its competitors. The PDS has therefore been able to find a niche for itself as the *Anwalt der Ostdeutschen* (advocate of eastern Germans).[1]

Chapters five and six build on the notion that the western German parties have lost the power to set the agenda in the East, and with it their 'control' of the political system. The natural tendency of political parties is to attempt to control the political process by channelling the requirements of diverse groups within society into their programmatic positions. This is a point of key strategic importance to the PDS – new political parties have to wrestle agenda-setting functions away from the 'major' parties in order to create a place for themselves in every-day political discourse. The electoral viability of 'new' parties depends initially on possessing the capacity to exceed the thresholds imposed by the electoral system, and the chances of a new party doing this are greatest when there is a large increase in the size of the electorate, a new clientele emerges, a particular set of events activate an existing social or attitudinal group, and loyalties to (or alignments with) established parties decline.[2]

Leadership

Curiously, the very lack of a clear and definable eastern German regional elite has not hindered eastern Germans from viewing themselves as 'Easterners'. Elites are generally held to be essential players in the mobilisation of regional sentiment and awareness, and to prevent political action being based upon 'national' themes and issues. Charismatic leaders are, therefore, important in ensuring that territory remains a salient issue in political debate; articulate elites tell people just why a regional party is needed within a particular political system. In eastern Germany the reverse has happened. The lack of a group of prominent actors advocating eastern German interests ensured that a vacuum existed in terms of expressing eastern German particularity in the political process. Western German politicians still continue to dominate political life in Germany, and eastern Germans themselves see very few Easterners in positions of power. Easterners tend, therefore, to view elites as a whole as both distant and inherently selfish.

The election of Angela Merkel, from Mecklenburg, to lead the CDU early in 2000 did appear to represent a shift in emphasis Eastwards, although in reality very few Easterners have managed to obtain prominent positions in political, economic or cultural life. Wolfgang Thierse (SPD – the President of the *Bundestag*), and a handful of other party politicians have national profiles, but they are the exception to the rule that sees western Germans remaining in the political ascendancy. Hence 'eastern German elites' remain noticeable very much by their absence.

Be this as it may, political competition in the eastern states is still strongly influenced by personalities – more so than is the case in western Germany. In a society where the conventions of political competition are not deeply ingrained, the importance of personalities in shaping political debate and party competition increases. This has been evident in a number of elections in the eastern states since 1990. For example, the *Land* elections in Brandenburg and Saxony in 1994 coincidentally fell on the same day, and the political and economic environments in the two states were very similar. Yet two different parties registered absolute majorities – results based principally on the positive ratings of their leaders – Manfred Stolpe (SPD) and Kurt Biedenkopf (CDU). Biedenkopf, in particular, was a trump card for the Saxon CDU, enjoying almost unparalleled levels of popularity both in 1994, and in the next state election five years later. In 1999, 71 per cent of all Saxons said that they would prefer Biedenkopf to continue as Saxony's Prime Minister, while a mere 5 per cent favoured his SPD opponent Karl-Heinz Kunckel. An amazing 89 per cent of Saxons were of the opinion that Biedenkopf had car-

ried out his functions as Prime Minister well – 96 per cent of CDU supporters, 88 per cent of SPD supporters and even 82 per cent of *PDS supporters*
were satisfied with his work.[3] Biedenkopf, a largely unsuccessful western
CDU politician of the 1980s, has transformed himself into a Saxon
Landesvater who has come to be associated with the Saxon *Land* itself. His
popularity has much to do with his strong defence of 'Saxon' interests and his
high-profile tussles with western heavyweights such as Helmut Kohl.[4] In the
Brandenburg state election of 1994, meanwhile, Manfred Stolpe was able to
benefit from a similar, if less statistically impressive, wave of popularity.
Eighty-one per cent of all Brandenburgers wanted to see him continue as
Minister President. Stolpe was able to refute allegations that he worked along-
side the East German secret police before unification, profiling himself as an
Easterner fighting against imported western norms and values. His
'Easternness' is subsequently seen very much as an electoral asset. Even at the
September 1999 state election, which took place as the SPD was going
through a period of considerable unpopularity, 58 per cent of
Brandenburgers said that they would prefer *Landesvater* Stolpe to continue as
Prime Minister. A mere 13 per cent of citizens wished to see his CDU com-
petitor, Jörg Schönbohm, replace him.[5]

While the PDS does not possess such widely popular figures, the reformers within the party are articulate and, in the eastern states, well-known and
largely viewed sympathetically. They are perceived as politicians who stand up
for particularly eastern German concerns. The four main examples are Lothar
Bisky, André Brie, Hans Modrow and, of course, Gregor Gysi. In the early
1990s Gysi became the most sought-after talk-show participant in all
Germany.[6] His sharp wit and telegenic nature enabled him to become the
party's undoubted figurehead, and PDS supporters and critics alike acknowledge the important role that he has played in improving and modernising the
PDS's image away from that of a party packed with stuffy former SED functionaries. Gysi's departure from his position as leader of the PDS in the federal parliament poses the question of how the party will replace its figurehead
and fill the void that he is bound to leave behind.

Lothar Bisky, leader of the party between 1993 and 2001, has come to represent the reformist, hard-working, down-to-earth nature of the PDS in eastern Germany. Bisky is not a spectacular figure; his presentational skills are not
like Gysi's. He impresses less with charisma and style, and much more with his
dedication and his workmanlike manner. This has led him to be described as
the 'good man of the PDS',[7] or even the '*Integrations-Opa*' (Grandfather of
integration) within the party, on account of his success at mediating between
the party's different wings and ideological factions.[8] This appealed to the east-

ern electorate after much of the hope and anticipation of the immediate unification period dissipated.[9] Bisky also receives credit as a result of being
regarded as *aufmüpfig* (rebellious) before 1989. As Vice-Chancellor of the
Filmhochschule in Potsdam he fought for films to be shown in the GDR that
SED bureaucrats were vehemently against. He was also known to be 'pro-
Gorbachev': ensuring that as the *Wende* approached he was viewed as anything
but an SED die-hard.[10]

André Brie, the long-time election manager of the PDS, who left this position to become a Member of the European Parliament in the Summer of
1999, is a much more controversial figure within the party, but this has not
detracted from his public profile as a reforming intellectual. Brie seeks to
move the party away from its more dogmatic tendencies, and to break with
the traditional ideological rigidity of Marxist/Leninist political thought. Brie
is not scared to break internal taboos (particularly with regard to criticisms of
the GDR[11]), and his election campaigning style, with its tendency to throw
light on controversial issues, has ensured that the PDS remains focused on the
problems of (eastern) Germans today, and not just on ideological disputes
behind closed doors.

Hans Modrow, the PDS's Honorary President and the last leader of the
GDR, represents a very different figure to that of André Brie. Modrow represents the traditionalist wing of the party, and his presence is often seen as
being of comfort to the stalwart membership of the PDS that was socialised
in the GDR. He symbolises the defence of active participation in the GDR's
societal structures, and a strong reluctance to condemn the GDR *per se*. He
reassures the conservative membership that the reforming leadership will not
go too far in abandoning left-wing principles – and Gysi, Brie and Bisky are
well aware that alienating Modrow is likely to disillusion many of the conservative rank and file. However, Modrow's public appearances are carefully
orchestrated and there is a clear division of labour between Modrow, Brie and
the other members of the PDS leadership. Modrow's internal party support
is not necessarily reflected in the population at large: although this does not
appear to have directly affected the electoral performances of the PDS in the
eastern states.[12]

During the 1998 Federal Election campaign, the PDS continued its long-
standing strategy of fielding high-profile candidates in strategic constituencies. Following the author Stefan Heym's successful campaign in Berlin Mitte
in 1990,[13] the PDS once again attempted to persuade high-profile candidates
to stand on its 'open lists'. The most prominent of these was Gustav-Adolf
'Täve' Schur, who became the *Spitzenkandidat* of the PDS in Saxony, as well as
the direct candidate in Leipzig South. Schur, a popular former cyclist, remains

a well known figure in the eastern states[14] and the PDS clearly attempted to use him in an attempt to increase the party's popular profile. Schur was openly aware of his symbolic importance to the PDS, and he made no secret of his willingness both to call on his sporting background, and to profile himself as a man of the (eastern German) people.[15] As he once observed:

> I know about life here … (in eastern Germany). Those people in Bonn don't, and they are the ones who want to make our decisions for us – to decide what is good for us and what is bad for us … These people … (in Bonn) … who decide for the Eurofighter, who are prepared to spend millions on military intervention in Bosnia while they simultaneously rip huge holes in the welfare system, they are not going to bring me into line. My vision of a democratic socialism is very real.[16]

Schur represents a hero from a bygone age and, despite having sat in the *Volkskammer* from 1958 to 1990, is still remembered for his sporting exploits. At information stands Schur remained an exceptionally popular figure, as PDS supporters and critics alike came to see one of the legends of GDR sport. Schur never claimed to be a great politician as such, rather he chose to emphasise his hard-working ethic and the importance of ordinary people being actively involved in the political process. Schur is never likely to progress to the higher organisational ranks of the party, and a number of commentators have claimed that the PDS will have to continue to look for new leaders if it is to 'stabilise' itself.[17] Under the tutelage of Gysi and Bisky the PDS has been on a continuous path of development with the aim of stabilisation within the German party system.[18] The next few years will highlight how successful the likes of Gabriele Zimmer, Petra Pau, Roland Claus, Helmut Holter and Dietmar Bartsch are in fulfilling this task. Gregor Gysi is clearly aware of the role that both he and Lothar Bisky have played in the PDS's development in the 1990s, but he has also articulated his concern that the party move on from this base, and stabilise itself within the German polity:

> I am of the opinion that Lothar Bisky and I have performed historically important functions within the party that have enabled the PDS to successfully arrive in the Federal Republic. The next generation are now faced with the challenge of making the PDS a *Bestandteil* (component) within German society.[19]

Despite (and often as a result of) its elderly membership, the PDS is also keen to promote younger members of the party into the public limelight. Angela Marquardt, a young punk from Ludwigslust in Mecklenburg Western Pomerania, became a member of the party Executive at the tender age of 19, and, by 23, she was one the PDS's deputy leaders (*stellvertretende Parteivorsitzende*). Marquardt, now also a member of the *Bundestag*, is one of a group of young, eloquent and sharp-tongued PDS politicians who present a very different, alternative image to the eastern electorate. As is often the case, the PDS is offering eastern Germans something a little different, and it is no coincidence that the PDS attempts to promote and support younger politicians, in order to try to dispel its image as an 'old' party. At the lower levels of political representation, the PDS also actively seeks to present a younger face in eastern state parliaments, on city councils in the eastern German communes. Roughly a quarter of the candidates on the first 30 places on the PDS list for the Saxony state election in the Autumn of 1999 were under 35, while the average age of the candidates on the entire list was a mere 43.[20] The PDS lists in other states have a similar age-profile. Within the middle and upper echelons of its eastern *Land* organisations the PDS is also able to call on a broad and gifted generation of 35–50 year olds with considerable intellectual competencies,[21] and more than two-thirds of the membership of PDS *Kreis*- and *Landesvorstände* are between the ages of 40 and 50.[22] Most of these elites came to prominence with very limited reform proposals as the GDR was collapsing in the late 1980s. They tended to belong to well educated groups within society who would, should the GDR have continued to exist, slowly have progressed into the leadership hierarchy of the East German state. Yet, as the GDR collapsed, they often showed remarkable foresight in balancing tradition and modernisation, by placing themselves at the forefront of the efforts to regenerate and transform the SED into the PDS. This subsequently gave them every opportunity of influencing the party's future direction. They represent clear evidence of the party's attempt to present both a much younger public profile, and to offer younger citizens an opportunity to actively enter the political process.

The ideological and historical background of the PDS elite therefore lends the party a unique public profile. It is this 'differentness', combined with their eastern roots, that allows them to articulate the feelings of many eastern Germans in the political process. PDS elites are adept at touching on broader undercurrents of opinion, whether this be in an aggressive and witty way (Gregor Gysi), a straightforward, workmanlike way (Lothar Bisky) or in an alternative, almost cheeky fashion (Angela Marquardt). PDS elites are not burdened by the responsibility of having taken part in the governmental attempts to improve the eastern economic and social landscape since 1989, and, despite talk to the contrary,[23] the PDS is not likely to allow itself to become part of a federal coalition until at least after the 2006 Federal Election – hence it can afford the luxury of playing, for the most part, the role of the political *Außenseiter* (outsider).

The PDS remains the clearest and most vocal advocate of what it (alongside many Easterners) sees as blatant discrimination within Germany today, and the rhetorical sharpness of PDS politicians on such themes increases the party's profile. The typology in chapter three suggested that some regional parties are built around the personality and beliefs of one figure: and while to say this of the PDS would be to exaggerate the importance of Gregor Gysi, it is clear that he plays a pivotal function in fostering a quick-witted, snappy image for the party. This is complemented by poster campaigns and election material[24] as well as the other PDS elites around him.

Party organisation

To complement the talented leadership figures that it possesses, the PDS has developed a strongly hierarchical and decentralised party organisation. This offers the PDS two key tools for maximising its political effectiveness in eastern Germany: firstly, its large and highly motivated base of members and activists is easily (and frequently) mobilised to conduct both official and unofficial (in terms of 'spreading the word') party work, and, secondly, it has a considerable presence in eastern Germany's communal parliaments and town halls, increasing its visibility at the micro-levels of eastern German political life.

The federal structures of the FRG offer PDS members and activists ample opportunity to participate in political activity, and the PDS encourages its large membership to do just this. In eastern Germany, the PDS has 6,506 *Basisorganisationen* (local party organisations) meeting once a month. Membership numbers vary, but each *Basisgruppe* discusses issues and problems that have been brought down from higher bodies, before sending delegates to one of the 122 *Kreis- Stadt-* or *Bezirksvorstände* to contribute to the formulation of policy proposals at the communal-local level and/or to discuss issues that need to be dealt with at *Parteitage* (conferences). This gives members the opportunity to actively shape and be involved with party activity. The *Landesvorständen* (regional executives) also fulfil a mediating role in this process by formulating and coordinating policy at the state level. The *Vorstand* (executive), comprising 18 members, is the PDS's highest organisational body, and is largely responsible for directing the party at the federal level.[25] The PDS also has both working groups and interest groups that discuss policy issues (i.e. ecology, peace, religion, and so forth), as well as 'Platforms', that are based on ideological orientation (i.e. the Communist Platform, the Marxist Forum).[26]

The horizontal and vertical membership structures of the PDS correspond with those of other regional parties. They enable the membership to feel that they are contributing to the party's success, and encourage high levels of commitment and motivation. However, highly committed memberships must also be, particularly in modern times, well supported by effective campaigning at the regional and national level, so as to ensure the party has a marketable image. Enthusiastic participation must not lead to internal disagreements over the 'big picture', as this inevitably leaves the impression that the party is split, or that it is close to splintering into an uneasy bundle of factions. The PDS has (often) been perceived as being on the brink of just such a split, as disputes between ideological and pragmatic wings of the party periodically come to the surface. But the strong core leadership around Gysi, Bisky and Brie has acquired and retained enough agenda-setting powers to continue to dictate general policy direction. This does not mean, however, that the members of the PDS are 'powerless'. Debates within party forums, and at national and regional *Parteitage*, illustrate that the leadership often has to drag the membership along, and, as was particularly evident at the Münster conference of April 2000, it is not unknown for the leadership to be defeated by the more conservative *Basis*.

Over and above party structure, it is clear that the PDS makes very good use of the advantages it possesses in terms of membership numbers, activist numbers, the use of modern technology and extra-parliamentary activity. The most effective and efficient study of the organisational structures of the parties in the eastern states was carried out in 1995 by researchers at the *Zentralinstitut für sozialwissenschaftliche Forschung* in Berlin (published in 1996).[27] Their detailed analysis highlights that although membership numbers, funding and facilities do not correlate directly to electoral success, such assets are helpful in developing a public profile of a party, and making it visible at key times. The PDS competes with, and often surpasses, even the CDU in terms of effective party organisation. This fits the pattern which sees regional parties as having slick, organised and efficient structures. They are often organisationally superior, or at the very least organisationally competitive, when compared to their national opponents. *Bundesgeschäftsführer* Dietmar Bartsch has emphasised that the PDS uses its organisational structures all-year round, not just as and when elections are contested. He claimed, as other PDS politi-

Table 5.1. Party Membership in the eastern states as at 1 January 1995

State	CDU	SPD	FDP	Alliance 90/ Green	PDS
Mecklenburg Western Pomerania	10,217	3,452	3,220	375	**14,154**
Brandenburg	9,505	6,750	3,848	492	**18,258**
Saxony Anhalt	15,461	6,207	5,908	478	**18,270**
Thuringia	19,685	6,012	6,138	470	**16,173**
Saxony	22,932	5,304	6,635	1,007	**32,853**
Total	77,800	27,725	25,749	2,822	**99,708**

Source: Zentralinstitut für sozialwissenschaftliche Forschung, 1996, p.41.

Table 5.2. The level of organisation of political parties in the eastern states at 1 January 1995

State	CDU	SPD	FDP	Alliance 90/ Green	PDS
Mecklenburg Western Pomerania	0.7	0.3	0.2	0.03	**1.0**
Brandenburg	0.5	0.3	0.2	0.03	**0.9**
Saxony Anhalt	0.7	0.3	0.3	0.02	**0.8**
Thuringia	1.0	0.3	0.3	0.02	**0.8**
Saxony	0.6	0.1	0.2	0.03	**0.9**
Average	0.7	0.3	0.2	0.03	**0.9**

Source: Zentralinstitut für sozialwissenschaftliche Forschung, 1996, p.42.

Table 5.3. The strength of membership at the *Kreisebene* in the eastern states – 1995 (per cent)

Members	CDU	SPD	FDP	Alliance 90/ Green	PDS
Up to 40	0	0	1	84	**0**
41-180	5	39	53	16	**1**
181-400	21	42	43	0	**18**
401-700	33	19	3	0	**42**
Over 701	41	0	0	0	**39**

Source: Zentralinstitut für sozialwissenschaftliche Forschung, 1996, p.45.

Table 5.4 Party membership in eastern Germany 1995–1998

	Alliance 90/Greens	SPD	FDP	CDU	**PDS**
1995	2,827	27,177	24,569	71,804	**101,033**
1996	2,753	26,863	21,212	65,923	**102,976**
1997	2,949	27,441	16,213	67,703	**96,097**
1998	3,150	27,527	15,590	61,046	**94,447**

Source: Bundesgeschäftsstellen der Parteien, December 1998.

Table 5.5. The level of organisation of political parties in the new states 1995–1998

	Alliance 90/Greens	SPD	FDP	CDU	**PDS**
1995	0.02	0.20	0.18	0.53	**0.74**
1996	0.02	0.20	0.16	0.48	**0.76**
1997	0.02	0.20	0.12	0.50	**0.71**
1998	0.02	0.20	0.11	0.45	**0.72**

Source: Hough, 2001, chapter 4.

cians have done, that 'the PDS is not just a party for election day, it is a party for every day'.[28] This is a regular rallying call in PDS discourse. The KSPW survey has illustrated that not only does the PDS possess more members than any other party (see table 5.1), but it also scores more highly in their index of levels of organisation (table 5.2).[29]

The PDS is able to call on the services of more citizens in every eastern state than any other party except the CDU in Thuringia, and this is one of the main reasons why the PDS is viewed as being both more visible and more active. Table 5.3. highlights how the PDS has a broad base of *Kreisparteien* each with a substantial membership.

This is particularly important when one considers the organisational ratings of the SPD, the party against which the PDS is competing most vigorously for votes. The most recent data reveals that the PDS remains in an advantageous position vis-à-vis all other parties in eastern Germany (tables 5.4 and 5.5).

To understand the true meaning of these figures it is important to consider exactly who the members of the party are. The PDS does not only have more members than other parties, it can also mobilise more of them, more often. This is of great importance in fostering face-to-face contact at the grass-roots level – a weakness that Angela Merkel, the leader of the Christian

Table 5.6. Party membership in the CDU, SPD and PDS in each of the eastern states

State	CDU		SPD		**PDS**	
	1996	1997	1996	1997	**1997**	**1998**
Brandenburg	7,927	7,974	6,778	6,868	**ca 15,000**	**14, 950**
Mecklenburg Western Pomerania	9,150	8,729	3,311	3,470	**11, 926**	**10, 614**
Saxony	19,205	18,516	5,989	6,091	**ca 25, 000**	**24, 333**
Saxony-Anhalt	12,567	12,130	5,123	5,233	**13, 861**	**12, 107**
Thuringia	17,074	16,342	5,662	5,589	**12, 950**	**12, 210**

Sources: Schmidt, 1998, pp.49–50; Werz, 1998, p.97; Moreau, 1998, p.97; http://www.pds-online/sonnenklar/mit-gliederzahlen.htm

Democrats, admits her party will have to live with over the medium and long term. As she has observed: 'We simply have not been able to build sustainable bridges to the most important societal groups – the trade unions, the churches and other similar associations'[30]. Of the PDS's total membership in May 1997, a mere 2 per cent were 29 or younger, 7 per cent were 30–39, 24 per cent were 40–59 and 67 per cent were over 60 years of age.[31] While this is undoubtedly worrying for the future *Nachwuchs* (next generation) of the party,[32] the large number of retired and early-retired members ensures that the hard graft, the *Knochenarbeit*, of grass-roots politics is well served.[33] The members of the PDS are exceptionally active and their work has enabled the PDS to establish a considerable presence in eastern German micro-politics. As Dietmar Wittich has observed 'the public perception of the PDS at the grass-roots and regional levels is defined above all by the groups who have taken early retirement and pensioners. They are the ones that are seen at public events and at the information stands'.[34] In Rostock alone, there are 121 *einschlägige Basisgruppen*, with approximately 2,600 members,[35] and every one of the groups serves one particular street or group of streets, ensuring that no letter box remains devoid of PDS literature and information.[36] Leipzig, meanwhile, has 51 *Ortsverbände* and *Basisorganisationen* and, at the beginning of 1999, a membership of 2,909. Of this membership, 71.2 per cent were either 61 or over, and a mere 3.9 per cent were 35 or under – once again indicating a reservoir of members who are likely to be able to dedicate time to PDS activities.[37] Peter Christian Segall *et al.* note that the electoral campaigning done by the PDS in 1998, as was also the case in 1994, was centrally organised and aimed at stressing the party's appreciation of the needs of the 'every-day man'. As they observe: 'the centralisation is channelled into an almost militant activism by the PDS, not only at the state and communal level but also at the micro-level in the new states. Such activism is only possible by virtue of the political strength of the PDS at the regional level'.[38] This is because the PDS is served by a loyal, committed (often through personal linkages to the party, fostered by many years of activity within the SED/PDS) and enthusiastic membership, united in its activism by a conviction that it is doing the 'right thing'. Helmut Holter is certainly very much aware of the importance of such *Basisarbeit* (grass-roots work), and he stressed this in 1998 when he observed that:

> the work of our members in chats over the garden fence, around the table in the pub, while having coffee with friends, as well as the many different forms of engagement that the members of our party who are retired undertake, cannot be regarded highly enough.[39]

The PDS '*Turborentner*'[40] (literally translated, 'Turbo-pensioners') are a unique phenomenon in (eastern) German politics, as they remain a cohesive and enthusiastic group of party servants the like of which other parties can only dream of possessing. Recording how many members man *Infostände* (information stands), stuff letter boxes and actively take part in political activity is virtually impossible,[41] but Lothar Probst, in his micro-study of the PDS in Rostock, estimates that in towns and cities with a considerable number of *Trabantenstädte*, the PDS is at a clear and conspicuous advantage thanks to its ability to organise and mobilise its membership in an almost military fashion. Up to 500 of the so-called *Altgenossen* ('old comrades') ensure that households in Rostock are regularly serviced with PDS literature. The nature of the high-rise flats ensures that tens of thousands of households can be reached in an impressively short period of time.[42]

The KSPW survey of 1995 also reveals that member mobilisation is high. The number of people who work for the PDS in an *ehrenamtliche* (voluntary) position is a telling indicator of how the PDS mobilises sympathetic supporters (table 5.7).

Ehrenamtliche work takes place where the parties do not pay supporters to work for them, but the supporters still actively assist in the party's activities. It is clear that the PDS possesses an impressive human reservoir of helpers. This, however, is not the only thing that contributes to organisational efficacy. The KSPW survey highlights the strengths and weaknesses of all of the main parties in eastern Germany in terms of constituency offices, fax machines, computers, printers and newsletters. The PDS is seen, at the *Kreisebene*, to be making good use of the district newsletter (87 per cent of the PDS *Kreisparteien* have one, compared to 37 per cent of CDU and a mere 12

Table 5.7. The presence of voluntary workers in political parties in eastern Germany in 1995 at the *Kreisebene* (per cent)

	CDU	SPD	FDP	Alliance 90/ Green	**PDS**
None	42	62	20	15	**0**
1-5	49	35	72	78	**29**
6+	9	3	8	7	**71**

Source: Zentralinstitut für sozialwissenschaftliche Forschung, 1996, p.49.

per cent of SPD parties), even though it is not quite as well catered for as the CDU in other areas. In terms of computers and fax machines the PDS remains well fitted out, as it does in terms of the number of *Wahlkreisbüro* (election offices) and *Geschäftsstelle* (administrative offices) that it possesses. However, the PDS is lagging behind in terms of *besoldete Mitarbeiter/innen* (paid employees): the CDU has at least one paid activist in 68 per cent of *Kreise* in eastern Germany: the PDS in just 31 per cent. This is, however, largely compensated for in the number of *ehrenamtliche* forces that the PDS can call upon.[43]

The PDS has also been eager to associate itself with numerous other associations within eastern German civil society. It sees advantages in spreading its scope of influence as broadly as possible, and as such it makes a concerted effort to be prominent in every-day life in eastern Germany. According to Segall *et al.*, the PDS 'was and remains ubiquitous in most of the structures of cultural and associational life in the eastern states',[44] with, in 1999, 110 associational groupings being affiliated to the party. Peter Porsch, the PDS leader in Saxony, has described the PDS's position within eastern German civil society thus:

> In the eastern states the PDS is deeply anchored in society. The party is known through the faces of its politicians at the communal level, in the *Wohngebiete* (residential areas), in the clubs and associations, in the trade unions and in the *Bürgerinitiative* (citizen's initiatives). In the East we are clearly the party for the *Alltag*, the party that people feel they can approach.[45]

It is, therefore, clear that the organisational strength of the PDS offers it clear advantages over its rivals. Furthermore, the 1998 federal election 'revealed a clear mathematical correlation between the areas where the PDS was very well organised and its best election results' – illustrating that it is a plausible hypothesis that the PDS's efficient organisation is leading to improved election results.[46] The party's organisational strengths have also enabled it to create a culture where people look towards it for support. As Thomas Lutze has observed:

> election and regional offices as well as *Landesgeschäftsstellen* are genuinely places where citizens can head for when they need information and assistance. They are places where those who are interested can simply pop in to drink a cup of tea or coffee, or to borrow a book. They are not places that are somehow hard to find, or large, expensive and imposing offices that on occasion might appear more akin to an archive … .[47]

For many Easterners the PDS is, in this sense, more than just a political party. The open and friendly manner in which the PDS conducts itself presents, for many, a refreshing change. It is a point of reference in a confusing world.

Communal politics

The PDS is well represented in communal politics. Over 6,000 eastern Germans sit in communal parliaments as PDS representatives. At the end of 1997, 1,074 PDS politicians were active in *Kreistage*[48] and *Stadträte kreisfreier Städte*[49], as well as the 195 politicians who were active for the PDS in Berlin's *Bezirksverordnetenversammlungen*[50]. In the 84 towns with more than 25,000 citizens, the PDS had 911 seats, plus a further 5,000 seats in the *kreisangehörigen Städten und Gemeinden*[51]. In total, the PDS had 191 Mayors as well as 2 *Oberbürgermeister*, 73 of which were in Mecklenburg Western Pomerania, 42 in Saxony-Anhalt, 39 in Brandenburg, 20 in Thuringia, 13 in Saxony and 4 in Berlin.[52] In 1998 the PDS tried to offer specific support to its communal politicians (who often work for no financial recompense) by organising various activities that aid them in learning from others, and in carrying out their duties in as efficient and effective way as is possible. These activities ranged from a conference for mayors, two weekend seminars for leaders of PDS groupings in communal parliaments, a *Kommunalpolitische Konferenz* in Leipzig, as well as sittings of the federal party with communal politicians. These are all in addition to the 'communal-political day' of the PDS (19 March 1998 in this case), when communal politicians were invited to a special conference in Saxony Anhalt.

The highly mobile membership and considerable presence in eastern German parliaments offers the party the perfect tool for establishing a strong presence on eastern German streets. This fact is not lost on the PDS activists themselves. The January 1996 party conference in Magdeburg settled on the motto of 'Kommunen stärken, Gesellschaft von unten verändern' (Strengthen the communes, change society from below) and the PDS has achieved greater visibility at the communal level not just because of the large number of activists it mobilises at election times, but also because of the effort and enthusiasm that the party puts into communal political activity all year round. As Heiko Grohe observes:

> Without its politicians at the communal level, the PDS would clearly not be the party that it is today ... competence, reliability and high personal commitment on social issues have become in many places the trademarks of PDS communal activity.[53]

In Saxony Peter Porsch stresses that:

> Our political representatives in the communal parliaments have actively ensured that the PDS remains visible, that everywhere in Saxony the PDS is seen to have a face and that citizens are able to trust the PDS. The PDS's communal politics, with its emphasis of political activity being brought as near to the citizen as is possible, is the basis of our success, and this is going to remain so in the future.[54]

The retention of as many local jobs as is possible, *Kindertagestätten*, Youth centres, communal housing and libraries, fighting for affordable services and rent issues etc. are all areas where the PDS retains a particular prominence at the communal level. It is precisely by doing this that the PDS is able to take advantage of its strengths: as a membership party, as a milieu party as well as a pragmatic representative of eastern interests and of eastern protest.[55] Furthermore, the PDS has proved itself to be totally integrated into the parliamentary procedures and mechanisms of communal governance. PDS politicians remain much more pragmatic and *sachorientiert* (issue-oriented) than, for example, their party fellow-representatives at either the regional or federal levels. Local politicians have to be much less ideological than their national equivalents, and they have carefully cultivated the image of politicians who are much more interested in finding solutions to problems than in ideological conflict.[56] In Mecklenburg Western Pomerania, for example, the SPD–PDS coalition is seeking to reform communal political activity in order to give communal authorities more power to control their own affairs. The

PDS actively campaigns against proposed forced amalgamation of particularly small communes, claiming that so long as the communes are financially
viable, it should be up to the citizens of the communes themselves as to what
happens to them.[57] This is part of the PDS strategy of bringing democracy
close to the citizenry, in order both to enrich democratic activity and dispel
some of the cynicism towards politics in general. Article 182 of the coalition
agreement in Mecklenburg Western Pomerania clearly states that:

> In the medium term, the coalition is striving to change the com-
> munal constitution (*Kommunalverfassung*). Communes are going
> to be given more competencies, as well as the opportunity to
> exert more control over their own affairs ... the right of citizens
> to be involved in the political process, as well as the use of
> *Bürgerinitiativen* (citizens' initiatives) will be expanded. The rights
> of *Ortsteilen* (city districts) and their administrations are going to
> be broadened. Children and young people will have the right to
> participate in communal activities that directly affect them.[58]

The PDS works closely with the *Kommunalpolitisches Forum* (Communal political forum) in the eastern states. The Forum is open in its proximity to the
PDS[59] and aims to conduct studies and hold seminars on social and educational issues for communal politicians, as well as for the general public.
Further to these attempts to educate citizens, the Communal political forum
aims to defend and expand the power and scope of communes everywhere in
Germany.

The PDS is well aware that the communes in both the eastern and western states (although this is particularly true in the East[60]) often suffer from
acute financial shortages. Both income tax and the *Gewerbesteuer* (trade tax) are
no longer available as sources of income to communes – yet the communes
have been delegated more responsibilities from not just the *Land* level, but
also the federal and European ones as well. If the communes are to function
properly, and to contribute to a reconstruction of trust in public institutions,
then they have to have a sound financial basis. As a result of this, the PDS
proposed in May 1996 a thorough reform of communal finances.[61] It also
pressed for extra subsidies for the particularly poor eastern communes.[62]
Having largely failed in 1996, the PDS repeated demands in October 1999 for
a fundamental reform of communal finance, in order to enable the communes to stabilise their precarious financial positions.[63] It has called for the
establishment of an Enquete-Kommission into reform of Communal finance
(*Reform der Kommunalfinanzierung*)[64] in a further effort to strengthen their finan-

cial basis across all of Germany. It has also attempted to increase financial support given directly to cities, municipalities and rural districts.[65]

> In particular the eastern German communes are dependent on the financial payments given them by the *Länder*, since they have hardly any financial resources of their own. With a fundamental and far-reaching finance reform, as the PDS Parliamentary party proposes, the public purse would have to be redistributed in favour of the communes.[66]

The communal level of political activity is, therefore, of great importance to the PDS. It is the political arena where it is most able to illustrate its close links with the institutions of eastern German civil society, and where its politicians can best demonstrate their considerable political know-how. It, therefore, goes almost without saying that empowering the communes is a fundamental part of the PDS's policy package: something that is discussed in greater detail below.

The PDS mobilising community: eastern German identity and the PDS

> The Federal Republic of Germany swallowed the GDR whole. And now she is causing the FRG to have quite a stomach ache![67]

The process of identity creation in eastern Germany has been crucial in creating an environment where sociocultural and economic issues increase in political importance. Empirical electoral research in Germany has long attempted to ascertain to what extent the PDS is perceived as having the capacity to articulate feelings of eastern German identity within the political arena, and whether PDS voters cast their vote for the party primarily on this basis. Wolfram Brunner & Dieter Walz claim that 85 per cent of citizens who voted for the PDS in 1998 did so because the 'PDS comes from the East, and is the party which most clearly represents eastern German interests.'[68] Detlev Pollack and Gert Pickel, meanwhile, claim that PDS voters tend to be better politically informed, and that they possess a self-identification that is different from that of Germans as a whole ('stehen in einer gewissen Distanz zu einer gesamtdeutschen Identität')[69] – i.e. they have an identity that is characterised by their socialisation and life experiences in the GDR and, following unification, in eastern Germany. This *Abgrenzungsmentalität* (mentality of demarcation) or *internaliserte Identitätsbegrenzung* (internalised limited identity) is specific to citizens of the eastern states, and PDS voters are highly likely to possess such an identification.[70] Pollack and Pickel conclude by stating that:

> the PDS is the clear beneficiary of the existence of an eastern German identity, and the nature of this identification ensures that the PDS acts as a catch-all home for voters who wish to give political voice to the subjective degradation of 'all' eastern Germans.[71]

For its part, the PDS attempts to make political capital out of its eastern German heritage, as well as what it sees as differences of attitude and experience between eastern and western Germans. PDS politicians shy away from deliberately discussing what an eastern German identity might be, as they believe that the publicity given to such a debate will diminish the PDS's chances of developing into an all-German party. If the PDS were willing, as Christine Ostrowski and Ronald Weckesser suggested in 1996,[72] to concentrate on what it does best (i.e. give specific voice to eastern Germans within federal and regional parliaments), then not only would the PDS be able to concentrate all its efforts on its key strength, but it would also have a long-term perspective in eastern German politics, as it hones its policy orientations to the specifically eastern environment.

Rhetorically, PDS politicians are more than willing to reflect feelings of eastern German dissatisfaction and they subsequently are much more 'radical' in their discourse than politicians of other parties. PDS politicians are not constrained by western party organisations anxious to preserve a large western electoral base, hence they can give polemical voice to eastern German feelings of dissatisfaction and difference. Two examples illustrate this explicitly. At the January 1999 Berlin party conference, Gregor Gysi, the master of the eastern German soundbite, observed that:

> I want to know: when is the Easterner who is on benefits, the Easterner who has to pay the same prices as a Westerner, going to at least be able to claim the same levels of social support? When is the Easterner who is unemployed going to be able to claim the same levels of unemployment benefit? When is the state, in the form of employees working in the public sector, going to pay the same rates to Easterners as it does to Westerners?[73]

PDS politicians know that they have not been responsible for any governmental decisions since 1990 – hence they can excuse the party of responsibility for the economic malaise and social dissatisfaction in the eastern states
today. They concentrate on stressing that the PDS is now a party with a
unique eastern German self-understanding. This is in spite of the fact that the
party continues to portray itself as a *national* party. In the 1998 Federal
Election manifesto, however, the PDS stressed its willingness to continue
articulating eastern German interests within the political process:

> ... the ... (PDS is) ... the party that for years has consistently
> represented eastern German interests, thereby forcing the other
> parties to address eastern concerns. Every form of discrimina-
> tion of eastern Germans that has been conceptualised in the
> federal parliament has been brought up at the behest of the
> PDS ... without the PDS eastern Germany would not be men-
> tioned in a political context in the *Bundestag* at all.[74]

In spite of claims in election programmes that the PDS unambiguously
embraces eastern German *interests*, the PDS still shies away from directly discussing what an eastern German identity should or could be. This remains, as
a concept, a divisive topic within the ranks of the party. The PDS is insistent,
and explicit, in its assertion of eastern Germans' self-perceptions as being
'different' to West Germans, and of being able to contribute valuable experiences towards the creation of a socially just, more egalitarian and 'fully
employed' Germany.[75] This is in terms of attitudes, expectations and values,
and although the words eastern German identity are not normally used, it is
clear that PDS politicians are referring to precisely this phenomenon. The
PDS demands that the subjective differences between East and West be
respected and not seen as hindrances on the way towards 'inner unity'.[76]

The left-wing bias and the emphasis on eastern German interests evident
in the PDS programme reflects a current of underlying attitudinal difference
between eastern and western Germans. Hence, the statist rhetoric of the PDS
finds an echo not just amongst its own supporters, but also amongst eastern
Germans who, for reasons to do with the PDS's past, or the practicality of the
PDS's policy alternatives, choose to vote for other parties. For many PDS voters, the PDS stands as a common denominator in terms of their general political orientation – much as the Catholic church has traditionally done for the
CDU in western Germany, and, above all, for the CSU in Bavaria.[77] By being
broadly more supportive of socialism, Easterners have (perhaps subcon-
sciously) taken on board an identity marker that is in direct contrast to the

prevalent political culture in western Germany – as well as being a clear recognition of their state-socialist past. The PDS remains 'a piece of "Heimat" that many eastern Germans do not wish to lose'.[78]

It should, therefore, be no surprise that PDS politicians from both the left and right wings of the party acknowledge the existence of a specific form of eastern German self-understanding. Michael Benjamin, a prominent former member of both the PDS Executive and the Communist Platform (KPF), argues that Easterners have (often unconsciously) taken on board socialist values, and these values provide the basis of eastern German attitudinal difference. The KPF and the Marxist Forum (MF) further discuss the evidence of increased solidarity between eastern Germans with explicit reference to a *positive* identification with the GDR. The more extreme proponents of this approach such as Sahra Wagenknecht, Ellen Brombacher and Benjamin use the existence of an eastern German identity as a basis for drawing attention to the solidaristic tendencies that were also evident in the GDR pre-1989.[79] Uwe-Jens Heuer, a prominent member of the Marxist Forum, has observed, 'under the rubble of the GDR state, building blocks of a GDR identity are clearly visible'[80] – and he claims that Easterners see value in recalling some of the more positive elements of life in the GDR. Although the opinions of ideologically active members of the PDS's left-wing do not, as a general rule, enjoy wide public acceptance, it is clear that when PDS politicians make points on the issue of eastern identity they do reflect a broader cross-section of eastern German popular opinion.

The mainstream of opinion within the party is more pragmatic on the issue. The deep social, historical and psychological particularities of life in the GDR and of the transformation process are accepted as having spawned a complex feeling of community. Yet PDS politicians remain circumspect in defining this in a detailed fashion – the eastern *Trotzidentität* is, at both the academic and popular level, not an easily definable construct. PDS politicians are none the less skilled at calling on indisputable feelings of solidarity that exist between Easterners. Peter Christian Segall *et al.* summarise this accurately when they observe:

> In the last analysis the PDS profiles itself as the defender of the past of every single eastern German – not just the former members of the SED and the citizens who worked in the public services in the GDR. The PDS does this by claiming that the 'West' can only think and act destructively. The PDS instinctively plays on the identity of eastern Germans.[81]

The PDS stresses not just that Easterners are poorer than their western counterparts, but also that their voices are not heard and (they perceive themselves to be) powerless. The PDS does not wish to see the GDR regarded as a footnote in history, it does not wish to see Westerners tell Easterners how life in the GDR functioned and what was right and wrong with it, and it does not wish to see German politics existing over and above the needs and concerns of Easterners. The PDS is the only party that views the history of the GDR and the FRG on equal terms, and as such it is the only party that is perceived in the electorate at large as being a genuine *Ostpartei*.[82]

Ingrid Tschirch, a former PDS member of the Mecklenburg Western Pomerania state Parliament in Schwerin, demonstrates the knack that PDS politicians have of relating the specific experiences of the transformation process to an individuals own life-experiences:[83]

> ... the solidarity and trust in the future dissipated as the excesses of capitalism became apparent. This occurred when in 1991, the old structures in the economic sphere, in administration, culture and the sciences were dissolved. As unemployment and short-time work became more regular, as the insecurities not just in the world of employment, but also in the social system, in the unfathomable new masses of legal regulations and laws as well as the mountains of bureaucracy, the giant leaps in rents and tariffs, the claims for redistribution of eastern German land came flooding in, younger people saw their future prospects darken and the over-50s were consigned to the scrap-heap, doubts grew about the promises of politicians and the agreements that were set down in the unification treaty.

The PDS is open in its definition of this as 'discrimination' against Easterners. The parliamentary work and the programmatic initiatives of the PDS are subsequently unique in their attitudes towards the legal, social and political 'discrimination' of eastern Germans. The 1998 'Rostock Manifesto' leaves the reader under no illusions as to how such a position has come about:

> The results of eight years of constitutional unity are the results of political approaches that were wrong (*verfehlt*) from the very beginning. The political approaches pursued were ineffective (*unwirtschaftlich*), anti-social and undemocratic.[84]

In the 1998 Federal Election Programme the PDS was no less forthright, as it concentrated on the outcomes that have resulted from these processes:

> ... the PDS is left fighting against inequalities of income and pensions, the evictions from homes and properties, the reduction or abolition of legitimate subsidies, *Strafrente* (discriminatory pensions), *Berufsverbote* (exclusions from certain professions), political *Strafverfolgung* (criminal prosecution) and the abuse and discrediting of eastern German biographies.[85]

None of the other parties can defend widely perceived eastern German concerns about their qualifications, their previous working-lives or their 'biographies' in such strong words.[86] The PDS touches this uniquely eastern German perception by stressing feelings of societal exclusion that Easterners perceive. In the words of Gabi Zimmer, Gerhard Schröder and the SPD's rebuilding of the East (*Aufbau Ost*) '... needs to help to end the inequalities of incomes earned and the discrimination that citizens of eastern Germany still suffer'.[87] The 'discrimination' of eastern Germans is not emphasised at all by the CDU or the SPD, even though this is a widely held sentiment in the eastern population. The former leader of the PDS parliamentary party in Mecklenburg Western Pomerania, Catherina Muth, felt that the very nature of the unification process, dominated as it was by Westerners, with their structures, judgements and arrogant know-it-all attitudes meant that talk of solidarity existing between East and West was somewhat misleading. Muth expressed the opinion that Westerners have never shown the requisite social and psychological solidarity with Easterners as they were unwilling to accept that anything in 'their' Weltanschauung may need overhauling. Or, in her exact words, 'In order to see solidarity weakening, one presupposes that solidarity between the old and the new federal states did actually once exist!'[88]

PDS politicians do not recognise the huge financial subsidies that have come from western Germany[89] as being sufficient expressions of solidarity. PDS politicians and Easterners alike see no reason why they should accept lower levels of wealth and employment than those of Westerners.[90] It appears to both the PDS, and to a swathe of Easterners, decidedly unsolidaristic that Westerners continue to enjoy a higher standard of living than they do. Lothar Bisky articulated this point well by observing that 'the eastern German pensioner is not now being punished ... (it terms of lower pensions) ... just for his or her political orientation: nowadays the criterion of his or her heritage suffices!'[91] Only when living standards and opportunity structures within society are perceived as being equal will the PDS regard Easterners as having attained equality within Germany. Gregor Gysi, as is often the case, articulated these sentiments in a broader fashion in a 1996 Bundestag debate:

> German unity will be achieved on the day that the special legal treatment of eastern Germans has ceased, on the day that Easterners and Westerners earn the same, on the day that there are as many eastern Germans owning property on Sylt as there are currently western Germans owning property on Rügen and on the day that an eastern German becomes Prime Minister of a western German state – and on the day that all of these things do not interest anybody in the slightest. This shows how far this process still has to go.[92]

The quest for inner unity may not be completed, but the PDS remains adamant that eastern difference is not one of the problems that have prevented this from happening. The PDS is of the opinion that Westerners have to learn to accept that the East *is* different: that it is not the West, and it never will be – and this should not be seen in any way as a threat. The East must be regarded as different in the same way that Bavaria is – and not in the threatening, critical way that it is at the moment. The PDS regards itself as merely a representative of a different political culture and heritage, and it is time that citizens of East and West alike recognise the party as a representation of 'normality'. For, as Gysi puts it, 'those who want to see unity in this land will have to get used to both the PDS and to me. If people can't do this, then they are simply not going to get the unity they desire.'[93]

Playing into the PDS's hands: the CDU/CSU and SPD and eastern Germany

The comments and observations of (principally) western German politicians have also caused strong feelings of solidarity between eastern German citizens. CDU and CSU politicians have periodically advised, warned or threatened Easterners about supporting the PDS at the ballot box. The PDS has been variously described as the 'SED Konzentrat',[94] or the 'Stasis from yesterday',[95] while politicians within the CDU have demanded that the PDS be put 'morally on the same level as the DVU and the Republicans'[96] because the PDS is not capable of existing democratically in the FRG as it 'does not in truth accept the Basic Law'.[97] Edmund Stoiber (CSU) has even claimed that:

> the PDS conducts itself like the SED, and the situation is comparable to one where the NSDAP, under the leadership of Herman Göring, had simply re-named itself in 1946, and tried to carry on as normal.[98]

As such observations imply, a number of western politicians have tried to paint a picture of the PDS as the SED re-incarnate – a vision that has paradoxically contributed to increasing the PDS's share of the vote.[99] The PDS has been able to use such accusations to turn the tables on western parties who do not understand the complexities of the eastern electorate.[100] Former General Secretary of the CDU Peter Hintze became a particular figure of disdain, following a series of undiplomatic remarks on the development and political goals of the PDS. Hintze was the driving force behind both the red socks (in 1994) and the red hands (in 1998) election campaigns that attempted to demonise the PDS. PDS politicians have been able to take the moral high-ground by depicting CDU and CSU politicians as stooping to populist rhetoric in order to try and increase their profile – principally in the West, where the PDS is still a tool with which the conservative parties can mobilise support. Catherina Muth and Dietmar Bartsch have epitomised the reactions of both the PDS and Easterners to such campaigns when they responded by stating that:

> Through his 'red-hands' campaign, Herr Hintze has remained true to his virulent campaigning of yesteryear. Typically for the CDU, Herr Hintze is peddling old slogans and symbols. This is a sign that, on the one hand, he wants to divert the citizens of the eastern states from the economic and social problems evident within eastern Germany – the causes of which lie in the policies of his party, the CDU. On the other hand, it is patently obvious that he can't think of anything new on which to campaign. He is producing a dull and dreary spectacle. We, on the contrary, are going to conduct a campaign that is based on arguments and a discussion of the issues.[101]

Western politicians have regularly shown a misunderstanding of the political situation in the eastern states, as they try to conduct political activity on western terms. This leads to both resentment in the population at large, as well as support for the cheeky and resilient little *Ostpartei*. As Peter Porsch, the PDS leader in Saxony has observed:

CSU and CDU have once again proved themselves to be the organised arrogance of the western states towards the eastern ones, and concurrently the greatest danger on the path towards inner unity.[102]

Erwin Huber, the leader of Bavarian *Staatskanzelei,* caused particular waves in 1998 by demanding that if the PDS remained in government in certain eastern states, then financial transfers from the *Bund* would have to either be cut or stopped altogether. Huber was of the opinion that the PDS would simply waste the money on socialist projects that had no long-term future.[103] Furthermore, if coalitions continued to be formed in the East that were not to the CSU's satisfaction, he threatened that Bavaria would begin to pull its ministers out of federal committees and governmental bodies.[104] Huber's comments were backed by the leader of the CSU Parliamentary Party who observed that 'our friend Huber has articulated here a very widespread view among the Bavarian population'.[105] It is clear that this looked to many like a(nother) western attempt to dictate to eastern Germans. And it came as no surprise when Gregor Gysi, speaking for the PDS, offered Huber a sharp response:

> The threats issued by the CSU politician Huber indicating that financial support for the eastern states will be stopped, as, in his opinion, Easterners are not voting correctly, and the right parties are not coalescing in government, is nothing more than an attempt to alter the long-established right in the Basic Law stating that parties have the freedom to form coalitions as they think appropriate. People who want to replace politics with blackmail are only showing that they themselves are politically finished. The citizens of the eastern states are not, however, going to allow their electoral freedoms to be taken away from them – on the contrary, Herr Huber should perhaps pay a bit more attention to how many Bavarian firms make their profits through economic activity undertaken in the eastern states, only to pay their taxes in Bavaria – or not at all, as the case may be. None the less you are not going to hear me calling for a boycott of Bavarian firms who are active in eastern Germany.[106]

The disgust that comments such as those by Huber caused in the East was further illustrated by Dietmar Bartsch: 'We eastern Germans are humble in our thanks to Herr Huber that he has not hesitated to march into the eastern states and ensure that order is restored!'[107]

In April 1998 Roland Koch, the CDU Prime Minister in Hesse, indirectly supported Erwin Huber's claims by observing that financial support for the *Aufbau Ost* should only be guaranteed if 'political responsibility' could also be ensured. Koch further added that it was unfair to expect the western states to look on while 'red governments economically run down the eastern states'.[108] Dirk Wenz, a spokesman for the Hesse government further added that 'it is simply not fair that western German taxes are creating thousands of jobs in the eastern states, while the problems of the western states are pushed to one side'.[109] PDS politicians once again articulated eastern German ire at such perceived western German arrogance. Christa Luft branded such remarks 'undignified' (*unanständig*), and a demonstration of the lack of understanding that was shown by Westerners towards the eastern states.[110]

Attempts by western politicians[111] to characterise the PDS as a reincarnation of the SED or as a communist party play into the hands of the PDS, as it is able to illustrate how distanced these Westerners are from the political realities in the eastern states. A look at the PDS's communal political activity illustrates that the vast majority of PDS politicians behave in exactly the same way as politicians of other parties do at this level. Rhetorical attacks on the PDS also ignore the fact that Easterners remain in a unique position: they have experienced a state and a whole system that collapsed around them, and this makes them particularly sensitive when it comes to comparing one societal and economic system against another. Citizens who have spent much of their lives in a society stressing egalitarianism have, in spite of an undoubted appreciation of parliamentary democracy, individual freedom and the social market economy, a much finer feeling for evidence of power, arrogance, injustice, bureaucracy and corruption.

This does not necessarily mean that Easterners are unaware of the PDS's history and heritage. The PDS is widely (and correctly) perceived as being the *Nachfolgepartei* (successor party) of the SED, but this is not solely disadvantageous against a background of widely experienced social injustice and of broken and battered personal biographies. For segments of the eastern electorate this ostracisation represents a part of their own lives. The PDS is seen in certain sociocultural milieus as a *Weggefährte*, as a party or a group of people that has been affected by the irritations and uncomfortable experiences of the last few years – but is still able to articulate feelings of *Trotz* and Easternness within the political arena.[112]

Concluding remarks

Clearly, the PDS possesses the capacity to mobilise 'Easternness' within the political arena. It's leadership and organisation offer it a clear advantage over the 'western' parties in eastern Germany. By applying the second part of the typology developed in chapter three we have been able to recognise that the PDS is capable of mobilising territorial sentiment in a similar way (although of course in a nationally unique context) to other regional parties across the western world. The PDS has been lucky in that it possessed a telegenic and charismatic leader, Gregor Gysi, who managed to drag the PDS forward without disillusioning some of his more conservative supporters. His influence was of particular importance in the early 1990s, as the PDS sought to cement itself into eastern German political life, and his is an achievement that should not be underestimated. Gysi's appeal has enabled the PDS to go at least some way towards improving the party's popular image away from the SED and towards a form of 'normality'. Gysi, as well as the reformers in the PDS leadership who have been active around him, have been able to mould the structural strength of the PDS in the East into programmatic positions that placate a conservative membership yet still appeal to a broad spectrum of the eastern population.

The leadership of the PDS has also appreciated that the structure of the German federal system has enabled the PDS to offer enthusiastic and talented members the opportunity to take part in political activity. The PDS has created a leadership hierarchy that effectively accommodates all strands of ideological thinking within the diverse membership. Inner-party democracy flourishes, and members are given ample opportunity to exert influence both within the party, and for the party, within the parliaments and councils of the eastern German communes. The 'second tier' of leadership figures in the eastern German *Landtage* have proved capable of shaping the PDS's profile in the lower levels of eastern German politics, just as the large pool of 30–50 year olds who work for the PDS in *Landtage*, *Stadträte* and at other levels of communal politics are seen as being hard-working, genuine and approachable. It is for this reason that the communal politicians of the PDS remain one of the party's greatest strengths over and above other parties in eastern Germany.

Importantly for the PDS's *Basisarbeit* (grass-roots work), the PDS is also in possession of a network of active and enthusiastic members who ensure that the PDS's message is passed on to the wider eastern German community in less formal arenas. This can often be over the coffee-table, in the local supermarket or at the bus stop. The effective (and often almost banal) extra-parliamentary activity of the PDS at the micro-levels of eastern German politics enables it to foster an image as *the* party of eastern German interests. The PDS remains embedded deep in eastern Germany's civil society and has managed to foster an image of a caring, compassionate actor in a harsh and unforgiving (new) environment. The key common denominator remains territory – as eastern Germans from many different sections of society are attracted by the PDS's 'eastern Germanness'.

Most importantly, the PDS has also managed to present itself as the representative of a community: eastern Germans. It gives voice to the unique eastern German identity within the political process. No other party is in a position to do this, as no other party is as deeply rooted in eastern German society and political culture. The PDS skilfully makes use of its heritage and ideological orientation in voicing concerns that are evident in the eastern German identity of defiance. It does not shirk from using populist terminology in articulating these sentiments, and this plays an important part in ensuring that Easterners identify with the PDS as the party that is 'fighting their corner'. PDS politicians excel at rhetorically bringing concerns that are unique to the identity of defiance into everyday political discourse. The PDS, owing partially to its similar experiences in being forced to come to terms with a new multi-party political system, has been able to appeal to sentiments that are widely held across the eastern states (see chapter four) and has been able to act as a fellow-traveller along an uneasy path.

In order to further understand how the PDS garners support in eastern Germany we must move on and discuss how the PDS advocates eastern German interests within the political arena. This chapter has concentrated largely on the (effective leadership and party organisation) that assist the PDS in articulating eastern German interests, as well as highlighting how the PDS represents eastern German identity within the political process. Chapter six moves the discussion on further to highlight how the PDS has articulated eastern German difference in terms of the policies it has developed and attempted to implement in regional and national legislatures. The PDS has a strong core of specific policy proposals that reflect the uniqueness of territorial sentiment in the eastern states. This is the nature of the 'big idea' that has proven to be so fundamental to the success of regional parties in, and it is to this that the discussion moves next.

Notes

1   Spittman, 1994, pp.673–4. Infratest Dimap, 1998, p. 10.

2   Berrington, 1985, p. 449.

3   Forschungsgruppe Wahlen, 1999c, p. 38.

4   Forschungsgruppe Wahlen 1999c, p. 42.

5   Forschungsgruppe Wahlen, 1999a, p. 35.

6   Gysi appeared on Erich Böhme's high-profile 'Talk im Turm' political discussion pro-gramme a record fifteen times. He is also the only politician to have appeared twice in the RTL 'heißen Stuhl' (hot seat). See Bergsdorf, 2001, p. 41.

7   See 'Rente statt Revolution', in *Süddeutsche Zeitung*, 3 April 2000, p. 11.

8   See 'Und ewig lockt die Weltrevolution', in *Süddeutsche Zeitung*, 6 April 2000, p. 3.

9   Despite not winning a *Direktmandat* in the 1998 Federal Election, Bisky was able to reg-ister 7.3 per cent more 'first' votes in the seat of Köpenick-Treptow than the PDS's pro-portion of the 'second' votes. This is quite a considerable achievement, only bettered amongst PDS politicians by Gregor Gysi in Hellersdorf–Marzahn (14.1 per cent), Christa Luft in Friedrichshain–Lichtenberg (9.5 per cent) and Petra Pau (9.1 per cent in the high profile seat of Mitte-Prenzlauer Berg). Citizens of these constituencies were prepared to vote for the PDS with their first, constituency, vote, while switching to other parties with their second, 'proportional' vote. This indicates both active vote-splitting for tactical rea-sons and a likely resonance with the candidate in question. See Infratest Dimap, 1998, p.91.

10 See 'Rente statt Revolution', in *Süddeutsche Zeitung*, 3 April 2000, p. 11.

11 For a particularly detailed account of André Brie's position within the PDS see Sturm, 2000, pp. 51–96. For a discussion of André Brie's most controversial statements on the GDR and socialism today, see Fraude, 1999, p. 174.

12 Sturm, 2000, p. 316.

13 Heym was not a member of the PDS, rather he stood on one of the PDS's open lists. Heym's position as a leading intellectual in the GDR, as well as his standing as a respect-ed author, granted him a high profile in the campaign to win, possibly, the most high-pro-file constituency in Germany.

14 'Täve' is most widely known for his exploits in the *Friedensfahrt* (the Peace Race). Although the *Friedensfahrt* has enjoyed something of a resurgence in the eastern states in the late 1990s, the race enjoyed its heyday in the years before the *Wende*. The *Friedensfahrt* traditionally went through Poland, Czechoslovakia and the GDR, and was a magnet for the best riders from throughout the socialist world (and selected others from the West). Schur not only won the event twice (in 1955 and 1959), he was also twice world champi-on and, in 1990, was voted the most popular sportsman in the history of the GDR. See http://www.friedensfahrt.de

15 Huhn, 1998.

16 Täve Schur (PDS): in Maxi Wartelsteiner 'Täve kommt – und ist nicht mehr zu überse-hen', on http://www.pds-online.de/disput/9808/39292.html and in *PDS Disput*, Number 8, August 1998.

17 For evidence of this approach see Neugebauer, 2000, p.44.

18 See Horst Kahrs: 'Was kommt nach den 'Reformen' in der PDS?', in *PDS Disput*, Nummer 5, May 2000, on http://www.pds-online.de/disput/0005/03.htm

19 Gregor Gysi (PDS): 'Die PDS kann als Sekte untergehen', in *Süddeutsche Zeitung*, 11 April 2000, p. 8.

20 'PDS-Vorschlag für die Landtagswahl', in *Neues Deutschland*, 18 May 1999, p. 5.

21 See Probst, 2000, p. 12.

22 Probst, 2000, p. 28.

23 See Klaus Halting: 'Die PDS schielt nach der Macht' in *Die Zeit*, 17 January 1997; 'PDS will im Bund bis 2002 Koalitionsfähig werden', in *Süddeutsche Zeitung*, 6 December 1999, p.6; 'Minister Holter ragt Parteireform an', in *Süddeutsche Zeitung*, 9 November 1999, p. 5; 'Die PDS vor ihrem Bad Godesberg' in *Süddeutsche Zeitung*, 30 November 1999, p. 4.

24 The PDS has become well-known for its eye-catching posters at election time. They have ranged from short and simple messages like *PDS: Cool!*, *PDS: Geil!* (PDS: Sexy!), *Euro?:So nicht!* (Euro? Not like this!), *Kohl muß weg, Du muß her!* (Kohl has to go, you have to join in!) to *Drei Gründe PDS zu wählen: CDU, SPD und FDP* (Three reasons to vote PDS: CDU, SPD and FDP!) and *Der Osten wählt links* (The East votes left-wing). The PDS also uses posters of its key personalities like Gysi and Angela Marquardt. Slogans have tended to remain short and simple and have often give the impression of cheekiness, vitality and the PDS as a somewhat different sort of party.

25 See *Blickpunkt Bundestag – Forum der Demokratie*, April 3/99, p. 34.

26 For a detailed discussion on the work of these groups within the PDS, see Moreau, 1998, pp. 130–211.

27 Zentralinstitut für sozialwissenschaftliche Forschung, 1996.

28 Dietmar Bartsch: 'PDS: Kein Auslaufmodell', in *Schweriner Volkszeitung*, 16 April 1997.

29 The level of organisation is measured as the number of members in a party multiplied by 100 and then divided by the number of voters in that state. This enables one to see what percentage of a state's population each particular party is able to (actively) mobilise to its cause.

30 Angela Merkel: in Dieter Wenz: 'Ostdeutsche Knochenarbeit', in *Frankfurter Allgemeine Zeitung*, 7 October 1999, p. 20.

31 Segall *et. al.*, 1999, p. 122.

32 The PDS is under no illusions about this. For examples of this see 'Mangel an Mitgliedern plagt alle Parteien im Land', in *Schweriner Volkszeitung*, 19 October 1995, 'Startschuß für Wahlkampf auf dem PDS-Parteitag', in *Schweriner Volkszeitung* 23 June 1997.

33 Dieter Wenz: 'Ostdeutsche Knochenarbeit', in *Frankfurter Allgemeine Zeitung*, 7 October 1999, p. 20.

34 Wittich, 1996, p. 181.

35 Lothar Probst: 'Wer ist die PDS? Einblicke in den Alltag einer postkommunistischen Partei', in *Frankfurter Allgemeine Zeitung*, 1 September 1997.

36 Dieter Wenz: 'Ostdeutsche Knochenarbeit', in *Frankfurter Allgemeine Zeitung*, 7 October 1999, p.20. Lothar Probst indicates, however, that the figures quoted by Wenz refer to 1997, as by June 1998 the number of *Basisorganisationen* had dropped to 105. See Probst, 2000, p. 17.

37 Amazingly, in 1999, 73 members of the PDS in Leipzig were 91 years of age or older! PDS Stadtverband Leipzig: *Mitteilungsblatt*, Nummer 2/3, März 1999, pp.4–5. It is, however, worth remembering that the CDU is also a party with what many would regard as an 'ageing' membership, even if its situation is not as extreme as the PDS's. The average age of a CDU member is 56, while only 15.7 per cent of the party membership is aged between 16 and 39. Of these, only 1.8 per cent are under 24, while only a total of 4.7 per cent are 29 or under. See Escher and Müller: *Empfehlungen zur Erneuerung der CDU* (Bonn: Pressekonferenz der CDU am 7 Oktober 1998), p. 2.

38 Segall *et al.*, 1999, p .7.

39 Helmut Holter (PDS): in Lothar Probst: 'Die PDS: Zur Anatomie einer postkommunistischen Partei' (Schwerin: Paper given at a Konrad Adenauer Stiftung conference on the 10.3.98), p.13. Also quoted in Dieter Wenz: 'Ostdeutsche Knochenarbeit', in *Frankfurter Allgemeine Zeitung*, 7 October 1999, p.20. See also Dieter Wenz: 'Ein Land für Wählergemeinschaften', in *Frankfurter Allgemeine Zeitung*, 12 June 1999, p. 16.

40 Moreau, 1996, p. 236.

41 Michael Chrappa and Dietmar Wittich do, however, estimate that approximately 50 per cent of all PDS members participate in campaign activities, while roughly a third participate regularly in *Basiskonferenzen* and a quarter in PDS-organised demonstrations. Quoted in Tom: Strohschneider: 'Befragung zum Thema: Der PDSler, das unbekannte Wesen?', in *Neues Deutschland*, 21 May 2001, p. 2.

42 For a fuller analysis see Probst, 2000, p. 17.

43 Zentralinstitut für sozialwissenschaftliche Forschung, 1996, p. 48.

44 Segall *et al.*, 1999, p. 9.

45 Peter Porsch: 'PDS 2000 – Worauf es ankommt!', in *PDS Pressedienst*, Nummer 20, 19 Mai 2000, on http://www.pds-online/pressedienst/0020/15.htm

46 Segall *et al.*, 1999, p. 9.

47 Thomas Lutze, PDS *Landesgeschäftsführer* in the Saarland: 'Ohne Verstärkung an der Basis, keine Basis bei den Wahlen', on http://www.pds-online.de/disput/9812/39759.html and in *PDS Disput*, Nummer 12, Dezember 1998.

48 Terms used in German local government do not have exact English or American equivalents: the nearest term is 'local council'.

49 Town or city council not under local control.

50 Borough councils in Berlin.

51 Council of a town or city under local control.

52 Heiko Grohe: 'Anregungen und Vorschläge für die kommunalpolitische Arbeit der PDS 1998', in *Kommunal Spezial* (Schwerin: Kommunalpolitsches Forum Mecklenburg-Vorpommern e. V, March 1998), p. 5.

53 Grohe, 1998, p. 5.

54 Peter Porsch (PDS): 'Unsere Zukunft liegt nicht in der Gegenwart anderer Parteien, sondern in einer Partei als Netzwerk demokratischer Bewegung', speech at the sixth *Landesparteitag* of the PDS in Saxony, in *PDS Pressedienst*, Nummer 2, 14 January 2000. See also http://www.pds-online.de/pressedienst/0002/09.htm

55 Rochtus *et al.*, 1996, p 9.

56 Probst, 2000, p. 6.

57 Gabi Schulz (PDS): 'Zusammenschluß von Gemeinden darf nicht zu deren Last gehen' (Schwerin: PDS Presseerklärung, PDS Pressestelle, Nummer 70, 6 April 1999). PDS politicians in Mecklenburg Western Pomerania have, however, acknowledged that the unique structure of communal authority in Mecklenburg Western Pomerania means that there is a large number of very small *selbständige Gemeinden* that remain too expensive to continue financing. In mid-2000 there were 1008 *Gemeinden*, compared to just 544 in Saxony – a state with a much higher population. 440 of the *Gemeinden* in Mecklenburg Western Pomerania have fewer than 500 residents living there – a figure that both Arnold Schoenenberg and Klaus Böttger (both PDS *Landtag* MdL's) admit is far too high. See 'Zu viele Gemeinden im Lande? Debatte über freiwilligen Zusammenschluss oder Zwangsvereinigung', in *Neues Deutschland*, 11 April 2000, p. 5.

58 'Koalitionsvereinbarung IX. Selbstverwaltung der Kommunen ausbauen und ihre Leistungsfähigkeit sichern. Abschnitt 1: Kommunalpolitik' in *Koalitionsvereinbarung zwischen der Sozialdemokratischen Partei Deutschlands und dem Partei des Demokratischen Sozialismus* (Schwerin: Landtag Mecklenburg-Vorpommern, 1998). See also http://www.mv-pds-ltf.de/koalition/i00000.htm

59 Bärbel Kozian (Vorsitzende des Kommunalpolitschen Forums Mecklenburg-Vorpommern e. V.): 'Jahresversammlung 1997 zog positive Bilanz', in *Kommunal Spezial* (Schwerin: Kommunalpolitsches Forum Mecklenburg-Vorpommern e. V, March 1998), p. 2.

60 According to the PDS spokesman on communal affairs in the Bundestag, Uwe-Jens Rössel, 50 per cent of communes in both Saxony and Thuringia are insolvent (*Zahlungsunfähig*). See *PDS im Bundestag Presseerklärung: Kommunalreform, Nummer 2070, 11 March 1998.

61 *Deutscher Bundestag:* Drucksache 13/4597.

62 *PDS im Bundestag Presseerklärung:* Kommunalreform, Nummer 2070, 11 March 1998.

63 'Einstieg in eine umfassende Reform der Finanzierung der Städte, Gemeinden und Landkreise' (A Comprehensive Reform of the Financing of Cities, Municipalities and Rural Districts). *Deutscher Bundestag:* Drucksache 14/1302.

64 *Deutscher Bundestag:* Drucksache 13/984.

65 *Deutscher Bundestag:* Drucksache 13/4597. Both of these motions were rejected, but the SPD and the Alliance 90/Greens acknowledged the necessity of financial reform at the micro-levels of German politics. Alliance 90/Greens did eventually call for the establishment of a commission of experts to investigate finance reform for municipalities, and the SPD followed suit after the Saarland brought a similar motion forward in the *Bundesrat.*

66 Lothar Bisky (PDS): Speech at the Rostock Party Conference, 3 April 1998, in *PDS Pressedienst*, Nummer 15–16, 17 April 1998, p. 3.

67 Gregor Gysi (PDS): 'Das rote Gespenst', in *Der Spiegel*, Nummer 10, 1999, p. 25.

68 Brunner and Walz, 2000, pp. 92–3.

69 Pollack and Pickel, 2000, p. 136.

70 Pollack and Pickel, 2000, p. 136.

71 Pollack and Pickel, 2000, p. 136.

72 Christine Ostrowski and Ronald Weckesser: 'Ein Brief aus Sachsen', in *Neues Deutschland*, 8 May 1996, p. 1.

73 Gregor Gysi: Speech at PDS Conference in Berlin, quoted in *Neues Deutschland*, 21 January 1999, p. 10.

74 http://www.pds-online.de/wahlen/dokumente/bt-wahlprogramm/praeambel.htm

75 In the Rostock Manifesto the PDS specifically defines these particular experiences as equality for women in the workplace, inter-disciplinarity in universities, experiences of greater solidarity in society, the benefits of job security and so forth. See Das Rostoker Manifest, PDS Parteivorstand (1998): op. cit. p. 6.

76 Lothar Bisky (PDS) articulated this by stating that 'we want the people of eastern and western Germany in the Berlin Republic to act as a stimulus for each other in the knowledge that they have clear cultural differences … and these real-existing cultural differences should not be seen as a threat to anyone'. Lothar Bisky, in a speech to the PDS party conference in Berlin, 18 January 1999 in *Neues Deutschland*, 18 January 1999, p.4.

77 Dürr, 1996, p. 1352.

78 Half of eastern Germans would have regretted it if the PDS had not achieved parliamentary representation at the 1998 Federal Elections. See Infratest Dimap, 1998, p. 10.

79 Michael Benjamin and Sahra Wagenknecht are known in particular to hold very ambiguous positions on the building of the Berlin Wall and the nature of the GDR's achievements and legitimacy. See for example Wagenknecht, 1998; Wagenknecht and Brie: *Wie macht sich die PDS nicht überflüssig?* , 1996; Benjamin, 1996a; 1996b, pp.231–6, 1999, p. 1; Michael Benjamin: '7. Oktober – war da nicht was?', in *Junge Welt*, 7 October 1999, p. 2.

80 Uwe-Jens Heuer (PDS), in Benjamin, 1996a, p. 1

81 Segall *et al.*, 1999, p. 43.

82 See Christoph Dieckmann, 1999,: 'Das Bier von Hier', in *Die Zeit*, 14 October 1999, p.14.

83 Ingrid Tschirch (PDS): '83 Sitzung am 31. März 1998', in Landtag Mecklenburg-Vorpommern: *Zur Arbeit des Landtags in der 2. Wahlperiode 1994 bis 1998*, p. 5167.

84 Das Rostocker Manifest, PDS Parteivorstand, 1998, p. 4.

85 PDS: *Wahlprogramm der Partei des Demokratischen Sozialismus zur Bundestagswahl 1998*, p.31.

86 'Die Doppelbiograhie der Bundesrepublik. Zum Phänomen der deutschen Zweistaatlichkeit', *Dokumente zur Geschichte der PDS* (Thesenpapier der Historischen Kommission beim Parteivorstand der PDS, on http://www.pds-online.de/geschichte/9903/doppelbiograhie.htm). See also *PDS Pressedienst*, Nummer 13, 31 März 1999.

87 Gabi Zimmer (PDS): 'Neue Lösungen für den Osten statt Festhalten am "Nachbau West"', in *PDS Pressedienst*, Nummer 14, 7 April 2000, on http://www.pds-online.de/pressedienst/0014/16.htm

88 Catherina Muth (PDS): '83 Sitzung am 31. März 1998', in Landtag Mecklenburg-Vorpommern: *Zur Arbeit des Landtags in der 2. Wahlperiode 1994 bis 1998*, p.5159.

89 By the end of 1998 these sums amounted to DM 1369 billion! *Presse- und Informationsamt der Bundesregierung*: 'Deutschland von der Teilung zur Einheit' (Bonn: Bundesregierung, 1999) p. 158.

90 Uwe-Jens Rossel (PDS): 'Maßstab: Gleiche Lebensverhältnisse im Schwarzwald und im Erzgebirge', in *R(h)einblick*, Number 3, 2001, on http://www2.pds-online.de/bt/

91 Lothar Bisky (PDS): 'Streit um langsamere Rentenanpassung', in *Schweriner Volkszeitung*, 20 January 1996.

92 Gregor Gysi, speech to the Federal Parliament on 11 September 1996, in Gysi, 1998, p. 19.

93 Gregor Gysi, speech to the Federal Parliament on 23 May 1996, in Gysi, 1998, p.15.

94 Peter Hintze (CDU): in 'Inhaltliche Auseinandersetzung mit falschen Parolen', *Frankfurter Allgemeine Zeitung*, 21 October 1999, p. 2.

95 Bernhard Vogel (CDU): 'Vogel: 'Freistaat' heißt Unions-Domäne', in *Neues Deutschland*, 8 November 1999, p. 5.

96 Peter Hintze (CDU): 'Heftiger Streit in der Union über Haltung zur PDS', in *Süddeutsche Zeitung*, 20 October 1999, p. 1.

97 Helmut Kohl (CDU): 'Blühende Landschaften? 'Zu diesem Satz stehe ich nach wie vor" in *Rheinischer Merkur*, 3 November 1999. See http://www.merkur.de Kohl has also recalled Kurt Schumacher's famous phrase directed at East German communists by denouncing the PDS as 'red-painted fascists'. See Phillips, 1995, p.221.

98 Edmund Stoiber (CSU): quoted in *Bild am Sonntag*, 5 May 1991, p. 1.

99 Golz, 1998, p. 876.

100 Regardless of how well the western parties understand the parameters of political com-

petition in the East, it is also clear that they are not averse to using the issue of the PDS as a stick with which to try and beat each other. The CDU and CSU, in particular, use the PDS as a picture of the enemy with which to mobilise the more conservative elements of their electorate in western Germany. This is often in spite of the negative impression that it can leave in eastern Germany. For evidence of criticism of this approach see Richard von Weizsäcker: in *Die Zeit*, 10 November 1995.

101 Caterina Muth and Dietmar Bartsch (PDS): *Rote Socken und rote Hände haben keine Angst vorm schwarzen Mann* (Schwerin: PDS Presseerklärung, PDS Pressestelle, Nummer 1000), 27 Mai 1998.

102 Peter Porsch (PDS): 'Huber verläßt Boden des Grundgesetzes', in *PDS Pressedienst*, Nummer 2, 14 January 1999.

103 Erwin Huber (CSU) was quoted as saying that 'we are not going to permit money that is designated by the Bund and the federal states for the rebuilding of the eastern economy to be misused for the resurrection of the communist East'. See *Die Zeit*, 14 January 1999, p. 2.

104 See *Der Tagesspiegel*, 16 January 1999, p. 1.

105 Stefan Kuzmany: 'Kein schwarzes Geld für den roten Osten?', in *Die Tageszeitung*, 9 January 1999, p.6. See also 'Empörte Reaktionen auf Hubers Vorstoß zur Einstellung der Ost-Hilfen', in *Süddeutsche Zeitung*, 8 January 1999.

106 Gregor Gysi (PDS): 'Huber verläßt Boden des Grundgesetzes', in *PDS Pressedienst*, Nummer 2, 14 January 1999.

107 Dietmar Bartsch (PDS): 'Huber verläßt Boden des Grundgesetzes', in *PDS Pressedienst*, Nummer 2, 14 January 1999.

108 Roland Koch (CDU): 'Koch will für Kredite Erfolgsgarantie: Hessischer Regierungschef wirft Osten Misswirtschaft vor', in *Süddeutsche Zeitung*, 10 April 1999, p. 8 .

109 Dirk Wenz: 'Koch will für Kredite Erfolgsgarantie: Hessischer Regierungschef wirft Osten Misswirtschaft vor', in *Süddeutsche Zeitung*, 10 April 1999, p. 8.

110 Christa Luft (PDS): 'Koch will für Kredite Erfolgsgarantie: Hessischer Regierungschef wirft Osten Misswirtschaft vor', in *Süddeutsche Zeitung*, 10 April 1999, p. 8.

111 There are also examples of *Eastern* CDU politicians levelling dramatic accusations that tend to isolate themselves more than the PDS. Wolfgang Riemann, for example, claimed that 'if it had been down to the SED/PDS, then in Leipzig we would have had something akin to an East German Tiananmen Square massacre … and the Prime Minister of this state would have been in a concentration camp'. Wolfgang Riemann (CDU): '83 Sitzung am 31. März 1998', in Landtag Mecklenburg-Vorpommern: *Zur Arbeit des Landtags in der 2. Wahlperiode 1994 bis 1998*, p. 5168.

112 Wittich, 1996, p. 184.

6

The PDS: making policy for eastern Germany

Chapter five illustrated that the PDS has taken advantage of a number of factors in establishing itself as a representative of eastern German interests. It is a very well organised party, with an active and highly motivated membership, and has been lucky enough to have a group of leaders, epitomised by the witty and telegenic Gregor Gysi, with the vision to lead the party away from its dogmatic SED past towards a more pragmatic understanding of socialism. The PDS has also invigorated its policy making, shaping a political programme which, while not disavowing the party's 1989 heritage, has enabled it to adapt to the contours of contemporary German society and articulate the specific sentiments of eastern Germans within the political process – it is in this role that the PDS makes another unique contribution to political life in Germany.

The policy areas and programme initiatives discussed in this chapter encompass the main areas of attitudinal difference between eastern and western Germans. The PDS has developed political approaches and policy options that reflect the attitudes and opinions of a significant portion of eastern Germans; as such, it is perceived by the electorate at large as the party which gives voice to the interests and demands of many eastern Germans. The immediate viability of the policies that the PDS has developed is not an issue – it is more the rhetorical significance and uniqueness of their political appeal that render them effective. Even eastern Germans who do not support the party often recognise that the PDS performs the valuable task of ensuring that issues and worries prevalent to the eastern states remain high on the national political agenda.[1]

The PDS has discussed eastern German interests explicitly in a number of documents, the most prominent of which was the 1998 *Rostocker Manifest*

(Rostock Manifesto). The manifesto, written principally by Christa Luft, economics spokesperson of the PDS, was launched at the April 1998 conference: It is a contribution to the debate over the economic and social future of eastern Germany,[2] the most comprehensive attempt by the PDS thus far to articulate eastern German interests, and has as its overarching aim the economic and social rejuvenation of the eastern states. Further, arising from the activities of its working and interest groups and its work in local, regional and national parliaments, the PDS has produced and published in its election material a wide variety of literature on the nature of its commitment to improving the lot of eastern Germans. All of this is referred to in the analysis below.

Eastern Germany

Even a cursory glance at the programmes of the major parties in Germany shows that issues surrounding the social, economic and political rejuvenation of eastern Germany, as well as attitudes to life in the GDR, are not highly developed. Approaches to the solution of the economic and social problems of '*Ostdeutschland*' are often summarised in a few paragraphs, with little or no policy detail. The PDS, as one would expect, handles the issue of 'eastern Germany' in a way that sets it apart from the other major German parties. Harry Nick observes that it is *the* issue that distinguishes the CDU, the SPD and Alliance 90/Greens from the PDS most dramatically.[3] This distinction is not just in the area of economic and social policy approaches, but also in interpretations of the extent and causes of eastern Germany's economic and social difference. The PDS is adamant that eastern Germans are largely *ausgegrenzt* (excluded) from the political process, and that political activity in Germany runs on an exclusively western German agenda. As was claimed in the 1998 'Rostock Manifesto':

> The decision on whether something is good or bad is made with reference to whether it is good or bad for the western states. The majority of eastern Germans perceive themselves has having hardly any opportunity to influence decisions made in the FRG today. GDR heritage is often sufficient reason to be discriminated against … and the promise of blossoming landscapes has proven itself to be the biggest lie of the unification year.[4]

The emphasis that the PDS places on current governmental responsibility for the economic, social and political dissatisfaction in eastern Germany mirrors the popular feeling that the CDU and, to a lesser extent, the SPD are primarily responsible for the Easterners' current plight. The PDS does not mention the decrepit state of the GDR economy in 1989, and as such purposely relieves itself of any blame for the economic difficulties of the last ten years.[5] The PDS in Saxony Anhalt, for example, explicitly blames post-1989 CDU policies for the unhealthy economic climate that prevails in that state. As a declaration from the February 1999 conference observes:

> ... since the beginning of the second legislative period in Saxony Anhalt, the financial, economic and labour market performance has been persistently poor – and this is as a result of the policies of the *Treuhand* holding agency and the CDU-inspired deregulation of Saxony Anhalt's industrial base.[6]

The East's high rates of unemployment are seen as ensuing solely from the CDU-led Federal Government's pursuit of 'neoliberal' economic policies, which ensure that (allegedly) the rich get richer, while the poor get poorer.[7] The PDS articulates a widely held belief that the West has used and abused eastern German economic assets. As Catherina Muth, former parliamentary leader of the PDS in Mecklenburg Western Pomerania has observed:

> ... it is a mistake to believe that the Government was simply incapable of effectively tackling the problem of unemployment. Quite the opposite. The policies of the CDU/CSU and FDP have led to a nation-wide redistribution of wealth and power in the direction of employers.[8]

Peter Porsch reiterated a similar disdain for neoliberal, capitalist polices following the 1999 elections in Saxony:

> The voters of Saxony have entrusted us ... (the PDS) ... with the key role of being the principal opposition party to the neoliberal policies, representing the interests of a few large western German and foreign companies, of Kurt Biedenkopf and his CDU.[9]

Although the eastern electorate certainly has *not* acquitted the SED for its role in ruining the East German economy, many Easterners appear more eager to punish the mistakes of the last ten years than those of the previous forty. The PDS both reacts to and actively promotes such attitudes, and remains explicit in its demands for 'a better deal' for eastern Germany in general. It is exceptionally proficient in tabling motions and questions, at both the federal and regional levels, with the aim of highlighting (perceived) governmental failures in the eastern states, PDS options for improvements, or simply campaigns to bring issues and problems to the government's or population's attention. The PDS is able to talk about the 'big picture', and is also adept at breaking down its complex ideas into themed policy proposals in 'live' areas – the persistent underlying emphasis being on a 'fair' treatment for Easterners: Lothar Bisky phrases it thus:

> ... we want more powers to be granted to eastern Germans in the key questions of their development. We want to have the courage to enable Easterners to come up with their own innovative solutions to problems. We want to strengthen the eastern states as a prerequisite to strengthening federalism in Germany and in a Europe of the regions.[10]

He continues by adding that:

> we do not want any *Dekret* that lifts eastern Germany over and above western Germany or that differentiates the East from the West. We are not in the game of replacing the failed ideas about the 'historic mission of the working class and their Marxist-Leninist party' with the even more absurd idea of the 'historic mission of the *Ossi* and their PDS'. We want a relationship between East and West, put nice and simply, that is characterised by solidarity – where it is necessary – and fair and open competition – where it is possible – just like the relationship between the north and south of Germany.[11]

Without the PDS directly voicing the concerns of eastern Germans, many issues and problems would not have been raised or resolved in the federal parliament, as the other parties are unlikely to have dedicated time to them. Some issues have only been placed on the agenda by the western parties after years, on occasion, of pressure from the PDS. The PDS is adamant that other parties frequently reject their policies *per se*, only to place them on the agenda themselves in succeeding months.[12]

With specific regard to eastern Germany, the PDS places many *kleine Anfragen* in the *Bundestag*, aimed at ensuring that the federal government has to answer specific questions relating to economic and political activity in the eastern states. Throughout the 1990s the PDS remained the most vocal party in forcing the federal government to defend its record in the eastern states: on 19 February 1999, for example, the PDS placed a catalogue of questions in front of the SPD-led administration, demanding to know how the key priority of rebuilding eastern Germany was proceeding. Among the questions they posed were:

- How had the cost of living, as well as average wages and salaries in the eastern and western states, progressed since 1990, and how did the government view these developments with regard to their avowed aim of equalising living standards?
- Which academic qualifications and other certificates of achievement obtained in the GDR were not presently recognised in the FRG? Did the federal government see any opportunity for increasing the number of qualifications that could be recognised in the future?
- When would eastern German doctors and other health workers, artists, scientists, railway employees, postal workers and those in the public services, at both state and federal levels, be able to claim the *liquidierten Versorgungsansprüche* (entitlements that were annulled in 1990) that they had been due since GDR times?
- How high was the proportion, at the federal level, of civil servants within the public sector who were, on the 3 October 1990, citizens of the GDR? How many of these were in high-ranking positions of service, and how did the federal government aim to increase the number of eastern Germans in such positions?
- Article 44 of the Unification Treaty (which states that the rights that come into force with the unification treaty can be validated by citizens of the eastern states and Berlin) had not been, at that date, acted upon. How and where were these rights be implemented? Did the federal government see any necessity to elaborate on this article, to ensure clarity?

At the federal level, the PDS tabled a *große Anfrage* (parliamentary questions) on the subject of 'The Situation in Eastern Germany' (*Zur Lage in Ostdeutschland*), containing 232 individual (and very detailed) questions on the economic, social and legal position of the eastern states.[13] This was followed in April 1999 by another *große Anfrage* on the 'Development and Situation in Eastern Germany' (*Zur Entwicklung und zur Situation in Ostdeutschland*), containing 133 questions and demands.[14] On the 22 of June 1999 Gregor Gysi and the PDS *Fraktion* (parliamentary group) submitted an *Antrag* (parliamentary bill) titled *Fahrplan zur Angleichung der Lebensverhältnisse und zur Herstellung von mehr Rechtssicherheit in Ostdeutschland – 'Chefsache Ost'* (A Timetable for the Equalisation of Living Conditions and the Production of Greater Law Enforcement in Eastern Germany), containing detailed demands for more social justice, material equality and judicial 'fairness' for eastern Germans.[15] These initiatives were supplemented by numerous other motions on specifically eastern German issues (see table 6.1) as well as a proposed 'Economic and Ecological Alternative Programme in the Eastern States'.[16]

The work of the PDS in regional parliaments also illustrates the PDS's ability to conceptualise its political platform of eastern interests in terms of policy initiatives. In Saxony, Saxony Anhalt, Thüringia and Brandenburg the PDS remains a clear and consistent opposition *Fraktion*. Furthermore, it has established itself, by a considerable distance, as the party that forwards the highest number of parliamentary initiatives (see table 6.1.). Christine Ostrowski, a (former) PDS *Landtag* representative from Saxony managed to place over 100 *Kleine* and *Große Anfragen* on her own.[17]

The thematic areas that PDS initiatives refer to reflect the worries and insecurities that Easterners display. Their sheer volume ensures that the PDS is viewed as a party that is 'doing something'. In terms of social policy in the second legislative period, for example, the PDS concentrated on questions of rent levels and *Wohnungspolitik*, and on social assistance and pensions. These are interests that reflect the anxiety of Easterners about the cost of living, and the insecurities they have experienced since 1989. In the area of economics the PDS has persistently stressed the need to tackle high unemployment and the importance of rejuvenating the regional economy, while doing away with

Table 6.1. Parliamentary initiatives proposed by the PDS in the eastern German *Landtagen* and the *Abgeordnetenhaus* (state parliament) in Berlin

	Gesetzentwürfe	*Anträge*	*Große Anfragen*
Berlin	14	96	5
Brandenburg	15	130	12
Mecklenburg Western Pomerania	14	155	6
Saxony	19	186	24
Saxony Anhalt	15	158	6
Thuringia	9	123	6

Note: These figures relate to the period from the beginning of the second legislative period of the *Landtage* until 1 January 1997. See PDS Parteivorstand (Hrsg.): *Studien zur inneren Verfaßtheit der PDS* (Berlin: PDS, 1997), p.16.

high-cost prestige projects like the Eurofighter jet or the *Transrapid* train. This once again is a reflection of particular eastern sentiment. In terms of culture, the PDS has sought to retain eastern cultural uniqueness against the onset of western German domination,[18] while in the field of education the PDS has sought to expand the number of *Hochschulen* in eastern Germany and the number of training places available.[19] The PDS is consistent in its call for better financing of communal politics. In terms of *Innenpolitik*, it seeks equal rights for those discriminated against as a result of their activities in the GDR.[20] In addition to these broad areas of activity, the PDS is active and vocal in many fields of interest in all the legislative bodies of the eastern states.

Defending the GDR and East German history

Alongside its active representation of the perceived political and economic interests of contemporary eastern Germany, the PDS is also permanently ready to discuss the historical position of the GDR and the citizens of eastern Germany who used to live there. In the 1990–94 legislative period, for example, the PDS proposed parliamentary initiatives to secure more protection for officials who worked in the public sector in the GDR, the equal recognition of teachers from East and West Germany, a *Bestandsgarantie* (guaranteed right of existence) for companies that were to be revitalised and sold off by the *Treuhand* agency, and an amnesty for GDR spies.[21] The PDS is also keen, perhaps unsurprisingly, to draw a line under the GDR in terms of prosecuting officials who are accused of committing crimes before 1989.[22] This may seem mere political expedience for a party like the PDS, many of whose members are still embroiled in such cases, but none the less it finds a sizeable echo in society at large. Although there is little direct empirical data available on public opinion in this area, it remains clear that a sizeable proportion of eastern Germans are unhappy with the relentless attacks on 'their' state and 'their' lives in the pre-*Wende* period.[23] In this matter, the SPD, Alliance 90/Greens and CDU/CSU hold similar positions, opposing the PDS.[24] The PDS claims that, in view of the 60,000 judicial hearings and over 320 guilty verdicts, the German state should cease prosecuting those who held positions of authority within the GDR. The PDS proposed a law that would have ended the prosecution of GDR officials (*Strafverfolgungsbeendigungsgesetz*) on 27 June 1995[25] (although the party conceded that a clause allowing prosecution in exceptional cases could remain). This proposal was rejected.

Following the creation of the first SPD–PDS government in Mecklenburg Western Pomerania in 1998, the PDS negotiated an amendment to the *Regelanfrage* which examined the history of every citizen seeking to take up position in public service in the *Land* for evidence of contacts with the MfS in the GDR. Paragraph 161 of the coalition agreement between the SPD and the PDS stated that:

> The Government of Mecklenburg Western Pomerania will not require the *Bundesbeauftragten für die Unterlagen des Staatssicherheitsdienstes* (Office for the Investigation of the Stasi Files) to investigate any individual for activities relating to any work with the MfS (Stasi) unless there is reasonable suspicion of such contact.[26]

The PDS has, therefore, defended specific groups in eastern Germany against alleged discrimination at the hands of western Germans and the 'western German system'. It is vociferous in its attempts to substitute equality and fairness for the injustices that both it and significant portions of the eastern German population believe have been done to them since 1989. It has carried out direct, specialised attempts to revoke or review laws, as well as a broader strategy of representing eastern Germans *per se*. Broad-based discrimination against qualification or experience gained while living in the GDR is stringently opposed. As Lothar Bisky phrases it:

> We are continuing to fight for fair recognition of eastern German biographies. The discrimination and defamation of eastern Germans has to be stopped, as does the totally unnecessary humiliation of hundreds of people in the eastern states. We demand that everybody be treated equally. We demand an end to the political isolation (*Ausgrenzung*) of Easterners.[27]

The PDS is particularly keen to dismiss any attempts to equate the GDR dictatorship with that of the Third Reich. Conservative politicians, in particular, have tended to place the two dictatorships on a par. The PDS, while not seeking to legitimise the crimes and offences that were committed in the GDR, is vehemently against this. This was evident, for example, in 1992 when the constitution of Saxony was passed in the Saxon Parliament in Dresden. The PDS was the only party that voted against it precisely because the PDS believed that, in the preamble of the constitution, there was insufficient differentiation between the two German dictatorships of the twentieth century.[28] The PDS has not, however, been so enthusiastic in taking part in the institutionalised 'working through' of the GDR's history. This attitude of studied indifference also, perhaps curiously, represents popular sentiment in eastern Germany: the top-down approach to discussing the GDR in the Enquete Commission at the federal level left Easterners distanced from the process;[29] they felt that Westerners expected them to be unduly critical of their own past, while refusing to discuss the contradictions that may have existed in the FRG. The Commission itself was attempting to reveal an historical record, and as such its audience was the *Bundestag*, scholars and those citizens with the stamina and enthusiasm to sit through its lengthy and complex procedures.[30] Indeed, although it was a public event, and hearings were held all over eastern Germany, the statist nature of the commission ensured that its work was simply too dry, aloof and unexciting for many citizens.[31] Consequently, public interest in and knowledge about the Bundestag's Enquete Commission is not great. Furthermore, the Enquete Commission adopted a working brief that expressly indicated a preference for researching into the history and consequences *of the SED Dictatorship*.[32] This directly indicated that no attempt was to be made to analyse the history of the two German states, or even of the *Alltagsleben* within the GDR, although this second element was undoubtedly included, to a degree, in the Commission's remit. And while no rational individual would dispute that East Germany existed under dictatorial conditions, or that this had some gruesome consequences for the population, it is important to remember that the GDR was *not just* a Stasi state – a proposition which one could believe if some of the exaggerations about the role and influence of the Stasi were taken at face value. To many Easterners it appears very easy to overlook the fact that the GDR had more to its history than the single (albeit very important) characteristic of dictatorship.[33]

The PDS was highly critical of what it viewed as the party political nature (and in essence the western German dominance) of the Commission. Therefore it doubted very strongly whether the Commission would be able to remain above partisan concerns and avoid instrumentalisation by the political opponents of the PDS.[34] More specifically, the PDS was particularly keen to stress that the GDR should not be classified as an '*Unrechtsregime*'. The PDS was at pains to point out that the GDR was a 'recognised, sovereign state and member of the United Nations': hence the founding of the GDR in 1949 was legitimate within the unique context of the Cold War era.[35] The PDS demanded that the Commission be given a much more general remit, including the right to assess the history of the pre-1989 FRG. The PDS clearly wanted to stress its unique position within eastern German society. It aimed to do this by:

stressing the one-sided nature of the process, asserting that it was dominated by western German interests. Its intention was to use its reaction to the Commission as part of its strategy to assume the role of the only genuine party in opposition which represented eastern German interests.[36]

The PDS was not initially permitted voting rights, and it was excluded from the discussions that led to the proposal for a foundation to continue the process of working through the GDR's history. One can dispute whether these procedural decisions were legitimate; their outcomes remain clear: the *Außenseiterstatus* of the PDS meant that only the expressly eastern German party was denied an institutionalised voice in questions concerning the GDR. In a final statement on the Commission's work the PDS claimed that 'the Enquete Commission could not and would not avoid instrumentalisation by political parties',[37] adding that 'fundamental decisions on historical processes and developments, as well as on political and social systems cannot be decided by parliamentary majority'.[38] The PDS thus remained highly critical of the commission's motives, its procedures and of its conclusions.[39]

> The majority of members in the Commission expressed an anachronistic and militant anti-communism, whose prejudices, clichés and anti-liberal undercurrents were not suitable for reaching historically sound judgements or feelings of mutual understanding. The generalisations that the GDR was an *Unrechtstaat*, the condemnations of GDR history as being only about dictatorship and criminality and, above all, the attempts to place the SED regime on a par with the Nazi regime simply lead to new walls being erected and to history being falsified.[40]

The PDS has claimed that all of the western parties have disillusioned many Easterners – including parts of their own electorates – by dictating how the GDR should be perceived in popular discourse. The top-down nature of a process dictated by the western parties has ridden roughshod over the small, but significant, parts of life in the GDR that people wish to retain in their minds as positive recollections. The PDS has also been continually enraged by the refusal of western actors to carry out similar processes of historical self-reflection in the western states.[41] This would not be an attempt to de-legitimise the FRG, rather, the PDS claims, it would be a useful process on the path to inner unity, as the FRG comes to terms with controversial issues like the imperfect de-nazification process of the 1940s and 1950s, as well as the impact and treatment of left-wing terrorism in later decades.[42]

The PDS has drawn attention to what it described as a much more constructive and thoughtful attempt at working through the history of the GDR in Mecklenburg Western Pomerania.[43] This was the only *Land* to create its own Enquete Commission in order to record how life in the GDR functioned, what mistakes had been made and what could be learned from the experience of living in the GDR. The CDU and SPD *Fraktionen* decided at the *Landtag* session of 17 May 1995 to constitute an Enquete-Kommission under the title of '*Leben in der DDR, Leben nach 1989 – Aufarbeitung und Versöhnung*' (Life in the GDR, Life after 1989 – Working Through and Reconciliation). The PDS originally voted against the creation of the commission in this particular form, preferring to attempt to change the nature of the commission by submitting a motion to change the title from 'Working Through and Reconciliation' to 'Realities, Contradictions and Chances for a New Political Culture'.[44] The PDS put forward four other proposed alterations, all of which were aimed at neutralising the pejorative (in the opinion of the PDS) terminology used by the CDU and SPD when creating the commission, and the commission itself when it commenced its work.[45] Hence it quickly became apparent that although the PDS was prepared to praise at the federal level the workings of the commission in Mecklenburg Western Pomerania, it proved a difficult partner for the other political parties in the commission itself. From the beginning of the commission's lifespan, in 1995, the PDS, as it had done for the federal commission, stubbornly fought its corner about the legitimacy of the GDR, and the importance of recording not just *Stasi, Stacheldraht und Schießbefehl* (Stasi, barbed wire and orders to shoot) but also *alltägliches Leben* (everyday life). It was once again not prepared to see western Germans sit in judgement on eastern German life and lives.

The PDS was consequently very active within the commission, although it was obstructive on many occasions, and the fundamentally different understandings of the GDR that were represented, a positive view from the PDS, a critical one from the other parties , ensured that that PDS took every opportunity to insist upon a less derogatory tone in the discussion of the GDR.[46] One such example occurred as the commission was deciding upon which academics should research which particular issues:

> In the course of the discussion it has become evident that members of the CDU and the SPD have considered asking academics from universities outside eastern Germany to complete projects with regard to the work of this Commission, so as to

ensure as much competence and neutrality as possible. The PDS group cannot support this. We would much rather see the qualities of academics who have been '*abgewickelt*' since 1990, and have been through a process of unemployment, before finding new positions in newly founded research institutes, both recognised and rewarded as outstanding academic personalities.[47]

The PDS therefore still remained distanced from institutionalised attempts to 'work through' the history of the GDR. This is not to say that the party has not attempted to come to terms with the role that the SED played in the GDR, and the broader implications that this has both for the PDS's political future, and the wider political environment in the eastern states.[48] Easterners themselves remain unconvinced by the work of the Enquete Commissions as they were not given the mandate to consider genuinely the complexities and contradictions that life in the GDR entailed. The dominance of the western parties (even if eastern politicians and academics, particularly in Mecklenburg Western Pomerania, contributed to the process of coming to terms with the past – *Vergangenheitsbewältigung*) has also done nothing to increase their popular legitimacy.

In other spheres of daily life, the PDS has been active in defending eastern German symbols and unique characteristics. Examples of this are surprisingly numerous. The PDS was vocal in its defence of the *gruner Pfeil*, a traffic arrow allowing cars to turn right despite the traffic lights remaining on red – and the green arrow has now become a common sight on western German roads.[49] The PDS also fought successfully for the eastern German *Ampelmännchen*. Its campaigns argued that the eastern figure, with his sun hat and bouncy walk, attracted more attention and appeared more personable, and so more effectively alerted pedestrians to the dangers of crossing the road. PDS members could be seen on the streets wearing *Ampelmännchen* T-shirts and selling other *Ampelmännchen* memorabilia.[50] The PDS appropriated this peculiarly eastern symbol to remind and reassure voters that it too was from the East, and was prepared to fight any case where the West trampled eastern sensibilities. It also identified and resisted the imposition of western German norms – in this case in the form of a very stilted figure with an abnormally large head (which came to be known as 'bubble head'). Easterners, and the PDS, saw no reason to dispose of their little figures for the characterless western version – and the PDS benefited from its leadership of this long and hard fight.

The PDS has also strongly defended the *Jugendweihe* – the traditional, non-religious ceremony that many Easterners go through around the time of their fourteenth birthday. The *Jugendweihe* was first recorded as taking place in 1852, as a non-religious replacement for confirmation, and although it also existed in the early twentieth century, as well as in the Nazi period, it was only in 1954–5, when the SED designated it an official *Festakt*, that it became a widely practised ritual.[51] Against many predictions, the *Jugendweihe* has survived the collapse of the GDR,[52] and in recent years the number of Easterners who have been through the process has actually increased. The PDS remains the only party to *actively* support the retention of the ceremony, even though the other parties all have a majority of supporters in favour (table 6.2).

Much to the consternation of religious organisations, the PDS in Mecklenburg Western Pomerania has taken the unprecedented step of recognising the *Interessenverein Humanistischer Jugendarbeit* (The Interest Group for Humanistic Youth Work) as elegible to receive state subsidies to continue its role supporting and advising eastern German youngsters – and in supporting the institution of the *Jugendweihe*. As Andreas Bluhm from the PDS *Landtagsfraktion* in Mecklenburg Western Pomerania has stated:

> The *Jugendweihe* has existed for over 100 years. Even today it represents for youngsters and for their families a high-point on the way to adulthood. Alongside this there are numerous information and education events, as well as projects based on the most diverse of topics. This should not be confused with religious confirmations ... (but) ... every organisation that conducts work with the younger elements of society has the right to apply for financial subsidies. This is exactly what the religious institutions are also able to do for the work they put in with youngsters.[53]

Table 6.2. Are you of the opinion that the *Jugendweihe*, that stems from GDR times, should continue or should it be abolished? (Answers according to party preference (per cent).

	CDU/CSU	SPD	Alliances 90/Green	**PDS**
I think that it should continue	62	83	88	**100**
I think that it should be abolished	14	2	7	-
I am undecided/do not know	24	15	5	-
Total	100	100	100	**100**

Source: Noelle-Neumann and Köcher, 1997, p.587.

The SPD–PDS coalition in Mecklenburg Western Pomerania has also attempted to create an environment where Easterners support and buy products from eastern Germany. This encompasses products that are new and have appeared since unification, as well as older products that have survived or been revived from GDR times. While other parties in other states also attempt to support indigenous economic development, the governing parties in Mecklenburg Western Pomerania are unique in their inclusion of such an explicit clause in their coalition agreements.

> In order to increase the presence of eastern German products in national and international markets the state government, together with the federal administration, will organise sales subsidies in a much advantageous fashion for eastern products.[54]

These few examples illustrate how the PDS is keen to mobilise symbols of eastern uniqueness into its political platform. This is, of course, not always a straightforward task, as many symbols of easternness (coffee, cigarettes, washing powder, for example) do not easily lend themselves to political adaptation. But when a characteristic of eastern life is under threat or is seen as requiring a political advocate, the PDS is quick to jump to its defence. This naturally means that the PDS is not able to mobilise regional symbols and characteristics in quite such an enigmatic fashion as other regional parties. It cannot call on positive recollections or associations with 'nationhood', just as it does not resort to flag-waving separatism. But it is able, when the time and the issue is right, to support and advocate eastern German symbols that are threatened by western German norms and traditions.

Democratising democracy

Since the collapse of Nazi Germany in 1945, the Federal Republic has developed into one of the most stable democracies in the world. The reasons for this are easy to see. The Basic Law is accepted by almost all political parties (including most of the extremist fringe groupings) and freedom of speech, political pluralism and human rights are rarely issues in normal political debate. As such, few of Germany's parties make the issue of democracy a key plank of their party programmes. The PDS is the exception. It sees not only eastern Germans as being under-represented in the political process, it sees fundamental flaws in the democratic structures of the Federal Republic as a whole. It has, however, no intention of overthrowing either the regime or the constitution (contrary to the conclusions of some of the more excitable examinations of the PDS). It has committed itself completely to democratic means of political activity.[55] The PDS does, however, want to alter some of the mechanics of the way democracy in the Federal Republic functions. It seeks to bring citizens into the political process, and to give them the opportunity of having more control over more aspects of their daily lives. It looks to augment the parliamentary model of democracy with elements of direct, plebiscitary democracy.[56] It seeks to encourage 'bottom-up' democracy, through the introduction of referenda and the rejuvenation of communal politics by means of policies that it has broadly titled a 'democratisation of democracy'.

Unique amongst the parties of the Federal Republic, the 'democratisation of democracy' initiative of the PDS is a response to dissatisfaction in eastern Germany with the functioning procedures of democracy and its institutions.[57] Large sections of eastern German citizenry feel that they are excluded from political, cultural and economic decisions. The PDS has pleaded, at different times, for a new constitution,[58] a third chamber that deals specifically with social movements and eastern German problems and issues, and a thorough system of plebiscites.[59] All of these recommendations have been enthusiastically received in the eastern electorate.[60]

In their 1998 Federal Election programme the PDS devotes six pages to the issue of improving Germany's functioning democracy.[61] The reasoning behind this, according to the programme, is that:

> Many people no longer believe in the ability of democracy to change society for the better ... the threat is looming that power will simply become uncontrollable. In this situation, the necessity of democratic, public controls and the ability to shape democratic activity is urgent.[62]

The PDS realises that citizens of the eastern states feel shut out of the decision-making processes that shape their lives, at the political level, within the companies where they work, and within other organisations such as trade unions. In the Rostock Manifesto the PDS phrases its main aims thus:

> The PDS calls for: the power to decide *about* ... (my emphasis) ... the eastern states to be located within the eastern states instead of ... elsewhere. In order to make this possible, more powers have to be passed down from the federal level to the state and communal levels – as [part of a move towards increased] decentralisation in the federal structures of the

German state – so as to enable a politics of social justice and socioecological development to be implemented.[63]

The SPD–PDS state government in Mecklenburg Western Pomerania has sought to put this subsidiarity into practice.[64] In sections 184 and 185 of the 1998 coalition agreement they state:

> Functional reform is going to continue. The government will examine which powers can be passed down from the state level to the *Landkreise* and the *kreisfreien Städte* as well as which tasks can be passed down from these levels to the *Gemeinden*. In this context, the government will examine the case for the introduction of another level of communal government called the *Große kreisangehörige Stadt* ... the amalgamation of some smaller *Gemeinden* into more effective and modern units, on the basis of voluntary and democratic citizen participation will also be supported.[65]

The PDS also made this explicit in other elections: in Saxony, for example, the 1999 election programme for the *Landtagswahlen* referred to the need to lower the quorum for referenda from 450,000 signatures to 250,000, in order to facilitate more participation by the citizens in the democratic process.[66] The PDS is clear and consistent in both its calls for greater democratisation and citizen participation, and the SPD–PDS government in Mecklenburg Western Pomerania has made clear attempts to achieve this, reflecting eastern German dissatisfaction with the perceived deficiencies in the democratic methods and procedures of the German state.

Unemployment

Rather than attempt to tinker with the mechanics of the social market economy, the PDS believes that the only way to tackle crippling high rates of unemployment in eastern Germany is to adopt radical (when compared to the other parties) measures. The PDS remains the only party which voices parliamentary opposition to the structures of capitalist society: it promotes the idea that capitalism as an ideology is detrimental to the economic, political and social future of not just the eastern states, but the western ones as well.[67] The very nature of capitalism is seen as being the root cause of unemployment rates that remain so stubbornly high; the capitalist order imposed in the eastern states following unification is not only detrimental to the fundamental interests of the socially disadvantaged, but to *Easterners* per se.[68] The party has been consistent in its condemnation of the 'neoliberal'[69] policies of both the Kohl government and the Schröder administration that followed it. In the *Bundestag* Gregor Gysi claimed that the Kohl labour market policies were merely successful in creating extra work for staff in unemployment offices. His criticisms of the CDU/CSU–FDP government's record were unrelenting and unequivocal:

> If it were the case that the reductions in company taxes and the reductions in the amounts of social support that the state provides were stimulatory factors in creating new jobs – and that is the theory – then we should theoretically now be begging for foreign labour to come and fill all of our vacant employment positions; however, this approach, that the government has been pursuing for 15 years, has in reality led to over 4 million registered unemployed, *de facto* 6 million, in Germany today.[70]

As the number of Germans not employed in gainful economic activity has stabilised at worryingly high levels, the PDS has actively campaigned for radical changes in approach to the support and regulation of the labour market. This is clearly a sentiment that resonates in the eastern states, where the inability of the state to provide the population with employment is seen as a much greater 'sin' than it is in the western part of Germany – an attitudinal difference that is part of the socialist legacy of the GDR. Both the SPD and the CDU have attempted to create a dynamic impression in the eastern labour market, but the stubbornly high unemployment statistics have left many Easterners with the impression that the state is still doing too little to in create employment in eastern Germany. Hence the PDS has been the tub-thumper calling for a radical (if still somewhat unspecified) change of approach.

The PDS's policies for reducing unemployment

The PDS election campaign of 1998 centred on the need for a change of government at the federal level as a basic prerequisite for achieving any upturn in employment statistics. The only plausible way of achieving this goal was to support the replacement of Helmut Kohl's CDU by Gerhard Schröder's SPD. The PDS perceived its role as putting the centre-left coalition under pressure to remember its social conscience; it termed this '*Druck von Links*' ('pressure from the left'), intended to make sure the government remained committed to policies of social justice, increased employment, support for the socially disadvantaged and so forth. In practice, and despite the Keynesian tendencies of the Finance Minister Oskar Lafontaine, the PDS quickly proclaimed itself highly dissatisfied with the efforts of the SPD–Alliance 90/Green government with regard not just to employment, but all manner of governmental activity.[71] The Schröder government was quickly condemned as neoliberal and pursuing policies detrimental to Germans on lower incomes,[72] and to Easterners.

The PDS subsequently demanded socialist alternatives to the neoliberal 'hegemony'. It broadly advocated Keynesian doctrines of economic demand management, with the state having a fundamental responsibility to stimulate demand and to provide its citizens with employment. Like a number of socialist parties across Europe, the PDS aims to counter high levels of unemployment with policies such as legally enforceable reductions in the number of hours that employees are allowed to work, a reduction in the length of the working lifetime, and drastic reductions in the amount of overtime worked, both in Germany and the European Union.[73] These policies were encapsulated in a motion put forward in the *Bundestag* requesting a maximum working week of 35 hours and, in the long-term, a five day week of just 30 hours.[74] The PDS also claimed that drastic reductions in the 1.8 billion hours of overtime worked yearly in Germany could create a further 600,000 jobs.[75] Helmut Holter has described this basic economic prescription as being not only beneficial in terms of employment levels, but also in generating demand within the economy and of setting off a virtuous cycle of economic prosperity.[76] This populist approach to labour market strategy is seen in eastern Germany as a clear acknowledgement of the need to 'do something' to reduce unemployment levels.

The PDS makes no bones about demanding the return of full employment.[77] It holds that this is not merely desirable but vital for the restoration of citizens' self-respect and for the good of society as a whole. It also believes that such an aim is a viable one, even if only in the long-term. Lothar Bisky puts this position thus:

> When we make the claim to a society with full employment, we make it very seriously. The right of every citizen to work if they wish to is, in our opinion, a human right that has to be fought for. If ever-fewer people have to work ever-longer hours, while at the same time essential tasks in society cannot be successfully completed, then work clearly has to be divided up anew, and employment that benefits society as a whole newly defined.[78]

The PDS is not scared of saying how it would go about doing this. The SPD–PDS government in Mecklenburg Western Pomerania states:

> (Active) … employment policies and the programme 'Work and Qualification for Mecklenburg Western Pomerania' (AQMV) are, in the current period of mass unemployment, indispensable. Job-creation schemes, further education and re-education, as well as the wage costs subsidy programme, will form the backbone of our active unemployment policy in the future.[79]

The PDS is careful not to promise to solve Germany's large unemployment position overnight,[80] though it does claim to have new and different strategies for tackling the problem. The PDS in Mecklenburg Western Pomerania has, since it entered government in 1998, tried to give the *Land*'s labour market policies a sense of dynamism, activity and energy,[81] and it has not been shy from investing, despite the considerable costs involved, in employment-creation programmes. The PDS in Greifswald, for example, proposed a regional 'Alliance for Jobs', with the aim of bringing together universities, research bodies, companies and trade unions under the supervision of the state in order to work together to increase employment.[82] It also proposed to expressly favour companies from the region when public contracts are distributed, as well as subsidising the development of small and medium-sized businesses.[83] Such an alliance is supported by PDS '*Fraktionen*' throughout the eastern states. The PDS in Mecklenburg Western Pomerania hopes that, even if unemployment figures do not drop drastically in Germany's north-east, it will be given credit at the next state election in 2002 for its willingness to try new approaches in tackling what seems an intractable problem.

The 'Pilot Projekt Ost"

This PDS-proposed pilot project in eastern Germany has become a key element of the party's entire employment policy package. It is intended to prompt regional economic development in the eastern *Länder*, to encourage investment in technologically advanced industries and, most importantly, create employment. The SPD–PDS coalition in Mecklenburg Western Pomerania phrases it thus:

> The state government of Mecklenburg Western Pomerania will attempt, in the medium term, to promote conditions that will enable the creation of sustainable employment at the federal

level in the form of a publicly subsidised employment sector (ÖBS).[84] The state government of Mecklenburg Western Pomerania will support the federal government in an attempt to reform employment subsidies. Possible savings in the AQMV as a result of the employment policies at the federal level will be used to finance the creation of an ÖBS. Priority will be given to creating 1,000 jobs in the areas of youth social work and school social work.[85]

Even though the PDS is open in admitting that the initial aims of the '*Pilot Projekt*' are limited, it is convinced that the project is the most important component of its policies to deal with economic difficulties in the eastern states, and is a new approach towards 'social, political and cultural rejuvenation' in all of Germany.[86] The three key thematic priorities of the *Pilot Projekt* are improvements in social justice, sustainable economic development and democratic subsidiarity to the eastern states.[87] It is an approach that clearly differentiates the PDS from other parties, and is something that the PDS at all levels is attempting to help construct.[88] In terms of economic policy, the state is encouraged to be active in attempting to alleviate economic difficulties. This, once again, is an articulation of widely held eastern German sentiment. Helmut Holter puts it thus:

> The construction and support of regional networks of economic activity is of primary importance for economic development in the eastern states. Reviving regional co-operation in the economic sphere and linking it to new, environmentally-friendly employment structures opens up future roads to prosperity in the eastern states.[89]

An example of this is the strenuous efforts that the PDS has made at both the regional and federal levels to try to attract new technologies to eastern Germany. The PDS was vociferous in its attempts to attract Airbus to Rostock in Mecklenburg Western Pomerania, with the aim of creating 2,000 high-technology new jobs. The PDS MPs Gregor Gysi, Rolf Kutzmutz, Christa Luft and Dietmar Bartsch tabled a joint motion on 9 November 1998 in the *Bundestag*, expressly calling for active support from the government for the new Airbus factory to be located near Rostock.[90] The PDS was keen to stress that such a development would also be beneficial in sending a signal to the industrial world that the eastern states were an attractive place to invest.

The PDS has very specific ideas on how to encourage increased employment within the public sector. These include the creation of the non-profit sector – the so-called *öffentlich geförderten Beschäftigungssektor* (publicly subsidised employment sector) – and programmes to support the expansion of the industrial and service base. While the non-profit sector proposal formed only a relatively small part of the coalition's labour market strategy in Mecklenburg Western Pomerania, its unprecedented nature ensured that it received more than its fair share of attention.[91] Christa Luft, the main force behind the *Pilot Projekt*, describes the logic and principles behind the PDS's 'non-profit sector' thus:

> … communal service agencies hive socially, culturally and eco-logically worthwhile tasks into the public sector at the *market price* (my emphasis), in order to distribute them to public bodies and private actors. The service agencies would buy up the tasks in order to sell them on to the consumers, who would take advantage of these services at *politically* (my emphasis) set prices. The prices for the people or organisations who make use of these services would be orientated towards their ability to pay. The state would make up the difference between the price at which the service is sold and the price at which it has been bought. This will prove more cost-effective than funding mass unemployment and crippling social security benefits … the intention is to create a regular employment sector alongside the normal profit-orientated private economy and the publicly run companies and services that exist for the well-being of the com-munity as a whole.[92]

The ÖBS (Non-Profit Sector) within the '*Pilot Projekt*' is, therefore, intended to be an approach that offers the opportunity of bypassing the profit-making imperative. It is an articulation of eastern German scepticism towards capi-talism. It is also part of the PDS's call for large-scale subsidiarity and grass-roots democracy – an approach that a number of post-communist parties have since chosen to take. The SPD–PDS coalition in Mecklenburg Western Pomerania is the first state government to be faced with putting the PDS's employment policies into practice. This has proved particularly difficult in Mecklenburg Western Pomerania, as the financial constraints of the govern-ment remain great, while the economic problems in Germany's poorest *Land* mount. In 1999 the SPD–PDS government had DM 164 million less at its dis-posal than in the previous year. None the less, Helmut Holter, the deputy Prime Minister and Construction Minister was still insistent that 8,000 extra

jobs could be created.[93] Holter stressed that the process of reducing unemployment was going to be a long one, but he still predicted that the *Öffentlich
geförderten Beschäftigungssektor* would be able to create 3,500 jobs in the medium
term.[94] Angelika Gramkow (PDS Parliamentary Leader in Mecklenburg
Western Pomerania) has, however, admitted that this is still something of a
drop in the ocean:[95]

> 3,500 is not a large number of jobs … but in view of the high
> unemployment here in Mecklenburg Western Pomerania, it is a
> representation of the realities in this *Land* that work that is useful
> to society … (in the non-profit sector) … but remains unprof-
> itable, is still recognised across society and is also affordable.

Indeed, in view of the excessive rates of unemployment in Germany's north-
east, the PDS had to look for 'innovative ways in terms of labour market policies'[96] – and these take time to conceptualise. The SPD does (begrudgingly)
support this key plank of the PDS economic strategy and, according to
Harald Ringstorff, the Prime Minister of 'Meck-Pomm' it is a 'further building block in our labour market policy'.[97] By May 1999, the leader of the PDS
faction within the *Landtag* claimed that DM 10 million had been invested in
the creation of the 'third labour market' over the first six months of the
SPD–PDS coalition[98] – although the project can only be effectively evaluat-
ed after a much longer period of time.

The PDS is, however, very aware of the need to remain credible on this
issue. It is one thing to promise to reduce unemployment by a considerable
number, but it is another altogether to achieve it. Dr Christian Westphal,
leader of the PDS in Rostock city council, made it clear that all of the jobs in
the non-profit sector have to be financially viable in the long-term. The ÖBS
cannot be an initiative that supports *Prestigeobjekte*, rather it must help improve
services in schools, hospitals etc. in and around the local community.
Westphal stressed that Easterners had been promised flourishing landscapes
before, only to be let down by the CDU – and this was not a mistake that the
PDS could afford to make in either Rostock or Mecklenburg Western
Pomerania as a whole.[99] The SPD–PDS state government is particularly keen
to create employment for younger members of society. By 2 November 1999,
it reported that it had been able to create 1,000 positions for 'Youth, School
and Social Workers' within the non-profit sector.[100] This is in tune with the
PDS's policy of providing every school-leaver throughout Germany with a
training place – something that the PDS has also tried to have enshrined in
the Basic Law.[101]

Methods of financing the ÖBS seem fanciful at best: but this has not (yet) stopped the PDS from attempting to push the project through. The financial basis of the ÖBS rests on attaining levels of full employment that have not been seen in western countries for a number of decades. Rather than spend billions of Deutschmarks on funding unemployment (DM 163 billion was spent on unemployment benefit in 1996, rising to DM 180 billion in 1997[102]), work that is directly beneficial to society should be encouraged. When this is coupled with a redistribution of wealth based on a re-shaping of the tax system, the PDS is of the opinion that an ÖBS is affordable. This is a clear function of the widely held eastern belief that income differentials between the rich and the poor are too large. The PDS espouses populist economic policies, simplistic and solve-all in nature, safe in the knowledge that it will not have to implement them at the federal level.

In more concrete terms, the PDS intends to finance its employment policies by :

- Levying a one-off tax (*Vermögensabgabe*)[103] on large sums of money, as well as on private wealth (*Grundvermögen*). This would apply both to private capital and capital owned by insurance institutes and banks.[104]
- The introduction of a 'Wealth Tax' (*Vermögenssteuer*).[105] The PDS estimates that a wealth tax will enable the state to raise between DM 9 Billion and DM 30 billion.[106] This would be complemented by a reform of inheritance taxes (*Erbschaftssteuer*).
- A closure of tax loopholes.
- Increased tax revenues as more people are employed, and more people pay into the tax system.
- Increases in the social contributions of companies, based on profits made.[107]

The PDS also supports active labour market policies to reduce the number of young people in Germany without gainful employment. This is a particular problem in eastern Germany, where high levels of youth employment encourage a tendency for young people to lean towards right-wing political activity in the form of sub-cultures in towns and cities.[108] A PDS *Sofortprogramm* (immediate programme) aims to offer every young person an *Ausbildungsplatz* (training place) when they leave full-time education, and after this a full-time job.[109] It argues for a change in the constitution to give every citizen the right not just to a job, training placement and education, but also the right to accommodation.[110]

Implementation of these policies is not something that the PDS is likely to have to worry about in the near future. The PDS is only a coalition partner in one eastern Government, and these policy approaches do not, as yet, meet with overwhelming support in the electorate. It is unlikely that the PDS will have to test its policy agenda further against the realities of governmental participation. Even in Mecklenburg Western Pomerania, the PDS openly admits that the opportunities for implementation of such radical plans are small. This is no bad thing for the party; it enjoys a position where it can voice loud criticism of the federal government without having the obligation to do a better job itself. Further, the PDS is not seen as a party of much governmental competence.[111] But surveys by the Konrad Adenauer Foundation reveal that none of the parties enjoy particularly large support in terms of *Problemlösungskompetenzen* in eastern Germany.[112] However, the reforming leadership of the PDS has clearly understood that if it is to remain an important proponent of eastern German specificity, then issues of democracy and employment are key battlegrounds. And the PDS has benefited in the last few years by having a distinctive profile on these issues. Helmut Holter is clearly aware of this: 'The PDS will have to make the future nature of work and the democratisation of society its key issues in order to be the main political alternative.'[113] This remains the case, in spite of the questionable practicality (particularly from a financial point of view) of the PDS's programme initiatives; the party sees the issues of democracy and employment as its two strongest policy areas – because they both clearly correspond to the wishes and goals of many eastern Germans.

Social justice

'Above all, we ... (the PDS) ... are needed as the party of social justice'.[114]

Like a number of post-communist parties in central and eastern Europe, the PDS has actively sought to take on the mantle of the protector of the poor, weak and socially disadvantaged.[115] In concrete terms, the PDS articulates this by campaigning for more social justice within Germany and Europe as a whole. This emphasis on social affairs corresponds strongly with eastern German feelings of egalitarianism and personal 'social injustices'. While the PDS sought to play this role throughout the 1990s, it is really only since the Federal Election of 1998, and the creation of the first SPD–Alliance 90/Green government at the federal level, that the PDS has been able to profile itself effectively as the party of social justice. The reasons for this are relatively straightforward. The attempt by the SPD–Alliance 90/Greens federal administration to restructure and 'balance the books' entailed Finance Minister Hans Eichel pushing ahead with a package of savings measures. This gave the PDS the opportunity to put itself forward as the only German party that proposed to protect the socially disadvantaged from the excesses of both global capitalism and the misguided (in the opinion of the PDS) policies of the SPD-led Government. Throughout 1999, therefore, the PDS increasingly stressed its commitment to 'social justice' – mirroring eastern Germans' clear preference for social equality rather than individual economic freedoms. Eastern Germans also came to perceive, and consciously appreciate, the PDS's policy positions, consequently rejecting the SPD as a party that was not prepared to alter the structures of capitalism radically in order to help the less well-off. Lothar Bisky claimed that the PDS was also widely seen as the party of social justice in society at large, while both the CDU and SPD were no longer seen as being credible on the issue.[116] The extent of this was shown by an Allensbach survey carried out in the eastern states in April 2000, which revealed that 56 per cent of Easterners saw the PDS as the 'party of social justice'. Only 23 per cent were of the opinion that the SPD was the party that would most effectively strive for this (admittedly fuzzy) ideal.[117]

Despite the persistent refusal of the PDS to define what it understood by the term 'soziale Gerechtigkeit' (social justice),[118] the issue remained highly prominent in all PDS literature published in 1999 and 2000. The front cover of the 1999 Communal election *Wahlprogramm* in Leipzig urged voters to 'Zukunft sozial gestalten' (shape the future socially),[119] while the PDS in Bad Doberan (Mecklenburg Western Pomerania) called its Communal election programme 'For Social Justice and Human Rights'.[120] These are representative of the election programmes that the PDS produced in all the eastern states in 1999. The PDS is adamant that ' … (in view of) … the dominant political discourse, we have developed suggestions, proposals and campaigns with the aim of increasing the amount of social justice in Germany today', and that it is the only party that can be trusted to look after the interests of pensioners, the ill and infirm, the unemployed, those on social security benefits, those on lower incomes, those not in a position to defend themselves and those who feel anxious about the capitalist world around them.[121] Easterners, because of their disadvantageous economic situation (in terms of levels of unemployment, wage levels and spending power) and self-perceived disadvantageous social situation, generally place themselves within this bracket, or at least tend to have sympathy with the PDS's ideals.

The PDS has energetically complained that the federal government takes money away from those who need it most, and has also claimed that the government is reluctant to tax corporations and richer citizens. During the 1999 European election campaign, and the state elections of the same year, the PDS was never slow to stress its role as the protector of the socially disadvantaged. It also urged voters, on campaign posters, to 'sozial wählen' (vote socially) – a clear response to the SPD's alleged move towards the centre-ground.[122] The political system in the eastern states, functioning largely around the socialist sub-culture that the PDS represents, and the social-market sub-culture represented by the CDU, has offered the PDS the opportunity to call for a radical redistribution of wealth in the direction of the poorer segments of society. Lothar Bisky has further recognised that the widely held public perception of the PDS as 'on the left' and the CDU as 'on the right' has contributed to a polarisation of the eastern political system on all social issues. As he phrased it:

> The differing options on the issue of social justice are those proposed by the CDU and the PDS. If the elector wants to see improvements in the *Standort Deutschland* under the guidance of an economic party (*Wirtschaftspartei*), then the elector votes for the CDU. If he or she wants to see improvements and reforms guided by the principle of social justice, then they decide for the PDS.[123]

The PDS's anti-capitalist stance has won it recognition as the party that continues to fight for the 'little man'. It has adopted an open and provocative attitude towards issues of social justice, as it realises that the populist rhetoric it espouses is well-received in the eastern electorate at large, and it is unlikely to have to fulfil any of the demands that it encourages. The PDS also attempts to use social justice as a means by which it can increase contact with other societal groupings – so spreading its influence across society as a whole. The PDS executive has explicitly called for discussions to take place on the issue of social justice between the DGB, individual trade unions, the farmers' associations, the Christian churches and even the *Zentralrat der Juden* – all under the leadership of PDS politicians.[124] Regional and local politicians are encouraged to work with other societal actors, explicitly trade unions, *Betriebs- und Personalräten* to introduce new models of employment and to accept the responsibility of providing the fundamentals of a socially secure existence for citizens.[125] The parliamentary motions put forward by the PDS at federal and state level also foreground issues of social justice. In Mecklenburg Western Pomerania, for example, the PDS *Anträge* have centred on the defence of social rights of citizens: examples of this include attempts to guarantee lower rents and housing, labour market policies that aim to maximise employment through the creation of more jobs in the areas of care-work and social assistance, criticism of the policies of the *Treuhand* successor organisation, and attempts to save the Rostock shipping yards.[126] At the federal level the PDS is also not slow to campaign for more funding for housing and social issues instead of for 'prestige objects'. Klaus-Jürgen Warnick (a PDS MdB) observed, commenting on the final budget of the CDU/CSU–FDP government in 1998, that the federal government persistently appears to get its priorities wrong – at the expense of the socially disadvantaged eastern Germans:

> Our proposals (supported by the SPD and Alliance 90/Greens) to increase the funds for *sozialen Wohnungsbau* (the construction of social housing) by DM 2.6 billion and for *Städtebauförderung* (subsidies for construction in towns) in eastern and western Germany by DM 1 billion were rejected. But there still appears to be enough money for unnecessary expenditure like the *Transrapid*, the Eurofighter, over-priced parliamentary and governmental buildings in Berlin, as well as tax breaks for the purchase of property.[127]

The PDS adopted the slogan 'Reichtum begrenzen, Armut bekämpfen' (limit wealth, fight poverty) in the 1998 election campaign, emphasising the importance of the 'social' in its platform. And this emphasis clearly had a resonance in eastern German society at large. In the October 1999 state elections in Berlin, 77 per cent of Easterners who voted for the PDS did so in the hope that the PDS would be able create a more socially just society.[128] This was further highlighted after the publication of the Blair–Schröder paper in 1999. The PDS roundly condemned the SPD's shift rightwards, and while the joint paper caused only mild consternation amongst western social democrats, it caused widespread disillusionment within both the SPD and the PDS in the East – illustrating the differing political consciousness of eastern and western Germans.[129] The publication of the paper allowed the PDS to present the SPD as saving for saving's sake, and put itself forward as the only trustworthy protector of the less well-off. Gregor Gysi subsequently published a paper listing twelve reasons why social justice was a modern concept, attacking the western parties for negating on their obligations to protect the socially disadvantaged.[130] The PDS is also not averse to flaunting its more populist colours when it talks about this issue, stressing the huge income differentials between rich and poor, relating this back to the relative equality (with obvious exceptions) of citizens' incomes in the GDR. Gregor Gysi polemically commented in the Bundestag that:

Between 1983 and 1989 the number of citizens who earn over DM 1 million in Germany rose from just over 33,000 to around 56,000. Since 1989 the Federal Statistical Office has stopped announcing these figures publicly. Meanwhile, the number of citizens earning over the million mark has risen by around 40 per cent, and now there are roughly 100,000. Of these 100,000 people, roughly 1,000 earn more than DM 10 million a year. Can anyone explain to me how anybody can put in so much work that they should merit a wage of over DM 10 million a year?! There is simply no justification for this, even if they were to work all day and all night and never sleep.[131]

The PDS remains a vocal and visible advocate of 'equality' rather than 'economic freedom', and 'social justice' as opposed to 'economic individualism'. The PDS has taken advantage of the SPD's weakness in eastern Germany to profile itself in direct opposition to the CDU. As a result, the PDS appears to be the only party articulating the considerable eastern dissatisfaction with the social and economic realities of the German state. It represents a distinctively eastern articulation of the social need for fairness, equality and solidarity within the political process.

NATO, Kosovo and foreign affairs

The PDS articulates a specifically regional critique of much of Germany's foreign policy. Eastern Germans, mainly as a result of their anti-Western socialisation within the GDR, are much more sceptical about the role of NATO and the WEU, and in their appreciation of what role (if any) German soldiers should play in international (peace-keeping) affairs. Falling as they did in the Summer and Autumn of 1999, the elections to the European Parliament and to the *Landtage* in Saxony, Brandenburg, Thuringia and Berlin offered the PDS the ideal opportunity to project itself as an 'anti-war' party, the more so since the controversial Kosovo War took place in the early months of the same year. The PDS incorporated this into the title of its 1999 European election programme by claiming that 'The Europe of the 21st Century needs Peace, Employment and Democracy'[132] and one of the key slogans of the PDS election campaign subsequently became 'Europa schaffen ohne Waffen' ('Create a Europe without weapons'). The PDS claimed that its position as an anti-war party was simply not up for discussion.[133] The 1999 bombing of Yugoslavia by NATO planes, with the active participation of

German forces, strikingly highlighted the differences of opinion in eastern and western Germany on a number of aspects of foreign policy. Apart from the PDS, all parties in the Bundestag were in favour of the attacks.[134] The PDS, calling on the pacifist traditions of the *Friedensbewegung* (Peace Movement), as well as the clear popular reluctance of a majority of eastern Germans to support the bombings, spent the duration of the war condemning the actions of what it viewed as western imperialism. As Hans Modrow observed at the Münster party conference in April 2000, 'it is down to the red–green Government that Germany, for the first time since 1945, has waged war against another European country, contravening both the Basic Law and the 2+4 Treaty in the process'.[135] The PDS organised peace demonstrations,[136] public displays of popular dissent,[137] the distribution of anti-war newspapers and other 'peace-orientated' literature. Lothar Bisky illustrated how clearly the PDS was able to distinguish itself on the issue of Kosovo when he observed that:

> the opinion polls that the federal party has commandeered prove unequivocally that it is not just we, the PDS activists, who are against this form of military activity by German soldiers. Our party is against it. The vast majority of PDS voters are against it. And the majority of Germans are against it.[138]

In the opinion of Modrow, the unswerving opposition of the PDS to the bombing of Yugoslavia gained the party considerable credit in the public at large,[139] while Gregor Gysi further illustrated the straightforwardness of the PDS's position at a special sitting of the Bundestag on the issue of the Yugoslavian War, on 15 April 1999, when he bemoaned the ineffectiveness of war as a policy instrument.

> You cannot avoid one simple truth about this war. Not a single bomb that has been directed at Yugoslavia has been of any help at all – I have seen[140] some of those people who have been injured by them, some of the factories that have been ruined by them, the buildings that have been destroyed by them as well as a heating plant that has been put out of action by them – and now 200,000 people are freezing in a city with no warmth.[141]

The Kosovo crisis was an unambiguous case of the PDS standing alone as a representative of distinctive eastern German sentiment. It alone represented the majority opinion in the eastern states that rejected the NATO attacks on

Yugoslavia. For the PDS, the need to demilitarise international relations and to insert a civilian dimension to global conflict solution has the highest priority. The PDS clearly rejects any transformation of the WEU into a military arm of the EU, and the party is of the opinion that Europe needs to be an area completely devoid of nuclear weapons. The weapons industry should be transformed into an industrial sector geared to improving 'civilian production' capacity, while NATO should be abolished altogether and Russia incorporated into a new European security order. Eastern Germans displayed deep unease at NATO's willingness to launch attacks unilaterally on Yugoslavia in 1999, and the PDS repeatedly argued that if NATO was to have any role, it must be under the auspices of the UN. The PDS continually stresses that international law must be adhered to at all times.

It is the opinion of the PDS that the OSCE also needs to be broadened into an organisation that fosters a non-military security structure across Europe, while the United Nations needs to be given much increased powers to enable it to effectively keep the global powers (principally the USA) in check.[142] The UN and the OSCE must, together, be the foundation of new European security structures (particularly in light of the proposed abolition of both NATO and the WEU). The role of the *Bundeswehr* should also be severely restricted: principally to defending German territory, rather than as a part of an *international Einsatztruppe* (international rapid-reaction force).[143] The PDS envisages both the abolition of national service and a 65 per cent reduction in the number of *Bundeswehr* troops to around 100,000.[144] It is, therefore, articulating the pacifist leanings of a citizenry that lived in a highly militarised state (the GDR) and is inherently more sceptical about the need and legitimacy of armed combat in general, and German participation in such events in particular, than is the case in western Germany.

The Euro and the European Union

Eastern Germans remain more 'eurosceptic' than western Germans, both towards the institutions of the EU and the processes of European integration and enlargement. This came to a head very publicly in the immediate run-up to the introduction of the Euro in 1999, although this should not overshadow the fact that scepticism of the integration process has been persistently more evident across the eastern states than in the West. The PDS defines itself as a 'European socialist party' within the context of the European Union,[145] but this assertion, mirroring the sentiment in eastern Germany, is certainly not unequivocal: the PDS is quick to point out that it is highly critical of the EU in its present form.[146] Alonso Puerta observes, for example, that the PDS politicians are 'critical Europeans that are of the opinion "Europe? Yes, but not like this!"'[147] Or, in the words of the PDS *Spitzenkandidatin* at the 1999 European election, Sylvia-Yvonne Kaufmann, 'the political nature and shape of the EU of the future is not yet known, and it is this that offers a left-wing party like the PDS the opportunity to exert influence on the future Union'.[148]

The issue of the Euro became a barometer of this opinion. While the PDS supported the idea of a European-wide currency in principle,[149] it was exceptionally critical of the restrictions, in the form of the economic convergence criteria, that were placed on European economies in order to make them 'lean' enough to enter. The PDS chose to stress the importance of creating what it describes as a 'social union' in order to protect Europeans against rising unemployment and increased economic insecurity – and to encourage an ecological, social and democratic process of European integration. The PDS was the only party in the Bundestag to vote against the implementation of the Euro, articulating considerable popular sentiment in the eastern states. It saw the advantages that were to be gained through a single currency as accruing mainly to large companies, enabling them to compete at a transnational level. Such companies can be, and often are, more mobile than workers, and it is these companies that benefit from economies of scale. Hence, the PDS demanded increased social protection from the forces of international economic competition. While accepting that these advantages were helpful to industry, the PDS consistently voiced concerns about the 'social' effects of the impending currency union. It predicted that downsizing and increases in economic efficiency would inevitably lead to increases in unemployment, a decrease in wages (in the long-term) and a decrease in job security.[150] This corresponds to the negative feelings that many Easterners have with regard to future economic development in the eastern states. Small and medium sized companies will, according to the PDS, find themselves in an increasingly competitive market place – resulting in more job losses, as competition forces streamlining. The social 'safety net' will need to be drastically diminished, in order to reduce companies' costs, so keeping them economically viable, and to enable countries to put an end to budget deficits in order to cut national debts. All of these effects are likely to be more pronounced, according to PDS politicians, in the East.

> The eastern states are already a test-bed in terms of neoliberal economics. Eastern German employees are already told that if they do not work under the agreed wage agreements, then the

firm will go bust. This process will simply be transposed onto the European level when the Euro highlights the fact that differing wage levels are paid for the same work on a Europe wide basis.[151]

At its most populist, the PDS claimed that Europe was on the verge of a violent dumping competition drivng down wages and social standards, as capitalism ravaged the weaker sectors of the European economy.[152] Hence, the PDS is vocal in its call for more citizens rights in the area of social policy – a policy that became a central plank of the PDS's election campaign in 1999.[153] The PDS was the only German party, in the words of Lothar Bisky, that 'put issues of social protection, labour market policy and ecological politics ahead of the Euro', emphasising eastern German angst both about the social and economic environment, and the wisdom of joining the Euro-zone under prevailing conditions.[154] The 'social union' that the PDS calls for is aimed at 'preventing competition to provide the lowest wages, the weakest forms of social protection and the most ineffective social and trade union rights', and represents clear eastern German demands for increased security in every-day life as well as a defence of the working classes.[155] EMU needs to be, in the minds of the PDS, regulated by the combined forces of not just a social union, but also an employment and ecological union – all flying in the face of the neoliberal logic of the integration dynamic thus far.[156] The employment strategies advocated by the PDS at the European level mirror their national strategies: reductions in the number of hours worked by all individuals; a reduction in the permitted amount of overtime and so forth.[157]

The PDS also promotes issues that are of particular resonance in the eastern states, as a result of experiences gained in the transformation process, within the European arena. These include the lack of suitable democratic representation in the political process in Europe (as well as in Germany), disquiet at high rates of unemployment (across Europe) and the dominance of large companies in the (German and European) market-place. The PDS supports the introduction of a European constitution, one of the aims of its initiative to 'democratise democracy' at the European level.[158] It also stresses the need to make the EU more open to its citizenry, to democratise the EU's institutional structures and workings. 'Now more than ever before the European Union is suffering from insufficient democratic legitimisation' claimed the PDS in its 1999 European election manifesto, before continuing:

> The European Parliament was indeed given more powers in the Treaty of Amsterdam, but one is still not in a position where cit-

izens of the European Union can democratically take part in politics at the European level. The results of this are scepticism, mistrust and distance from the European Union and from the process of European integration.[159]

These calls correspond to the PDS's calls for a reform of the democratic procedures in the FRG, with a particular emphasis on increased citizen participation. The onset of ever-closer union has made the reform of the political structures of the EU ever more urgent, as:

> … it is now clearer than ever that it is vitally important to reform the European Union politically. This is in order to correct the imbalance that currently ensures a contradiction between the single market and economic and monetary union on the one hand, and the lack of democratic participation and a political union on the other.[160]

The PDS proposes to do this by:

- The inclusion of inviolable fundamental, human rights in European Union treaties.[161]
- The *Beseitigung* of the increasing centralisation of power within the Executive branch and the bureaucracy through increased representative democracy, above all in the European Parliament (EP) and the national parliaments. This would include giving the EP the right to elect the President of the European Commission and the European Commissioners, and the implementation of a single electoral system across all member states. It would also include giving national parliaments clear opportunities to participate in the decision-making processes at the European level.
- More opportunities for popular participation and for more direct democracy in European politics. In cases of fundamental importance to the future development of the EU, such as treaty changes and expansion plans, plebiscites would be held in all member states.
- The democratisation of employment and economic activity. This would mean increased, institutionalised rights for trade unions, and for citizens to have the right of consultation at the work-place.[162]

Blatantly populist language is also invoked on occasion. The PDS has, for example, called for the European governments and institutions to make a concerted effort to reduce stubbornly high rates of unemployment. In the words of Andreas Wehr the PDS suggests that:

> the aim of high levels of employment ... (should be taken) ... into consideration by the European Central Bank.[163] In the future this aim should be accorded at least the same priority as monetary stability. In the current situation, this means a clear drop in interest rates in order to stimulate demand.[164]

The PDS claims that the 'guidelines' that currently exist with regard to encouraging employment at the European level are far too weak to have any genuine effect, and must be lifted up to the level of high-profile aims that individual governments must fulfil or face financial penalties. Wehr provocatively claims, for example, that if the aim of reducing by half unemployment in each European state had been adopted as one of the convergence criteria for entry into monetary union (with appropriate financial penalties for non-achievement), then unemployment would not be at its current high levels.[165] Lothar Bisky further demands that the European Central Bank be placed under the political control of the European Parliament, so that coherent, transparent European-wide strategies can be developed, by accountable politicians, to tackle Europe's disastrously high unemployment figures.[166] Alonso Puerta adds that only a European government can ensure that the Europeanisation of economic policies can be democratically controlled.[167]

Thus, the PDS represents the deep-seated scepticism about the processes of European integration that is evident in eastern Germany. The PDS does not reject the EU as an institution, but has grave misgivings about the European Union's democratic credentials, its capitalist instincts and its manipulation by big business. European policy is an area where the PDS has been most successful in articulating territorial uniqueness in the eastern states. Western Germans have grown up with the European Union, and accept it as a fundamental necessity if Europe is to enjoy peace and prosperity in the future. Easterners, meanwhile, remain broadly pro-European, but take critical standpoints on many of the EU's shortcomings. The PDS is the only party that presents this view in the political arena, and it is always ready to represent the CDU and the SPD as being equally responsible for developing and supporting some of the EU's *Fehlorientierungen*.

Land reform

The PDS actively tackles the controversial issue of the *Bodenreform* (Land Reform). As a result of the Kohl government's policy of returning property confiscated during the SED dictatorship to its former owners, many eastern Germans have either lost what they perceived to be their property or are still unsure as to the future of what they currently own. The PDS is against the continued insecurity of property ownership, and unequivocally supports the retention of the law on land reform that was passed in March 1989 in the GDR. As the 1998 Federal Election programme states:

> We energetically condemn all attempts to reverse the law concerning the *Bodenreform*. The federal law on 'rights of property holders on property resulting from the *Bodenreform* of 6 March 1990' should be completely abolished.[168]

The PDS is particularly critical of the *Entschädigungs- und Ausgleichsleistungsgesetz* (EALG) of 1994, which it portrays as a fundamental contravention of eastern German rights. The PDS accuses the federal government of serving the interests of western capitalists, and neglecting the interests of eastern Germans who, in some cases, see their livelihoods compromised as a result:

> The facts of the matter are that this law ... (the EALG) ... opens the floodgates for former owners of property (*Alteigentümer*) to claim land in eastern Germany back for themselves. This leaves eastern Germans in a permanently disadvantageous position. The land is being taken literally away from underneath their feet. This is not a suitable balance of interests between different sides, this is politics on behalf of a distinct interest group.[169]

The PDS is, therefore, defending explicitly eastern German interests, in that it seeks to be the only political expression of eastern contempt for a policy that is seen to help western German former land-owners.[170] The PDS remains convinced that:

> only the concerted defence of the legally and judicially correct decision *not* too give back their land to the owners of property confiscated in the period 1945–1949, safeguards the livelihoods

of the many eastern German who have built up their lives, often over decades, on the basis of being the owners of this property. There still remain over 1.5 million hectares of fields, meadows, woods, heathland, that qualify as *Bodenreformland*. Everything else has long since got its western owner ... .[171]

Lothar Bisky has further added that:

The aggressive defence of the *Bodenreform* is not a nostalgic attempt to defend former East German 'achievements' (*Errungenschaften*). Rather, it is a defence of the legitimate interests of many eastern Germans – concurrently combined with a real opportunity to propagate something new for all of Germany.[172]

Klaus Bartl, a PDS member of the state Parliament in Saxony has further added that:

Thousands of citizens and families have been chased off their property and are having to pursue long-winded and expensive legal claims in order to fight off the restitution claims of *Alteigentümer*. The principle of *Rückgabe vor Entschädigung* ... (the return of property in preference to compensation) ... deprives eastern Germans of their rights and is the cause of much *Lebenstragik* (personal tragedy) in the eastern states.[173]

The northern areas of eastern Germany, such as towns and villages in Mecklenburg and Western Pomerania, have suffered particularly strongly from the policy of 'return rather than compensate', as their large agricultural sectors have seen numerous claims made upon them. This has led the PDS to be particularly active at all levels in Mecklenburg Western Pomerania, as it seeks to avoid more land passing into the hands of western German owners. As Günther Rogin, the PDS leader in the Ludwigslust *Kreistag* has claimed:

... (there is a need) ... to change the existing laws on the land reform in order to alter the bias towards the previous owner. The *Kreistag* condemns the new and rejuvenated attempt to revise the *Bodenreform*, in contravention of the rights and interests of eastern Germans, and in particular eastern German farmers. The implementation of this law would have negative consequences for citizens who live and work in the country, as well as deepening and cementing eastern German disadvantages in terms of property ownership. This is completely unacceptable – particularly in the context of German–German growing together and the future development of inner unity.[174]

The PDS is, therefore, articulating territorial specific sentiment with regard to property ownership: a vocal, though not particularly effective, supporter of eastern German property owners against western German claims.

Conclusion

The nature and scope of the policies that regional parties develop and articulate in the political arena depend on the regional context where they are active. In many cases, the policies will be presented in 'ethnonationalist', terms, an attempt to win improved rights and privileges for a particular ethnic group. In other cases their policy orientation may require a restructuring of the nation-state (this may, of course, also be an intrinsic aim of ethnonationalist parties), the defence of economic prosperity or the preservation of a unique culture. In any event, these policy demands have a particular territorial element, and reflect the wants, needs, worries and expectations of a large number of citizens in their region.

The PDS's policy package is based on the presentation of eastern German interests within the political arena. To succeed in this the PDS has understood what makes eastern Germans different and how best to take advantage of the structural assets it possesses; it has developed unique policy approaches that both differentiate it from other, all-German, parties and allow it to represent effectively the demands of a broad cross-section of the eastern German population in the political process. It is the only political party to conceptualise and express effectively the attitudinal and value differences illustrated in chapter four , in the national legislature as well as the regional and local parliaments in eastern Germany. The policies on which it has built its unique platform are specific representations of eastern German interests – and it is by successfully re-adapting to the contours of political competition in the eastern states that it has created a niche for itself that enables it to wrest agenda-setting functions from both the SPD and the CDU.

The PDS's policy package may well not be widely regarded as fit to solve the social and economic problems of eastern Germany, but there is a growing acceptance that in certain areas (the attainment of social justice, the articulation of of eastern German pacifism, for example) the PDS is regarded as a capable and effective political actor. It is taken seriously by electors as a party that seeks a 'better deal' for the citizens of eastern Germany. It represents through its policies, in a way that only a party with strong roots in the eastern German community can do, the feelings and dispensations of a large minority of eastern German society. It is the visible representative of the cleavage between the eastern and western *Länder*.

The PDS has moulded elements of continuity and change into its political platform. It has developed an agenda that neither rejects the GDR past, nor glorifies it. It manages to incorporate elements of theoretical continuity (i.e. egalitarianism, a rejection of NATO and capitalist economics) and clear change (i.e. the acceptance that the market must play some, largely undefined, role in economic management, proposals to 'democratise democracy'), incorporating key elements of the eastern German identity into its own platform.

Notes

1   Easterners have traditionally viewed the PDS as a 'normal party', campaigning on a legitimate political platform, in much greater numbers than western Germans have done. In 1995, for example, 73.8 per cent of Easterners were of the opinion that the PDS should be treated like any other 'normal party' (Forschugsgruppe Wahlen: ZA-Nr 2777, Politbarometer Ost 1995, p.111), whereas 52.5 per cent of Westerners were of this opinion (Forschugsgruppe Wahlen: ZA-Nr 2765, Politbarometer West 1995, p.98). By 1998, 60.9 per cent of Germans as a whole thought that the PDS was sufficiently normal to not merit any particular special treatment (Forschugsgruppe Wahlen: ZA-Nr 3160, Politbarometer 1998, p. 229).

2   Dellheim, 1999, p. 28.

3   Nick, 1998, p. 35.

4   Das Rostocker Manifest, PDS Parteivorstand, 1998, pp. 2–3.

5   'Die Doppelbiograhie der Bundesrepublik. Zum Phänomen der deutschen Zweistaatlichkeit', *Dokumente zur Geschichte der PDS* (Thesenpapier der Historischen Kommission beim Parteivorstand der PDS, on http://www.pds-online.de/geschichte/9903/doppelbiograhie.htm). See also *PDS Pressedienst*, Nummer 13, 31 März 1999.

6   Declaration of the fourth session of the fifth *Landesparteitag* of the PDS in Saxony Anhalt on the 6 and 7 February 1999 in Magdeburg. In *PDS Pressedienst*, Nummer 8, 26 Februar 1999, p. 7.

7   'Keine Unterstützung für CDU-light-Politik' in *PDS Pressedienst*, Nummer 45, 6 November 1998, p. 1. See also speech by Gregor Gysi at the fifteenth *Gewerkschaftstag der Gewerkschaft Handel, Banken und Versicherungen* in Bremen, 28 October 1998, in *PDS Pressedienst*, Nummer 45, 6 November 1998, p. 8.

8   Catherina Muth (PDS): '83 Sitzung am 31. März 1998', in Landtag Mecklenburg-Vorpommern: *Zur Arbeit des Landtags in der 2. Wahlperiode 1994 bis 1998*, 1998, p. 5160.

9   Peter Porsch (PDS): 'Unsere Zukunft liegt nicht in der Gegenwart anderer Parteien, sondern in einer Partei als Netwerk demokratischer Bewegung', speech at the sixth *Landesparteitag* of the PDS in Saxony, in *PDS Pressedienst*, Nummer 2, 14 Januar 2000. See also http://www.pds-online.de/pressedienst/0002/09.htm

10   Lothar Bisky (PDS): speech to the Rostock Party Conference, 3 April 1998, in *PDS Pressedienst*, Nummer 15-16, 17 April 1998, p. 4.

11   Lothar Bisky (PDS): speech to the Rostock Party Conference, 3 April 1998, in *PDS Pressedienst*, Nummer 15-16, 17 April 1998, p. 4.

12   An example of this came in September 1996, when the PDS placed a motion to retain extra payments to 80,000 poorer pensioners in the eastern states. The PDS was prompted to propose such motion as the CDU/CSU-FDP coalition originally proposed a bill ceasing extra payments to pensioners in the East who, from 1 January 1997, received more than DM647 a month. On the 5 December 1996 all parties in the *Bundestag* (with the exception of Alliance 90/Greens) voted against the PDS's motion. On the same day the CDU/CSU-FDP and the SPD proposed a bill guaranteeing elderly citizens in the East higher levels of social support – a demand previously made by the PDS, over and above the motion that had been rejected on the same day. See http://www2.pds-online.de/bt/themen/rb980802.htm A further example of this concerns a motion that the PDS proposed in order to try to introduce a yearly wealth report in 1996. After rejecting the motion, the SPD drew up an *Antrag* in mid-1997 calling for regular reports of both poverty and wealth to be drawn up. See *Deutscher Bundestag*: Drucksache 13/6527.

13   *Deutscher Bundestag*: Drucksache 13/8369. The CDU/CSU-FDP Government replied with a 130 page document in May 1998.

14   *Deutscher Bundestag*: Drucksache 14/860.

15   See http://www2.pds-online.de/bt/themen/9906/99062407.htm

16   The main points of this were the creation of a long-term investment programme; efficient implementation of public money with the aim of creating employment; support for science and research; democratic control of the implementation of contracts distributed by the *Treuhand* holding agency and so forth. See *Deutscher Bundestag*: Drucksache 13/7519.

17   See Ostrowski, 1999. See also Lang, 1998, p. 49.

18   For explicit reference to this see the PDS Party Programme, section 4.9. 'Kultur, Bildung und Wissenschaft befreien', on http://www.pds-online.de/programm/punkt409.htm. See also 'Kulturpolitische Positionen der PDS und Aufgaben für die laufende Legislaturperiode', on http://www.pds-online.de/politik/kultur/9905/positionen.htm

19   See for example PDS Parteivorstand: 'Ausbildung statt Ausbeutung', in *PDS Pressedienst*, Nummer 20, 14 Mai 1998, on http://www.pds-online.de/pressedienst/9820/24791.html. See also Stefan Grunwald (PDS): 'Ausbildung in der ländlichen Region stärken!', August 2000, on http://www.pds-online.de/pressemeldungen/0008/grunwald2.htm

20   PDS Parteivorstand, 1997, p. 18.

21   For an enlightening analysis of the PDS's parliamentary activities in the 1990–1994 legislative period see von Ditfurth, 1998, p. 238. See also *R(h)einblick*, the monthly newsletter of the PDS Bundestagsfraktion.

22   PDS Parteivorstand: *Fraktionsvorstand zu Schwerpunkten 2000: PDS schärft ihr Profil* (Berlin: PDS Pressemitteilung, Nummer 1156, 14 January 2000).

23   According to surveys carried out by Forschungsgruppe Wahlen, in 1995 61.8 per cent of eastern Germans were of the opinion that a *Schlußstrich* (line) should be drawn under East German history. More surprisingly, and perhaps typical of the contradictory data that opinion polls occasionally reveal, 55.8 per cent of western Germans thought that such a line should be drawn! See Forschungsgruppe Wahlen: ZA-Nr 2765, p. 152 and ZA-Nr 2777, p. 167. When a similar question was asked by Allensbach in June 1994, asking if too much time was spent 'working through' East German history, a similar divide was seen to exist between East and West, with more eastern Germans (44 per cent) than western Germans (38 per cent) believing this to be true. See Noelle-Neumann and Köcher, 1997, p. 591.

24   Nick, 1998, p. 36.

25   See *R(h)einblick*: http//www2.pds-online.de/bt/themen/rb980802.htm

26   'VIII Die Demokratie stärken und die persönliche und öffentliche Sicherheit gewährleisten. Abschnitt 2 Überprüfungen', in *Koalitionsvereinbarung zwischen der Sozialdemokratischen Partei Deutschlands und dem Partei des Demokratischen Sozialismus* (Schwerin: Landtag Mecklenburg-Vorpommern, 1998). See also http://www.mv-pds-ltf.de/koalition/i00000.htm

27   Lothar Bisky (PDS): Speech to the Rostock Party Conference, 3 April 1998, in *PDS Pressedienst*, Nummer 15-16, 17 April 1998, p. 11.

28   PDS-Fraktion im Sächsischen Landtag, 1997, p. 1.

29   Yoder, 1999, p. 72.

30   Yoder, 1999, p. 72.

31   Grix, 2000a, p. 63.

32   The full title of the commission was 'The Investigatory Commission on the Working-Through of the History and Consequences of the SED Dictatorship in Germany'. See Yoder, 1999, p. 71.

33   Bender, 1999, p. 8.

34   Barker, 2000, p. 85.

35   *Deutscher Bundestag*: Drucksache 12/2226.

36   Barker, 2000, p. 86.

37   'Zum Schlussbericht der Enquete-Kommission 'Deutsche Einheit' des Bundestages', in *Dokumente zur Geschichte der PDS* (Gemeinsame Erklärung des Parteivorstandes und der Bundestagsgruppe der PDS, on http://www/pds-online.de/geschichte/9806/schlussbericht.htm). See also *PDS Pressedienst*, Nummer 26, 25 Juni 1998.

38   http://www/pds-online.de/geschichte/9806/schlussbericht.htm See also *PDS Pressedienst*, Nummer 26, 25 Juni 1998.

39   For a further discussion of the considerable disagreement between the two PDS members of the Commission, as well as within the PDS itself, see Barker, 2000, pp. 86-88.

40   http://www/pds-online.de/geschichte/9806/schlussbericht.htm See also *PDS Pressedienst*, Nummer 26, 25 Juni 1998.

41   'Die Doppelbiografie der Bundesrepublik. Zum Phänomen der deutschen Zweistaatlichkeit', *Dokumente zur Geschichte der PDS* (Thesenpapier der Historischen Kommission beim Parteivorstand der PDS, on http://www.pds-online.de/geschichte/9903/doppelbiograhie.htm). See also *PDS Pressedienst*, Nummer 13, 31 März 1999.

42   http://www/pds-online.de/geschichte/9806/schlussbericht.htm   See   also   *PDS Pressedienst*, Nummer 26, 25 Juni 1998.

43   http://www/pds-online.de/geschichte/9806/schlussbericht.htm   See   also   *PDS Pressedienst*, Nummer 26, 25 Juni 1998.

44   Landtag Mecklenburg-Vorpommern: *Zur Arbeit des Landtags in der 2. Wahlperiode 1994 bis 1998*, 1998, p. 621.

45   Landtag Mecklenburg-Vorpommern: *Zur Arbeit des Landtags in der 2. Wahlperiode 1994 bis 1998*, 1998, p. 619.

46   Four members of the Enquete-Kommission resigned in the course of the proceedings, mainly as a result of the blocking tactics and ineffectiveness of the PDS in the Enquete-Kommission. Jürgen Pohl, the first person to resign, expressly stated that the blocking tactics of the PDS ensured that the Commission was not going to be able to carry out its work properly. He observed that is was not possible to work through history alongside people who were unable to look truth in the face. Landtag Mecklenburg-Vorpommern: *Zur Arbeit des Landtags in der 2. Wahlperiode 1994 bis 1998*, 1998, p. 633.

47   Landtag Mecklenburg-Vorpommern: *Zur Arbeit des Landtags in der 2. Wahlperiode 1994 bis 1998*, 1998, p. 626. In this instance, the PDS's claim was rejected – and on 23 May 1996 in a debate in the Mecklenburg Western Pomerania *Landtag* it was decided that the universities and polytechnics in the new *Länder* had been suitably 'cleansed' of GDR teachers, and that they most certainly could be trusted to carry out tasks that the commission set them. Unanimity couldn't however be reached on the proposal to do this.

48   For evidence of the PDS's discussions on the GDR, see http://www.pds-online.de/ geschichte

49   Statistics produced by the *Bundestag* indicate that 'Green Arrows' can be seen at between 400 and 500 crossroads in eastern Germany, and, since the new ruling allowing 'Green Arrows' in the western states was introduced on the 1st of May 1994, they are evident at around 160 in western Germany as well. See http://www.bundestag.de/aktuell/ wib95/895195.htm

50   The campaign was partly successful, as the *Ampelmännchen* are still visible in Berlin, Saxony, and Saxony Anhalt. See http://www.interactive.de/ampel.html

51   In 1955 less than 20 per cent of 13/14 year olds took part, but by 1989 this figure was over 90 per cent. In the FRG there were very, very few *Jugendweihe* ceremonies. See Meier, 1997.

52   70,000 youngsters had their *Jugendweihe's* in 1993 (or 30 per cent of eastern Germans of the relevant age). 80,000 did so in 1994, while 85,000 did so in 1995. 95,000 did so in 1996 (or just under 40 per cent of eastern children who were 13 and 14). See Meier, 1997, pp. 8–9.

53   Andreas Bluhm (PDS): *PDS für Anerkennung des Jugendweihevereins als Träger der freien Jugendhilfe* (Schwerin: PDS Presseerklärung, PDS Pressestelle, Nummer 73, 8 April 1999).

54   'Koalitionsvereinbarung II. Zukunftsfähige Arbeits- und Ausbildungsplätze schaffen und die Wirtschaftskraft stärken', Abschnitt 2 Teil 23: in *Koalitionsvereinbarung zwischen der Sozialdemokratischen Partei Deutschlands und dem Partei des Demokratischen Sozialismus* (Schwerin: Landtag Mecklenburg-Vorpommern, 1998). See also http://www.mv-pds-ltf.de/koalition/i00000.htm For support of attempts to protect eastern German products from the vagaries of international capitalism see Rolf Kutzmutz's speech to the *Bundestag* in the plenary sitting of 5th February 1997. 'Absatzförderung für Produkte aus Ostdeutschland', *Bundestag Plenarprotokoll* 13/216.

55 See the PDS's party programme on http://www.pds-online.de/dokumente/pro-gramm/punkt5.htm for details of this. Commentators who view the PDS as an extremist political organisation claim that the PDS's belief that *"extra-parliamentary activity is decisive"* (see the PDS Party Programme on the above mentioned website) ensures that commitments to bring about political change through parliamentary majorities are illusory. Such an analysis tends to lack empirical basis. The PDS uses the term 'extra-parliamentary' to mean engaging with groups within civil society. That the PDS seeks to mobilise these groups (trade unions, particular interest groups and so forth) to its cause is self-explanatory – and it is something that all political parties attempt to do, whether they admit it or not. It does not mean that the PDS aims to revolutionise society in order to overthrow the democratic order – as even the most cursory glance at the PDS's societal activity reveals.

56 As the constitutions of the eastern states were being drawn up in the early 1990s, the PDS made concerted attempts to have considerable measures of direct democracy included within them. These failed at the hands of the CDU/CSU and FDP. There are, however, lower thresholds for initiating petitions and referenda than there are in the West. See Gunlicks, 1996, p. 265.

57 It is not solely in the eastern states where such attitudes are visible. The *Süddeutsche Zeitung* of 23 November 1998 bemoaned the lack of, and consequently called for, a *"democratisation initiative in the eastern states"*, much along the lines of the policies that the PDS is advocating. See *Süddeutsche Zeitung*: 'Neue deutsche Lehrjahre', 23 November 1998, p. 3.

58 The PDS calls for a new constitution in its party programme of 1993. See http://www.pds-online.de/dokumente/programm/punkt401.htm

59 This claim has also received been repeated in the popular press. See for example 'Überall fordern Bürger Volksabstimmungen. Die Zeit ist reif für mehr Demokratie', in *Die Zeit*, 8 August 1998, on http://www.archiv.zeit.de/daten/pages/demokratie.txt. 19980408.html

60 Segall *et al.*, 1999, p. 38.

61 PDS, 1998, pp. 31–36.

62 PDS, 1998, p. 31.

63 Das Rostocker Manifest, 1998, pp. 7–8.

64 For a detailed English language analysis of the developments that led to the formation of the first SPD–PDS Coalition, as well as an initial assessment of its successes and failures see Olsen, 2000, pp. 557–580. See also Berg and Koch, 2000.

65 'Koalitionsvereinbarung IX. Selbstverwaltung der Kommunen ausbauen und ihre Leistungsfähigkeit sichern. Abschnitt 1: Kommunalpolitik' in *Koalitionsvereinbarung zwischen der Sozialdemokratischen Partei Deutschlands und dem Partei des Demokratischen Sozialismus* (Schwerin: Landtag Mecklenburg-Vorpommern, 1998). See also http://www.mv-pds-ltf.de/koalition/i00000.htm

66 See Jesse, 2000, pp. 69–87.

67 PDS, 1993, p. 6.

68 Dellheim, 1999, p. 32.

69 As has already been mentioned, 'neoliberal' is a term much used by PDS politicians, yet, bar ascribing it to the politics of the Conservative Coalition under Helmut Kohl, it is very rare to hear any sort of definition of what is precisely meant by the term. Cuts in social services and benefits as well as increases in unemployment are frequently mentioned in the same breath, but conceptualising the meaning of the term is rarely, if ever, attempted.

70　Gregor Gysi, speech to the federal Parliament on 14 June 1996, in Gysi, 1998, p. 17.

71　At the rhetorical level, the PDS articulated such criticisms within a matter of weeks, and within months the PDS was tabling parliamentary initiatives demanding to know what had happened to Chancellor Schröder's promises to make the *Aufbau Ost* his *Chefsache* (key priority). Such initiatives included one placed in the *Bundestag* on the 19 February 1999; one in March 1999 on the '*Entwicklung und Situation in Ostdeutschland*' (On the Development and Situation in Eastern Germany – *Deutscher Bundestag*: Drucksache 14/860) and one on the 22 June 1999 on the *Fahrplan zur Angleichung der Lebensverhältnisse und zur Herstellung von mehr Rechtssicherheit in Ostdeutschland – 'Chefsache Ost'* (a timetable for the equalisation of living conditions and for ensuring more *Rechtssicherheit* in eastern Germany – see http://www2.pds-online.de/bt/themen/9906/99062407.htm).

72　For a particularly clear example of this see Pia Maier: 'Auch unter Schröder gilt: Kampf gegen Arbeitslose statt Kampf für Arbeitsplätze', in *R(h)einblick*, Number 5, 2001, on http://www2.pds-online.de/bt/

73　PDS Mecklenburg-Vorpommern: 'Für eine andere Beschäftigungs- und Wirtschaftspolitik in Mecklenburg-Vorpommern. Beschluß der 4. Tagung des 4. Landesparteitages der PDS Mecklenburg-Vorpommern, Parchim, 15 and 16 Februar 1997', in *PDS Pressedienst*, Nummer 8, 21 Februar 1997, p. 8.

74　This has also been written in to the party programme. See PDS, 1993, p. 17.

75　*Deutscher Bundestag*: Drucksache 13/10015.

76　Helmut Holter (PDS): 'Arbeitsplätze gehen vor Profit', in *Schweriner Volkszeitung*, 27 May 1997.

77　Even André Brie, widely perceived as being on the social-democratic wing of the PDS, has concluded that full employment is both a legitimate and necessary goal. See André Brie (PDS): 'Erfordernis, Möglichkeiten, Schwierigkeiten und Inhalt eines Strategiewechsels der PDS', on http://www.pds-online.de/pressedienst/9951/06.htm See also *PDS Pressedienst*, Nummer 51, 23 Dezember 1999.

78　Lothar Bisky (PDS): Speech at the Rostock Party Conference, 3 April 1998, in *PDS Pressedienst*, Nummer 15-16, 17 April 1998, p. 2.

79　'Koalitionsvereinbarung II. Zukunftsfähige Arbeits- und Ausbildungsplätze schaffen und die Wirtschaftskraft stärken. Abschnitt 1 Teil 9: Arbeit und Ausbildung' in *Koalitionsvereinbarung zwischen der Sozialdemokratischen Partei Deutschlands und dem Partei des Demokratischen Sozialismus* (Schwerin: Landtag Mecklenburg-Vorpommern, 1998). See also http://www.mv-pds-ltf.de/koalition/i00000.htm

80　Helmut Holter stated that the aim of the SPD–PDS government in Mecklenburg Western Pomerania was to create between 15,000 and 20,000 new jobs within the state. Given Mecklenburg Western Pomerania's high rate of unemployment, this is perhaps not as many as the PDS originally would have hoped, but it is none the less a considerable commitment. See Helmut Holter (PDS): 'Sparkurs der Bundesregierung wirkt sich verheerend aus', in *Schweriner Volkszeitung*, 21 May 1999.

81　The PDS has made every attempt to give the impression that it is a party of dynamism and of action per se, and its election activity is particularly geared to being as visible and as energetic as possible. See Segall and Schorpp-Grabiak, 1999, p. 18.

82　PDS Greifswald: *Mit guten Leuten und neuen Ideen in der Bürgerschaft* (Greifswald: PDS, 1999).

83　PDS Greifswald, 1999.

84　The PDS has tended to use somewhat confusing terminology when referring to the publicly subsidised employment sector. In public debate and in the majority of PDS literature the term ÖBS is used. But in studies undertaken by the Mecklenburg Western Pomerania government in 1999, and in particular with regard to the implementation of this policy in certain cities (notably Rostock), the term 'gemeinwohlorientiertes arbeits-marktgefördertes Beschäftigungsprojekt' (GAP – subsidised employment project for the well-being of the community) has been preferred. Despite the different categorisations, the policy is the same. For details on the ÖBS in Rostock, see *Machbarkeitsstudie zu einem Öffentlichen Beschäftigungssektor in der Region Rostock*, 1998. PDS Rostock, 1999, p. 1.

85   'Koalitionsvereinbarung II. Zukunftsfähige Arbeits- und Ausbildungsplätze schaffen und die Wirtschaftskraft stärken. Abschnitt 1 Teil 11: Arbeit und Ausbildung' in *Koalitionsvereinbarung zwischen der Sozialdemokratischen Partei Deutschlands und dem Partei des Demokratischen Sozialismus* (Schwerin: Landtag Mecklenburg-Vorpommern, 1998). See also http://www.mv-pds-ltf.de/koalition/i00000.htm

86   Lothar Bisky (PDS): Speech at the Rostock Party Conference, 3 April 1998, in *PDS Pressedienst*, Nummer 15-16, 17 April 1998, pp. 3-4.

87   Dellheim, 1999, p. 36.

88   The ÖBS is mentioned in many election programmes of the PDS at the national, region-al and communal levels, stressing how the non-profit sector is going to create jobs in the socio-cultural area.

89   Helmut Holter (PDS): '83 Sitzung am 31. März 1998', in Landtag Mecklenburg-Vorpommern: *Zur Arbeit des Landtags in der 2. Wahlperiode 1994 bis 1998*, 1998, p. 5164.

90   *Deutscher Bundestag*: Drucksache 14/25.

91   The PDS put forward a motion attempting to create an ÖBS at the federal level which was, unsurprisingly, rejected by the *Bundestag's* other *Fraktionen*. The key difference between the SPD-Alliance 90/Greens and the PDS was that the other centre-left parties saw the ÖBS as, at best, a short-term solution. The PDS aims to see the ÖBS become a long-term institution within the German economy. See *Deutscher Bundestag*: Drucksache 13/7417.

92   Luft, 1998, pp. 102–103.

93   *Mecklenburg-Vorpommern Landtags Nachrichten*, 1999, p. 5.

94   *Mecklenburg-Vorpommern Landtags Nachrichten*, 1999, p. 5.

95   Angelika Gramkow (PDS): *Mecklenburg-Vorpommern Landtags Nachrichten*, 1999, p. 7.

96   Helmut Holter (PDS): *Mecklenburg-Vorpommern Landtags Nachrichten*, 1999, p. 5.

97   Harald Ringstorff (SPD): *Mecklenburg-Vorpommern Landtags Nachrichten*, 1999, p. 5.

98   Angelika Gramkow (PDS): 'PDS steht zu hoher Investitionsquote und zum Einstieg in den ÖBS' (Schwerin: PDS Presseerklärung, PDS Pressestelle, Nummer 82, 4 Mai 1999).

99   Interview with Dr. Christian Westphal, *Kreisvorsitzender* of the PDS Fraktion in Rostock, 29 April 1999.

100   'Soll und Haben in Nordosten': in *Neues Deutschland*, 2 November 1999, p. 2.

101   *Deutscher Bundestag*: Drucksache 13/8573.

102   Das Rostocker Manifest, 1998, p. 22.

103   The PDS committed itself to this at the 1997 Schwerin conference. The Alliance 90/Greens demanded in their election programme in 1998 a one off levy on assets of over DM2 million. The PDS demand levies that are spread over 10 years. For those with net assets of between DM300,000 and DM500,000 there would be a charge of 2 per cent a year, and for assets over this it would be 3 per cent. See http://www2.pds-online.de/bt/themen/rb980802.htm

104 The PDS has had a motion to this affect rejected in the *Bundestag* once. It involved the implementation of a 'luxury tax' (defined as being 6 per cent above the rate of value added tax) and a reduction in the rate of VAT for medication and for labour intensive services by 7 per cent. All other *Fraktionen* rejected this motion on 7 May 1998. See *Deutscher Bundestag*: Drucksache 13/9760.

105 The question of the (re)introduction of a wealth tax arises periodically in political discourse, even though the Federal Court declared such a tax to be illegal in 1997. Hence, since the 1997 party congress in Schwerin, the PDS has talked more (although not exclusively) of a *Vermögensabgabe*, where one-off payments are demanded on large sums of property and wealth. In December 1997 the PDS conceptualised this in the *Bundestag* by bringing a motion calling for the introduction of a capital transactions tax. See *Die Rote Schanze: Zeitung der PDS Ingolstadt*, 1998, p. 6.

106 Heide Knake-Werner (PDS), Arbeitsmarktpoltiische Sprecherin der PDS: 'Die gesetzliche Rente wird seit Jahren kaputt geredet', in *Neues Deutschland*, 3 November 1999, p. 3.

107 Das Rostocker Manifest, 1998, p. 22.

108 For evidence of 'German zones' see 'Breite völkische Bewegung', in *Schweriner Volkszeitung*, 2 November 1999 or 'Wie kriegen Euch alle', in *Schweriner Volkszeitung*, 15 July 1995.

109 "*The state Government will ensure that there is a training place made available for all young persons … the state government will also strive to offer every young person the opportunity of employment after their training has been completed*". 'Koalitionsvereinbarung II. Zukunftsfähige Arbeits- und Ausbildungsplätze schaffen und die Wirtschaftskraft stärken. Abschnitt 1 Teil 15 and Teil 16: Arbeit und Ausbildung' in *Koalitionsvereinbarung zwischen der Sozialdemokratischen Partei Deutschlands und dem Partei des Demokratischen Sozialismus* (Schwerin: Landtag Mecklenburg-Vorpommern, 1998). See also http://www.mv-pds-ltf.de/koalition/i00000.htm

110 PDS: *Farbe bekennen*, 1998, p. 1.

111 This is when figures collected by public opinion agencies are compared with those for the CDU and the SPD. Other sections of this chapter do illustrate that eastern Germans are, however, ascribing more and more *Problemlösungskompetenzen* to the PDS in certain areas. For example, in 1998 35 per cent of eastern Germans thought that the PDS would do the most towards equalising living standards between eastern and western Germany. 33 per cent thought that the PDS would do the most for families with children. A year later in 1999, around 20 per cent of the eastern German population thought that the PDS would be the most effective party in both these areas as well as in improving the situation of *Jugendliche*, and *soziale Sicherheit gewährleisten*. See 'Konrad Adenauer Stiftung, Bereich Forschung und Beratung, Kumulierter Datenfile', in Neu 1999, p. 4.

112 See Neu, 1999, p. 3.

113 Holter 1999, p. 2.

114 Hans Modrow (PDS): 'Erneuerung als einen ständigen Prozess verstehen und betreiben', in *PDS Disput/Pressedienst*, Nummer 4/15-16, April 2000, p. 3.

115 Kitschelt *et al.* 1999, p. 75.

116 Lothar Bisky (PDS): 'Weiter für das 'magische Dreieck': Opposition, Mitgestaltung, Widerstand', in *PDS Disput/Pressedienst*, Nummer 4/15-16, April 2000, p. 6.

117 See Toralf Staud: 'Ankunft im Modernen: Die PDS braucht ein neues Programm und einen neuen Chef', in *Die Zeit*, 6 April 2000, on http://www.archiv.zeit.de/zeit-archiv/daten/pages/200015.pds_.html

118 It is assumed that such calls for more social justice centre around a better working and social environment for the 'socially disadvantaged'. An underlying presupposition that universal standards of social justice both exist, and are attainable, is evident within the PDS's political rhetoric. But it remains clear that such standards are by no means universally acccepted – and the means and methods that different actors propagate in an attempt to achieve 'social justice' are therefore wide, diverse and often plain contradictory. The PDS remains skilled at articulating the worries of Easterners about their social and working environments, just as it is vociferous in its egalitarian, anti-capitalist rhetoric. Yet it (the PDS) is not willing to define its broad understanding of 'social justice' over and above basic calls for equality and more 'fairness'. But this is as it is not (yet) in a position where it is forced to – as only when it is required to implement the policies that it espouses will it be forced to consider the constraints and contradictions of governmental responsibility and idealist policy positions. For an analysis on the theoretical underpinnings of social justice, see Harvey 1993, pp. 41–66.

119 PDS Stadtvorstand Leipzig, 1999.

120 PDS Kreisvorstand Bad Doberan, 1999.

121 PDS Sachsen, 1999, p. 2.

122 The PDS has not been afraid to claim that it preserves the social democratic tradition in Germany better than the SPD is able to do. In view of the SPD's particularly poor showing in the Saxon state election of September 1999 the PDS unambiguously claimed, for example, that "the social democratic tradition is … better preserved by the PDS". Quoted in Patton, 2000, p. 158.

123 Lothar Bisky (PDS) in: 'Und dann das Meisterstück', in *Frankfurter Allgemeine Zeitung*, 20 November 1999, p. 12.

124 'Angebot zum Dialog über soziale Gerechtigkeit: Bericht von den Beratungen des Parteivorstandes', on http://www.pds-online.de/parteivorstand/berichte/991101.htm

125 PDS Mecklenburg-Vorpommern: 'Für eine andere Beschäftigungs- und Wirtschaftspolitik in Mecklenburg-Vorpommern. Beschluß der 4. Tagung des 4. Landesparteitages der PDS Mecklenburg-Vorpommern, Parchim, 15 and 16 Februar 1997', in *PDS Pressedienst*, Nummer 8, 21 Februar 1997, p. 8.

126 Werz, 1998, p. 95.

127 Klaus-Jürgen Warnick (PDS): *Wohnen ist Menschenrecht* (Bonn: PDS im Bundestag, Rundbrief Nr. 15, December 1997), p. 3.

128 Infratest Dimap, 1999, p. 12.

129 See http://www.pds-online.de/newsletter/9909/gysi.htm

130 Gregor Gysi (PDS): 'Gerechtigkeit ist Modern', Dokumente zur programmatischen Debatte on http://www.pds-online.de/programmdiskussion/9908/gysi-thesen.htm

131 Gregor Gysi, speech to the Federal Parliament on 27 November 1996, in Gysi, 1998, p. 19.

132 PDS, 1999.

133 Hans Modrow (PDS): 'Erneuerung als einen ständigen Prozess verstehen und betreiben', in *PDS Disput/Pressedienst*, Nummer 4/15-16, April 2000, p. 3.

134 Only Alliance 90/Greens showed any sign of being hesitant in showing their support although Foreign Minister Joschka Fischer eventually managed to persuade his party to follow his line.

135 Hans Modrow (PDS): 'Erneuerung als einen ständigen Prozess verstehen und betreiben', in *PDS Disput/Pressedienst*, Nummer 4/15-16, April 2000, p. 3.

136 *Friedensdemonstrationen* (peace demonstrations) were organised in the majority of eastern Germany's major towns and cities. Most were held weekly, although special weekend demonstrations in Berlin were also periodically organised.

137 The PDS in Mecklenburg Western Pomerania, for example, organised a concert in May 1999 called *Kunstler gegen den Krieg* (Artists against the War), where musicians and popular entertainers performed in the name of bringing the war with Yugoslavia to an end.

138 Lothar Bisky (PDS), speech to the *Landesparteitag* of the PDS in Saxony on the 11 April 1999 in Schneeberg. *PDS Pressedienst*, Nummer 15, 15 April 1999, p. 4.

139 Hans Modrow (PDS): 'Erneuerung als einen ständigen Prozess verstehen und betreiben', in *PDS Disput/Pressedienst*, Nummer 4/15-16, April 2000, p. 3.

140 In early April 1999 Gregor Gysi paid a personal visit to Yugoslavia to speak with the Yugoslavian President Slobodan Milosevic. His visit was strongly criticised in Germany, although Gysi and the PDS claimed that it was an attempt at engineering dialogue between Milosevic and the West.

141 Gysi, 1999, p. 8.

142 PDS, 1999, pp. 42–43..

143 'Für eine 100,000 Personen-Armee', in *Neues Deutschland*, 19 May 2000, p. 14.

144 'Der PDS reichen 100,000 Mann', in *Neues Deutschland*, 17 May 2000, p. 1.

145 PDS, 1999, p. 1.

146 PDS, 1999, p. 1.

147 Alonso Puerta (PDS): 'Der Kampf gegen das neoliberale Europa braucht alle Kräfte', speech at the PDS Conference in Suhl, March 1999, in *PDS Disput*, Nummer 3, März 1999, pp. 16-17.

148 Sylvia-Yvonne Kaufmann (PDS): 'Wir wollen Europa schaffen ohne Waffen', speech at the PDS conference in Suhl, March 1999, in *PDS Disput*, Nummer 3, März 1999, pp. 11-15.

149 The PDS does see advantages in a single currency: currency speculation between the currencies of European countries would be eliminated, granting investors more long-term security; costs of currency exchange would be abolished; it would be possible to directly compare the costs and prices of goods and services across the entire European Union, increasing economic transparency. See 'Euro? So nicht! Gemeinsame europäische Währung – Fragen und Antworten' in *PDS im Bundestag*, 1997.

150 For a detailed analysis of the PDS's position on the Euro, see Kaufmann, 1999. For discussion of the likely effects of the Euro's implementation on jobs, job security and the labour market see in particular pp. 116–117.

151 Kaufmann, 1999, p. 121.

152 'Euro? So nicht! Gemeinsame europäische Währung – Fragen und Antworten' in *PDS im Bundestag*, 1997.

153 The PDS produced a number of placards on this theme. They included "Demokratisch, Gerecht, Zivil. Für ein soziales Europa. PDS" (Democratic, Just and Civil: For a Social Europe. PDS), "Sozial und Solidarisch in Europa. PDS" (Social and Solidaristic in Europe. PDS) and "Europa für alle: PDS" (Europe for all: PDS).

154 Lothar Bisky (PDS): 'Ein gemeinsamer Wille und Geist des Politikwechsels muß unsere Wahlkämpfe bestimmen', speech to the PDS Conference in Suhl, March 1999, in *PDS Disput*, Number 3, März 1999, pp. 3–10.

155 PDS, 1999.

156 Kaufmann, 1999, p. 125.

157 PDS, 1999.

158 See André Brie (PDS): 'Zugunsten von Koalitionszwängen nicht Prinzipien aufgeben. André Brie über Bündnisse mit der SPD, Europapolitik und den Reformprozeß der PDS', in *Freies Wort*, 6 March 1999.

159 PDS, 1999.

160 PDS, 1999.

161 It is clear that the parties of the left remain the biggest critics of the Maastricht and Amsterdam treaties. The PDS, the French Communist Party, the Italian Communist Party, the Spanish Communist Party and, to an extent, the Portuguese Communist Party are all highly critical of the capitalist emphasis in these treaties. See Segall and Schorpp-Grabiak, 1999, p. 13.

162 http://www.pds-online.de/wahlen/dokumente/europawahlprogramm/02.htm

163 Sylvia-Yvonne Kaufmann has explicitly called for the European Central Bank (ECB) not just to have price stability as its key aim, but also to take into account specific social and employment goals – i.e. to aim for full employment Europe-wide, and to create the economic conditions suitable for achieving *nachhaltige Entwicklung* (sustainable growth). See Kaufmann, 1999, p. 125.

164 Andreas Wehr (PDS): 'Nach der Währungs- nun die Beschäftigungsunion?', on http://www.pds-online.de/disput/9811/39712.html See also *PDS Disput*, Number 11, November 1998.

165 Andreas Wehr (PDS),1998): op. cit.

166 Lothar Bisky (PDS): 'Ein gemeinsamer Wille und Geist des Politikwechsels muß unsere Wahlkämpfe bestimmen', speech to the PDS Conference in Suhl, March 1999, in *PDS Disput*, Number 3, März 1999, pp. 3-10. See also http://www.pds-online.de/wahlen/dokumente/europawahlprogramm/02.htm

167 Alonso Puerta (PDS): 'Der Kampf gegen das neoliberale Europa braucht alle Kräfte', speech at the PDS Conference in Suhl, March 1999, in *PDS Disput*, Number 3, März 1999, pp. 16–17.

168 PDS, 1998, p. 32.

169 Lothar Bisky (PDS): speech at the Rostock Party Conference, 3 April 1998, in *PDS Pressedienst*, Nummer 15–16, 17 April 1998, p. 13.

170 See Kersten Naumann (PDS): 'Ostdeutsches Land an kapitalkräftige Westdeutsche', in *R(h)einblick*, Nummer 2, 2001, on http://www2.pds-online.de/bt/

171 Lothar Bisky (PDS): speech at the Rostock Party Conference, 3 April 1998, in *PDS Pressedienst*, Nummer 15–16, 17 April 1998, p. 13.

172 Lothar Bisky (PDS): speech at the Rostock Party Conference, 3 April 1998, in *PDS Pressedienst*, Nummer 15–16, 17 April 1998, p. 14 .

173 Klaus Bartl (PDS): in PDS-Fraktion im Sächsischen Landtag, 1997, p. 8.

174 Günther Rogin (PDS): in *Kommunal Spezial* (Schwerin: Kommunalpolitsches Forum Mecklenburg-Vorpommern e. V, March 1998), p. 3.

Conclusion:

'Vorwärts immer, Ruckwärts nimmer' …

The PDS and the future

Despite its electoral successes in the 1990s, the future of the PDS is, as it has periodically seemed to be, uncertain. As the GDR imploded in 1989 and 1990, for example, few observers believed that the SED, the SED/PDS, and eventually the PDS, had any realistic hope of long-term survival. The external environment was too hostile, the party membership too intrinsically reform-shy, and the PDS's electoral potential insufficient for it to get over the 5 per cent barrier consistently. Hence, imminent death seemed the only logical conclusion. Even when the PDS re-entered the Bundestag and performed well in both the European and *Land* elections of 1994, the party was largely viewed as having reached its political and electoral zenith. The PDS was expected to disappear from the political scene as and when eastern Germans became more 'satisfied' with the wider environment within which they lived.

It was only after the PDS achieved full *Fraktion* status after the 1998 Federal Election that it dawned on many that the party might not be the transitory political phenomenon that they had anticipated. Encouraged by continued strong showings in *Land* elections in eastern Germany, the PDS was able to cement itself as a vocal, visible and, particularly at the micro-levels of politics in the eastern states, competent political actor. Given this, one would expect that questions on the immediate future of the PDS would dissipate. The PDS is making slow strides away from a pure party of opposition towards becoming a party of government – originally dipping its feet in Saxony Anhalt as early as 1994, before diving full-length into a coalition with the SPD in Mecklenburg Western Pomerania in the Autumn of 1998. Although these developments prompted considerable discussion, and no little consternation within the party itself, the SPD–PDS coalition in Meck-Pomm has proved to be remarkably unspectacular, as the PDS learned to cope with the different matrix of problems that face a party of government.[1] Given these developments, the future of the PDS appears more rosy than at any time since unification.

But PDS politicians and supporters are well aware that the PDS has to remain 'ahead of the game' if it is to continue securing parliamentary status at the federal level, and if it is to genuinely contribute to shaping public policy in contemporary Germany. The resignations of Lothar Bisky and Gregor Gysi have added a new dimension to the debate on 'where does the PDS go from here?', as, devoid of the two politicians who so successfully came to define the party through the 1990s, it discovers the necessity of explaining why it is still needed in the German party system at all. Gysi and Bisky successfully accomplished a task that few people thought they were up to in 1990 – that of estabilishing the party in the German party system – but it is now up to other individuals to shape and refine the PDS's policy package to enable it to expand its voter base in the light of the resignations of the two star performers. Without these two there is an urgent need for new, energetic and effective replacements to be found. The performances of Gabi Zimmer, Roland Claus, Petra Pau, Helmut Holter and Dietmar Bartsch will be crucial in building on the foundations that Gysi and Bisky laid. Although the schooling of the PDS elites in the structures of the GDR has enabled them to be effective party figureheads in the eastern German *Landtage*, it remains to be seen if they can do this at the national level, without the guiding hands of Gysi and Bisky to assist them.

The PDS's long-term aim therefore remains that of regularly achieving 5 per cent of the popular vote at the national level, and the party leadership is well aware that, given the boundary changes that have taken place in the run-up to the 2002 Federal Election in eastern Berlin, the importance of doing this is now greater than ever before. Only in Gregor Gysi's constituency (which has remained unaffected by the boundary changes) of Berlin Marzahn-Hellersdorf does the PDS appear to be favourite to win the most *Erststimmen* (first votes). In the high-profile constituency of Berlin Mitte, a seat that the PDS won in both 1994 (Stefan Heym) and 1998 (Petra Pau), the addition of *Westbezirke* Tiergarten and Wedding, and the omission of Prenzlauer Berg, would appear to render the PDS's chances of retaining this seat in 2002 extremely slim. The party faces a similar problem in Christa Luft's constituency of Friedrichshain/Prenzlauer Berg Ost. The addition of Kreuzberg (another *Westbezirk*), and the loss of Lichtenberg, is likely to make this seat 'unwinnable'. In Berlin Pankow the situation would appear to be similarly bleak, as the loss of Hohenschönhausen and the addition of Prezlauer Berg West (an area where the SPD tends to perform better than the PDS) is likely to wipe out Manfred Müller's 3,293 majority.

Of the constituencies that the PDS narrowly failed to win in 1998, three appear to offer the party some hope of achieving directly elected members of the *Bundestag*: in Berlin Treptow-Köpenick, where Lothar Bisky was narrowly run into second place in 1998, there have been no boundary changes and so the PDS candidate needs only a small swing to defeat the SPD; in Rostock, where Professor Wolfgang Methling was just over 4,000 votes behind Christine Lucyga (SPD) in 1998, the PDS is likely to invest considerable resources in an attempt to overturn the SPD's narrow advantage; while in the slightly reorganised Halle constituency, Roland Claus is likely to perform considerably better than in 1998, and the PDS remains hopeful of a large swing in its favour.[2]

The biological question

Given the importance of achieving 5 per cent of the popular vote in forthcoming national elections, the PDS will need to make the most of its robust organisational structures and its highly motivated, and politically active, membership base. The advantageous position that the PDS enjoyed through the 1990s, as the party leadership knows all to well, is not something that it can be sure to retain, and it will have to find an answer to the 'biological question' if it is not to crumble owing to its membership base eroding in the coming years. The PDS has consistently lost members, even if it has been able to retain a numerical advantage over both the CDU and the SPD (see chapter 5). As infirmity and death culls its ageing membership, this will not continue to be the case indefinitely, and, although estimates vary, it is clear that in the medium term the PDS will almost certainly lose (to the CDU) its position as the most prominent *Mitgliederpartei* in eastern Germany.

The loss of members is a negative development for all political parties, but for the PDS this is likely to be an even more traumatic experience. As with other former Communist parties in central and eastern Europe, organisational advantages stemming from pre-1989 hegemonic status have been eroded over time, to the advantage of political competitors.[3] The PDS will no longer be able to profile itself so strongly at the *Kreisebene*, as the ever-reducing number of members will ensure, firstly, that fewer people are prepared to stand on PDS lists and sit in Communal parliaments, and, secondly, the PDS's much-cherished image as the party that is visible on the streets, in the clubs and knocking at doors, will slowly slip. *Partei für den Alltag* perhaps no more? Financially, the PDS has also relied heavily on members' contributions, owing to its perpetual difficulties in finding sponsors and external investors; the dying-out of the membership is likely to acutely affect the party's ability to campaign in the way it did throughout the 1990s. Shrinking membership numbers may also affect the policy orientation of the party: the fewer party members there are, the more likely that the rump that remains takes on ideologically less integrative positions. In other words, the rejuvenative effect of new members with new ideas will be missing, offering the ideologically entrenched core the opportunity to drive the party away from modernisation and towards structural conservatism.

The PDS's competitors

The future of the PDS will, of course, not just depend on internal party dynamics, even if they inevitably play a key role in dictating the party's future direction. The PDS will also be affected by the strategies, tactics and policy successes (or failures) of its main competitors in eastern Germany: the CDU and the SPD. While the PDS is faced with the serious structural difficulties of a decreasing membership, a weaker financial base and ideological disagreements, these concerns may be at least partially counteracted by the inability of the PDS's competitors to take electoral advantage of the situation. Hence the PDS may still be able to continue profiling itself as a uniquely eastern German political actor, even if it is forced to re-adapt its electoral strategies in doing this.

The CDU

The PDS may have to contend with a revitalised and eastward-looking CDU, led by the *Mecklenburgerin* Angela Merkel. Merkel's moderate and conciliatory style is likely to considerably improve the electoral chances of what, particularly towards the end of the Kohl era, came to be seen as a gentrified and distant CDU. This may directly challenge the PDS on the key plank of its electoral strategy – the articulation of eastern German interests. However, if the CDU is going to deprive the PDS of votes in the eastern states, then it will have to appeal to Easterners in a way that the PDS has successfully done through the 1990s – not a task that the CDU will be able to accomplish easily. CDU politicians realise that political competition and political mobilisation in the eastern states take place in a very different structural environment to that in the western states, and the CDU will need to fundamentally re-invent itself if it is to beat the PDS on its own ground.[4] Paul Krüger, an eastern CDU MP in the *Bundestag*, for example, has been adamant that the CDU needs to fight the PDS with its own weapons, stressing that the CDU should positively emphasise the important function that specifically regional identities play within social and political life in the eastern states. He proposes that the CDU can only come to terms with the diverging differences within Germany by actively articulating them, seeking either to stress the virtues evident in diversity or, where applicable, to develop feasible political alternatives. He demands that eastern MPs in the CDU need to be more vocal and prepared to fight more vigorously for eastern German interests in times of conflict within the parliamentary party.

The lack of any Christian underpinnings to 'eastern Germanness' is also a clear and persistent worry to CDU politicians, as Christianity has traditionally been the bedrock of their political platform. Jörg Schönbohm, Deputy Prime Minister of Brandenburg, has stressed that even in eastern Germany, where only one- fifth of citizens classify themselves as Christians, the CDU needs to use the Christian world-view as an explicit feature of the process by which it develops policies to deal with contemporary problems. He speaks for a majority of CDU members when he emphasises that the Christian faith and conservative value structures are the 'moral basis for the future'.[5] Eckhard Rehberg, the leader of the CDU in the Mecklenburg Western Pomerania state parliament in Schwerin, stresses the same point in a slightly different way when he observes that:

> The Union has a hard task ahead of it, as it needs to sell a political package based on Christian values to a broadly atheist population[6].

The CDU will also have to reappraise its rhetoric on the issue of the GDR, as it will not attract the votes of current PDS supporters unless it softens its harsh position. As was illustrated in chapter 4, in 1998 72 per cent of Easterners felt that the GDR as a whole had at least as many good sides as bad sides. Nowhere in any CDU literature is one likely to find such a positive analysis of life in the GDR. On the contrary, the GDR is persistently and relentlessly condemned – inevitably leaving many Easterners with the impression that their experiences and views of the GDR are not valued in the same way as those of Westerners. The policy positions of the CDU also have little in common with much of the ideological underpinnings of the eastern German identity.[7] The core values and ideological basis of the CDU's platform, formed and developed in western Germany and largely unchanged since 1989, are far removed from eastern German interests and concerns. The PDS's supporter base does not identify with many of the key tenets of the CDU: a strong support for the social market economy, a firmly westward-ori-entated foreign policy, pro-Europeanism, and the adoption of morals and val-ues based firmly on Christian beliefs. The experience of living in the GDR, and experiencing the rapid *Wende* transformation process, has shaped the atti-tudes and preferences of eastern German citizens today – and, once the ini-tial alignment of broad swathes of the eastern electorate with the CDU sub-sided, the Christian Democrats have found it difficult to incorporate specifi-cally eastern value-structures and preferences into their all-German party platform.

The SPD

Although the SPD was swept to power at the federal level in 1998, the losses that it suffered in the European and *Land* elections of 1999 illustrated that it does not have strong alignments of consistent support in the eastern states. Voters can and do turn away from the CDU and SPD in eastern Germany just as quickly as they turn towards them. The SPD suffers from the structural dif-ficulties inherent in not genuinely 'fitting-into' the eastern German party sys-tem, which is dominated by the two pillars of the CDU and PDS: it is the dynamic between them that tends to dictate how much 'centre-ground' is left for the SPD to exploit. In 1998, the SPD successfully mobilised support around the 'Neue Mitte', based on the 'Third Way' between these two pillars, although its performances since illustrate that voters remain unconvinced about the long-term viability of its policies for eastern Germany. This is in spite of the fact that since 1998 the Schröder government has implemented a wide range of eastern-friendly policy alternatives, ranging from specific strategies aimed at counteracting high unemployment, to encouraging region-al economic development and recognising the achievements of Easterners in bringing down the GDR.

Yet while the SPD-led government, like the CDU government before it, has been active in attempting to help support and rejuvenate political and eco-nomic life in the eastern states, it, too, has been unable to profile itself as a party that genuinely caters for and forwards the interests of eastern Germans. The PDS has still been able to attract the support of a broad swathe of Easterners who would, one presumes, vote for left-of-centre parties (i.e. the SPD and/or Alliance 90/Green) in western Germany. Those eastern Germans who feel strongly about redistributing wealth downwards, achieving more social justice, advocating a less combative foreign policy and defending elements of life in the GDR still tend towards the PDS, as, firstly, the SPD is not perceived as having delivered in these policy areas, and, secondly, the PDS advocates a bundle of policies that clearly does represent the wants and desires of eastern Germans.

Vorwärts immer, Ruckwärts nimmer?'

It is clear that for as long as eastern Germans perceive the western parties as failing to represent their interests within the political process there will be a niche for an eastern German regional party. If Angela Merkel proves to be a good rather than a truly outstanding leader, if the 'new' PDS leadership proves capable of offering sufficient direction and enthusiasm, and if the party avoids major policy or rhetorical disaster[8], the future prospects of the PDS rest on it continuing to do what it does best: representing eastern German difference in the political arena. This book has highlighted that this is the role that the PDS has succeeeded in thus far. There is no guarantee that the social, cultural, economic and political differences that currently exist will continue; but for as long as attitudinal and value differences of the type discussed in chapter four do prevail – and there is every indication that they may endure well into the medium and long-term – then there will be scope for a party to articulate them in the political arena. The defiant nature of the eastern identity, and the region's attitudinal and cultural differences, indicate that a party with the PDS's ideological inclinations and heritage will remain in the best position to exploit them.

This is of particular importance to the PDS as the westward expansion of the party has met with such dismal failure. It has applied considerable resources to competing in western state elections and attempting to build a western base 'from the bottom up'; but to no avail. The *Land* elections in the western state of North-Rhein Westphalia in May 2000, where the PDS was hopeful that the substantial working class electorate would offer it the opportunity to jump out of the 1 per cent ghetto, proved yet another electoral disaster, with the PDS polling a mere 1.1 per cent of the popular vote. Despite the alleged 'move rightwards' of the SPD and the 'neoliberalisation' of not just German but European politics, the PDS is manifestly incapable of mobilising western Germans behind its claims that it is the party of social justice, economic equality, peace and progressive politics. The PDS's heritage (i.e. its previous life as the SED) prevents it from alleviating the impression that it is an *Überbleibsel* (left-over) of a failed and bankrupt regime. This must also be coupled with the fact that there appears to be no room for a socialist or communist political party to the left of the SPD. The failings of the KPD are the clearest example of this and no nationwide anti-capitalist party seems to have a sufficient electoral base, principally because the SPD has managed to incorporate left-wing political beliefs into its platform. In spite of the personalisation of politics and the alleged drift towards the centre this appears to have changed little after unification.

The federal system of governance allows, and in many ways positively encourages, regional representation within the political system. As a pragmatic actor within eastern German state and communal parliaments, the PDS has 'normalised' its position as an eastern German regional party. It has moved a long way towards 'normalising' relations with Germany's other political parties, and eastern German politicians and citizens no longer regard the PDS either as an extremist or dogmatic political actor. On the contrary, at the communal level the PDS exhibits political pragmatism and flexibility in seeking to find solutions to an array of complex problems. As an eastern regional party, working in unison with other political parties (although principally, one would presume, the SPD), the PDS is likely to be able to capitalise on its social and political strengths, and exert more influence, over the longer term, on German politics at the national level. Difficult though this may be for the PDS leadership and membership to accept, the realities of political competition in Germany indicate that the attempted westward expansion of the party is not likely to be successful – and so the PDS needs to stabilise its electoral support at around 30 per cent in the eastern states and/or seek to maintain the four directly elected MP's it already possesses. Only then will it be able to contribute to reforming the German state it claims is in such desperate need of an overhaul.

Notes

1   Berg and Koch, 2000, p. 108.
2   Eisel and Graf, 2001.
3   Gapper, 2002, chapter five.
4   Rehberg, 1996; Krüger, 1996.
5   Jörg Schönbohm (CDU): "Bewahren und Verändern - Mut zur Wertorientierung". Speech given by Jörg Schönbohm at the Konrad Adenauer Foundation sponsored event "10 Years of German Unity: Values and Value Change in East and West" on the 11. January 2001 at the Dorint-Hotel, Potsdam.
6   Rehberg, 1996, p. 23.
7   Hough, 2002, Forthcoming.

8   The PDS *Parteitag* in Münster in April 2000 was widely viewed in the (western) media as such a disaster, when the Party Executive was defeated in a motion regarding the deployment of UN troops in international activity. It remains, at the time of writing, to be seen if the eastern electorate, with its strong peace-orientated inclinations, will pass so harsh a judgement on the PDS.

Bibliography

Primary sources

Parliamentary papers and documents

Deutscher Bundestag: Drucksachen.

Deutscher Bundestag: Plenarprotokoll.

Landtag Mecklenburg-Vorpommern: *Leben in der DDR, Leben nach 1989 – Aufarbeitung und Versöhnung: Zur Arbeit der Enquete-Kommission*, (Schwerin: Landtag Mecklenburg-Vorpommern, Bands 1–10, 1997).

Landtag Mecklenburg-Vorpommern: *Zur Arbeit des Landtags in der 2. Wahlperiode 1994 bis 1998* (Schwerin: Landtag Mecklenburg-Vorpommern, 1998).

Ministerium für Arbeit und Bau des Landes Mecklenburg-Vorpommern: *Machbarkeitsstudie zu einem Öffentlichen Beschäftigungssektor in der Region Rostock* (Schwerin: Ministerium für Arbeit und Bau, November 1998).

Other primary sources

Bayerisches Landesamt für Statistik und Datenverarbeitung: http://www.bayern.de/lfstad/

Bayerisches Staatsministerium des Innern (Hrsg.): *Partei des Demokratischen Sozialismus* (München: Bayerisches Staatsministerium des Innern, 1997).

Bundesministerium des Innern (Hrsg.): *Verfassungsschutzbericht 1996* (Bonn: Bundesministerium des Inneren, 1996).

Bundesregierung: *Deutschland von der Teilung zur Einheit* (Bonn: Presse- und Informationsamt der Bundesregierung, 1999).

Emnid (1999): *Umfrage und Analyse*, Heft 3/4, p.7.

Forschungsgruppe Wahlen e. V. on http://www.aicgs.org/wahlen/elect98.htm

Forschungsgruppe Wahlen e.V.(1995): *Wahl in Berlin: Eine Analyse der Wahl zum Abgeordnetenhaus vom 22. Oktober 1995* (Mannheim: Forschungsgruppe Wahlen, Bericht 83, 1995).

Forschungsgruppe Wahlen e.V.(1998a): *Wahlergebnisse in Deutschland 1946–1998* (Mannheim: Institut für Wahlanalysen und Gesellschaftsbeobachtung der Forschungsgruppe Wahlen).

Forschungsgruppe Wahlen e.V. (1998b): *Wahl in Sachsen-Anhalt: Eine Analyse der Landtagswahl vom 26. April 1998* (Mannheim: Forschungsgruppe Wahlen, Bericht 89).

Forschungsgruppe Wahlen e.V. (1999a): *Wahl in Brandenburg: Eine Analyse der Landtagswahl vom 5. September 1999* (Mannheim: Forschungsgruppe Wahlen, Bericht 97).

Forschungsgruppe Wahlen e.V. (1999b): *Wahl in Thüringen: Eine Analyse der Landtagswahl vom 12.*

September 1999 (Mannheim: Forschungsgruppe Wahlen, Bericht 98).

Forschungsgruppe Wahlen e.V. (1999c): *Wahl in Sachsen: Eine Analyse der Landtagswahl vom 19. September 1999* (Mannheim: Forschungsgruppe Wahlen, Bericht 99).

Forschungsgruppe Wahlen e.V. (1999d): *Wahl in Berlin: Eine Analyse der Wahl zum Abgeordnetenhaus vom 10. Oktober 1999* (Mannheim: Forschungsgruppe Wahlen, Bericht 100).

Forschungsgruppe Wahlen e.V. (1999e): *Wahl in Mecklenburg-Vorpommern: Eine Analyse der Landtagswahl vom 27. September 1998* (Mannheim: Forschungsgruppe Wahlen, Bericht 92).

Infratest Dimap (1998): *Wahlreport: Wahl zum 14. Deutschen Bundestag 27. September 1998* (Berlin: Infratest Dimap).

Infratest Dimap (1999): *Wahlreport Berlin 1999* (Berlin: Infratest Dimap).

Institute für Arbeitsmarkt- und Berufsforschung der Bundesanstalt für Arbeit (IAB), Kurzbericht, Nr.1/26 Februar 1999.

Kommunalpolitisches Forum Mecklenburg-Vorpommern: 'Anregungen und Vorschläge für die kommunalpolitische Arbeit der PDS 1998', in *Kommunal Spezial* (Schwerin: Kommunalpolitisches Forum Mecklenburg-Vorpommern e. V, März 1998).

Landesamt für Datenverarbeitung und Statistik Brandenburg: http://www.brandenburg.de/lds/index.html

Mecklenburg-Vorpommern Landtags Nachrichten: Jahrgang 9, Nummer 2, 1999.

Politbarometer Mecklenburg-Vorpommern (Bielefeld: EMNID, März 1996, 6. Welle).

Politbarometer Mecklenburg-Vorpommern (Bielefeld: EMNID, Dezember 1996, 6. Welle).

Politbarometer Mecklenburg-Vorpommern (Bielefeld: EMNID, Mai 1997, 7. Welle).

Politbarometer Mecklenburg-Vorpommern (Bielefeld: EMNID, März 1998, 10. Welle).

Statistisches Bundesamt Deutschland: http://www.statistik-bund.de

Statistisches Landesamt Berlin: http://www.statistik-berlin.de

Statistisches Landesamt des Freistaates Sachsen: http://www.statistik.sachsen.de

Statistisches Landesamt Mecklenburg-Vorpommern: http://www.statistik-mv/projekte

Statistisches Landesamt Sachsen-Anhalt: http://www.stala.sachsen-anhalt.de

Thüringer Landesamt für Statistik: http://www.tla.thueringen.de

PDS literature

PDS: *Mitgliederzeitschrift Disput.*

PDS: *Pressedienst.*

PDS: *Programme of the Party of Democratic Socialism* (Berlin: PDS, 1993).

PDS: *Zur Programmatik der Partei des Demokratischen Sozialismus: Ein Kommentar* (Berlin: Dietz Verlag, 1997).

PDS-Fraktion im Sächsischen Landtag: *Sächsische Verfassung und Wirklichkeit: Eine Festschrift der PDS-Fraktion der Sächsischen Landtag zum 5. Jahrestag der Sächsischen Verfassung am 26. Mai 1997* (Dresden: PDS-Fraktion im Sächsischen Landtag, 1997).

PDS Greifswald: *Mit guten Leuten und neuen Ideen in der Bürgerschaft* (Greifswald: PDS, 1999).

PDS im Bundestag: R(h)einblick (Bonn/Berlin: PDS, 1990–2000).

PDS im Bundestag: 'Wohnen ist Menschenrecht', in *Rundbrief* (Bonn: PDS, Nummer 15, Dezember 1997).

PDS im Bundestag: 'Euro? So nicht! Gemeinsame europäische Währung – Fragen und Antworten' (Bonn: Arbeitsbereich Außen- und Friedenspolitik, 1997).

PDS Ingolstadt: *Die Rote Schanz: Zeitung der PDS Ingolstadt*, (Ingolstadt: PDS Stadtvorstand, Nummer 1, 1998).

PDS Kreisvorstand Bad Doberan: 'Für soziale Gerechtigkeit und Menschenwürde', *Wahlprogramm zu den Kommunalwahlen 1999* (Bad Doberan: PDS, 1999).

PDS Parteivorstand: *Ostdeutschland: Herausforderung und Chance* (Berlin: PDS, 1996).

PDS Parteivorstand: *Studien zur inneren Verfaßtheit der PDS* (Berlin: PDS, 1997).

PDS Parteivorstand: *Farbe bekennen* (Berlin: Parteivorstand der PDS, 1998),

PDS Parteivorstand: *Das Rostocker Manifest. Für einen zukunftsfähigen Osten in einer gerechten Republik* (Berlin: Parteivorstand der Partei des Demokratischen Sozialismus, 1998).

PDS Parteivorstand: *Beiträge zur Wirtschaftspolitik: Grenzen des Wachstums heute* (Berlin: Arbeitsgemeinschaft Wirtschaftspolitik beim Parteivorstand der PDS, Januar 1999).

PDS Parteivorstand: *Beiträge zur Wirtschaftspolitik: Globalisierung oder Regionalisierung?* (Berlin: Arbeitsgemeinschaft Wirtschaftspolitik beim Parteivorstand der PDS, Februar 1999).

PDS Parteivorstand: 'Die Doppelbiographie der Bundesrepublik. Zum Phänomen der deutschen Zweistaatlichkeit', *Dokumente zur Geschichte der PDS* (Thesenpapier der Historischen Kommission beim Parteivorstand der PDS, on http://www.pds-online.de/geschichte/9903/doppelbiographie.htm).

PDS Parteivorstand: 'Angebot zum Dialog über soziale Gerechtigkeit: Bericht von den Beratungen des Parteivorstandes', on http://www.pds-online.de/parteivorstand/berichte/991101.htm

PDS Parteivorstand und Bundestagsgruppe: 'Zum Schlussbericht der Enquete-Kommission 'Deutsche Einheit' des Bundestages', in *Dokumente zur Geschichte der PDS* (Gemeinsame Erklärung des Parteivorstandes und der Bundestagsgruppe der PDS, on http://www/pds-online.de/geschichte/9806/schlussbericht.htm).

PDS Rostock: *Kommunalwahlprogramm der Rostocker PDS 1999* (Rostock: Rostocker PDS, 1999).

PDS Sachsen: 'Ein Land für die Menschen. Veränderung beginnt vor Ort', *Wahlprogramm 1999* (Dresden: PDS, 1999).

PDS-Stadtvorstand Dresden: *Querschnitt: Sonderausgabe* (Dresden: PDS, 1996).

PDS Stadtverband Leipzig: *Mitteilungsblatt* (Leipzig: PDS, Nummer 2/3, März 1999).

PDS-Stadtvorstand Leipzig, AG Geschichtsaufarbeitung: *Der lange Weg vom Bekenntnis über Rechtfertigung bis zum kritischen Umgang: Dokumentation zur Basiskonferenz 'Geschichtsaufarbeitung' am 25 Februar 1995* (Leipzig: PDS, 1996).

PDS Stadtvorstand Leipzig: 'Leipzig 2000 – Zukunft sozial gestalten', *Wahlprogramm zu den Kommunalwahlen* (Leipzig: PDS, 1999).

PDS Wahlbüro: *Wahlprogramm der Partei des Demokratischen Sozialismus zur Bundestagswahl 1998: Für den politischen Richtungswechsel! Sozial und solidarisch – für eine gerechte Republik* (Berlin: Wahlbüro der PDS, 1998).

PDS Wahlbüro: 'Für einen Kurswechsel in Europa. Das Europa des 21. Jahrhunderts braucht Frieden, Arbeit und Demokratie', *Europawahlprogramm der Partei des Demokratischen Sozialismus* (Berlin: Wahlbüro der PDS, 1999).

SPD and PDS: *Koalitionsvereinbarung zwischen der Sozialdemokratischen Partei Deutschlands und dem Partei des Demokratischen Sozialismus* (Schwerin: Landtag Mecklenburg-Vorpommern, 1998). See also http://www.mv-pds-ltf.de/koalition/i00000.htm

Press releases

Bluhm, Andreas (PDS): *PDS für Anerkennung des Jugendweihevereins als Träger der freien Jugendhilfe* (Schwerin: PDS Presseerklärung, PDS Pressestelle, Nummer 73), 8 April 1999.

Gramkow, Angelika (PDS): PDS steht zu hoher Investitionsquote und zum Einstieg in den ÖBS (Schwerin: PDS Presseerklärung, PDS Pressestelle, Nummer 82), 4 Mai 1999.

Muth, Caterina and Bartsch, Dietmar (PDS): *Rote Socken und rote Hände haben keine Angst vorm schwarzen Mann* (Schwerin: PDS Presseerklärung, PDS Pressestelle, Nummer 1000), 27 Mai 1998.

PDS Parteivorstand: *Fraktionsvorstand zu Schwerpunkten 2000: PDS schärft ihr Profil* (Berlin: PDS Pressemitteilung, Nummer 1156), 14 Januar 2000.

Rössel, Uwe-Jens (PDS): *Kommunalreform* (Bonn: PDS im Bundestag Presseerklärung, Nummer 2070), 11 März 1998.

Schulz, Gabi (PDS): 'Zusammenschluß von Gemeinden darf nicht zu deren Last gehen' (Schwerin: PDS Presseerklärung, PDS Pressestelle, Nummer 70), 6 April 1999.

Secondary sources

Abromeit, Heidrun, 1993: 'Die 'Vertretungslücke'. Probleme im neuen deutschen Bundesstaat', *Gegenwartskunde*, 42(3), 281–92.

Agnew, John A., 1981: 'Structural and dialectical theories of political regionalism', in Burnett and Taylor, 1981, pp. 275–89.

Agnew, John A., 1985: 'Models of spatial variation in political expression: The case of the Scottish National Party', *International Political Science Review*, 6(2), 171–96.

Ahbe, Thomas, 1999: 'Ostalgie als Laienpraxis', *Berliner Debatte INITIAL*, 10(3), 87–97.

Ahbe, Thomas, 2000: 'Hohnarbeit und Kapital: Westdeutsche Bilder vom Osten', *Deutschland Archiv*, 33(1), 84–9.

Alber, Jens, Nübel, Christina and Schöllkopf, Martin, 1998: 'Sozialstaat/Soziale Sicherheit', in: Schäfers and Zapf, 1998, pp. 622–32.

Allardt, Erik and Littunen, Yejö (eds.), 1964: *Cleavages, Ideologies and Party Systems* (Helsinki: Academic Bookstore).

Allen, Christopher S. (ed.), 1999: *Transformation of the German Political Party System: Institutional Crisis or Democratic Renewal?* (New York: Berghahn).

Almond, Gabriel and Verba, Sidney, 1963: *The Civic Culture. Political Attitudes to Democracy in Five Nations* (Princeton, New Jersey: Princeton University Press).

Anderson, Christopher J., Kaltenthaler, Karl and Luthardt, Wolfgang, 1993: *The Domestic Politics of German Unification* (London: Lynne Rienner Publishers).

Anderson, Christopher J. and Zelle, Carsten (eds.), 1998: *Stability and Change in German Elections: How Electorates Merge, Converge or Collide* (London: Praeger).

Arzheimer, Kai and Falter, Jürgen W., 1998: 'Annäherung durch Wandel? – Das Wahlverhalten bei der Bundestagswahl 1998 in Ost–West-Perspektive', *Aus Politik und Zeitgeschichte*, 52, 33–44.

Arzheimer, Kai and Klein, Markus, 2000: 'Gesellschaftspolitische Wertorientierungen und Staatszielvorstellungen im Ost–West-Vergleich' in Falter *et al.*, 2000b, pp.363–96.

Assman, Jan, 1999: *Das kulturelle Gedächtnis. Schrift, Erinnerung und politische Identität in frühen Hochkulturen* (München: Verlag C.H.Beck).

Backes, Uwe and Jesse, Eckhard, 1993: *Politischer Extremismus in der Bundesrepublik Deutschland* (Berlin: Prophyläen).

Barker, Peter (ed.), 1998a: *German Monitor*, 42: *The Party of Democratic Socialism. Modern Post-Communism or Nostalgic Populism?* (Amsterdam: Rodopi B.V).

Barker Peter, 1998b: 'From the SED to the PDS: continuity or renewal?' in Barker, 1998a, pp.1–17.

Barker, Peter, 1998c: 'The Party of Democratic Socialism in Germany: modern post-Communism or nostalgic populism?', *German Politics*, 7(2), 211–15.

Barker, Peter (ed.), 2000a: *German Monitor, The GDR and its History: Rückblick und Revision* (Amsterdam: Rodopi, 2000).

Barker, Peter, 2000b: '"Geschichtsaufarbeitung" within the PDS and the Enquete-Kommissionen', in Barker, 2000a, pp.81–95.

Bardi, Luciano and Ignazi, Piero, 1998: 'The Italian party system: the effective magnitude of an earthquake', in Ignazi and Ysmal, 1998, pp.91–109.

Barth, Frederick, 1969: *Ethnic Groups and Boundaries: The Social Organisation of Cultural Difference* (London: Allen and Unwin).

Barthel, Wilfred *et al.*, 1995: *Forschungsbericht Strukturen, politische Aktivitäten und Motivationen in der PDS – Mitgliederbefragung der PDS 1991* (Berlin: Trafo-Verlag).

Bartolini, Stefano and Mair, Peter, 1990: *Identity, Competition and Electoral Volatility* (Cambridge: Cambridge University Press).

Bastian, Jens, 1995: 'The *enfant terrible* of German politics: the PDS between GDR nostalgia and democratic socialism', *German Politics*, 4(2), 95–110.

Bastian, Jens, 1996: 'The process of social unification: more by default than by design', *German Politics*, 5(2), 297–303.

Baylis, Thomas A., 1999: 'East German leadership after unification: the search for voice', in Merkl, 1999, pp.135–46.

Beinert, Heinz (ed.), 1995: *Die PDS – Phönix oder Asche?* (Berlin: Aufbau Verlag).

Bender, Peter, 1992: *Unsere Erbschaft. Was war die DDR – was bleibt von ihr?* (Hamburg: Luchterhand).

Bender, Peter, *et al.*, 1999: *Zeichen und Mythen in Ost und West* (Rostock: Universität Rostock, Rostocker Philosophische Manuskripte).

Bender, Peter, 1999: 'Deutsche Legenden seit 1990', in Bender *et al.*, 1999, pp.7–18.

Benjamin, Michael, 1996a: *Ostdeutsche Identität und ihre sozialen Grundlagen. Gedanken über linke Politik* (Berlin: Marxistisches Forum der PDS, Heft 6).

Benjamin, Michael, 1996b: 'DDR-Identität und PDS' in Bisky *et al.*, 1996, pp.231–6.

Benjamin, Michael, 1997: *Konsens und Dissens in der Strategiedebatte* (Berlin: Helle Panke e.V., Pankower Vorträge, Heft 5).

Benz, Arthur and Holtmann, Everhard (Hrsg.), 1998: *Gestaltung Regionaler Politik: Empirische Befunde, Erklärungsansätze und Praxistransfer* (Magdeburg: Landeszentrale für Politische Bildung Sachsen Anhalt).

Benz, Arthur, Crow, Kimberley and Holtmann, Everhard, 1998: 'Regionen und regionale Politik', in Benz and Holtmann, 1998, pp.15–32.

Benz, Wolfgang, 1998: 'Einheit durch Spaltung?', *Blätter für deutsche und internationale Politik*, 6, 739–46.

Berg, Frank and Koch, Thomas, 2000: *Politikwechsel in Mecklenburg-Vorpommern? Die SPD–PDS-Koalition fünfzehn Monate nach ihrem Amtsantritt* (Berlin: Dietz).

Bergsdorf, Harald, 2001: 'SPD/PDS zwischen Dichtung und Wahrheit', *Die Politische Meinung*, 379, 41–7.

Berrington, Hugh, 1985a: 'New parties in Britain: why some live and most die', *International Political Science Review*, 6(4), 441–62.

Berrington, Hugh, 1985b: 'Centre–periphery conflict in British politics', in Meny and Wright ,

1985, pp.171–206.

Betz, Hans-Georg, 1999: 'The evolution and transformation of the German party system', in Allen, 1999, pp.30–61.

Betz, Hans-Georg and Welsh, Helga A, 1995: 'The PDS in the new German party system', *German Politics*, 4(3), 92–111.

Beyer, Achim, 2000: 'Über den Umgang mit Biographien: Die Täter verwöhnt, die Opfer verhöhnt', *Deutschland Archiv*, 33(1), 82–4.

Beyme, Klaus von, 1993: *Das politische System der BRD nach der Vereinigung* (München: Piper).

Bisky, Lothar, 1997: *Die PDS trägt Dissens und Konsens seit ihrer Gründung in sich – und sie lebt davon!* (Berlin: Helle Panke e.V., Pankower Vorträge, Heft 5).

Bisky, Lothar *et al.*, 1993: *'Rücksichten': Politische und juristische Aspekte der DDR-Geschichte* (Hamburg: VSA)

Bisky, Lothar *et al.* (eds.), 1996: *Die PDS – Herkunft und Selbstverständnis* (Berlin: Dietz).

Bisky, Lothar, Stobrawa, Gerlinde and Vietze, Heinz (eds.), 1998: *Unmittelbare Demokratie zwischen Anspruch und Wirklichkeit* (Potsdam: Kolloquium der PDS-Fraktion im Landtag Brandenburg).

Blank, Thomas, 1997: 'Wer sind die Deutschen? Nationalismus, Patriotismus, Identität – Ergebnisse einer empirischen Längsschnittstudie', *Aus Politik und Zeitgeschichte*, 13, 38–46.

Bleicher, Joan, 1989: 'Die kulturelle Konstruktion sozialer Identität am Beispiel Schottlands', in Haferkamp, 1989, pp.328–46.

Bluck, Carsten and Kreikenbom, Henry, 1991: 'Die Wähler in der DDR: Nur issue-orientiert oder auch parteigebunden?', *Zeitschrift für Parlamentsfragen*, 22, 495–502.

Bluck, Carsten and Kreikenbom, Henry, 1993: 'Quasiparteibindung und Issues', in Gabriel and Troitzsch, 1993, pp.455–70.

Boll, Bernhard, 1999: 'Germany: regional aspects of the 1998 National Elections', *Regional and Federal Studies*, 9(2), 89–97.

Boll, Bernhard, Crow, Kimberly, Hofmann, Bernd and Holtmann, Everhard, 1999: 'Sozialprofil und Einstellungen der Mitglieder von Parteien in Ostdeutschland am Beispiel Sachsen-Anhalts', *Aus Politik und Zeitgeschichte*, 12, 34–45.

Boltho, Andrea, Carlin, Wendy and Scaramozzino, Pasquale, 1995: *Will East Germany Become a New Mezzogiorno?* (Berlin: Wissenschaftszentrum für Sozialforschung, Social Science Research).

Bortfeldt, Heinrich, 1992: *Von der SED zur PDS: Wandlung zur Demokratie?* (Bonn: Bouvier Verlag).

Bortfeldt, Heinrich, 1994a: 'Auf daß der Wind sich drehe', *Deutschland Archiv*, 27(4), 342.

Bortfeldt, Heinrich, 1994b: 'Die Ostdeutschen und die PDS', *Deutschland Archiv*, 27(12), 1283–7.

Bowler, Stephen, 1999: 'Ethnic nationalism: authenticity, atavism and international instability', in Brehony and Rassool, 1999, pp.51–69.

Brand, Jack, 1987: 'National consciousness and voting in Scotland', *Ethnic and Racial Studies*, 10(3), 334–48.

Brandenburgische Landeszentrale für Politische Bildung: 1994 *Die real-existiernede postsozialistische Gesellschaft: Wissenschaftliche Konferenz der Brandenburgischen Landeszentrale für politische Bildung* (Berlin: Gesellschaft für sozialwissenschaftliche Forschung und Publizistik GmbH).

Brehony, Kevin J. and Rassool, Naz (eds.), 1999: *Nationalisms Old and New* (Basingstoke: Macmillan).

Brie, André, 1996: *Wählerpotential der PDS: Erkenntnisse, Tendenzen und Möglichkeiten* (Berlin: PDS-Grundsatzkommission).

Brie, Michael *et al.*, 1994: *Schiff ohne Kompaß? Marxistische Gesellschaftswissenschaften und sozialistische Politik* (Berlin: Grundsatz Kommission der PDS).

Brie, Michael, Herzig, Martin and Koch Thomas, 1995: *Die PDS – Empirische Befunde und kontroverse Analysen* (Köln: Papyrossa Verlag).

Brie, Michael, 1995: 'Das politische Projekt der PDS – eine unmögliche Möglichkeit' in Brie, Herzig and Koch, 1995, pp.9–38.

Brie, Michael and Klein, Dieter (eds.), 1991: *Umbruch zur Moderne* (Hamburg: VSA Verlag).

Brie, Michael and Woderich, Rudolf (Hrsg.), 2000: *Die PDS im Parteiensystem* (Berlin: Dietz).

Broughton, David and Donovan, Mark (eds.), 1999: *Changing Party Systems in Western Europe* (London: Pinter).

Brown, Alice *et al.*, 1998: *Politics and Society in Scotland* (Basingstoke: Macmillan).

Brunner, Wolfram and Walz, Dieter, 1998: 'Totgesagte leben länger – aber *wie* lange ganz genau? Zur Situation der PDS im Wahljahr '98 und darüber hinaus' in Pickel, Pickel and Walz, 1998, pp.81–96.

Brunner, Wolfram and Walz, Dieter, 2000: 'Zwischen Parteiidentifikation, Kandidatenbewertung und Issueorientierung. Bestimmungsfaktoren der Wahlentscheidung 1998', in Pickel, Walz and Brunner, 2000, pp.101–8.

Buelens, Jo and Van Dyck, Ruth, 1998: 'Regionalist parties in French-speaking Belgium', in De Winter and Türsan, 1998, pp.51–69.

Bull, Martin J. and Newell, James L, 1993: 'Italian politics and the 1992 elections: from "stable instability" to instability and change', *Parliamentary Affairs*, 46(2), 203–6.

Bürklin, Wilhelm and Klein, Markus, 1998: *Wahlen und Wählerverhalten – Eine Einführung* (Opladen: Leske und Budrich).

Burnett, Alan D. and Taylor, Peter. J (eds.), 1981: *Political Studies from Spatial Perspectives* (New York: John Wiley and Sons).

Busch, Ulrich, 1998: 'Sieben Fette Jahre? – Kritische Bemerkungen zu Charakter und Umfang der Transfers', *Berliner Debatte INITIAL*, 9(2), 89–103.

Busch, Ulrich, 1999: 'Solidarischer Finanzausgleich. Wie hoch ist der Solidaritätsbeitrag der alten für die neuen Länder?', *UTOPIE Kreativ*, 100, 15–28.

Butt-Philip, Alan, 1975: *The Welsh Question: Nationalism and Politics 1945–70* (Cardiff: University of Wales Press).

Carlin, Wendy, 1998: 'The new East German economy: problems of transition, unification and institutional mismatch', *German Politics*, 7(3),14–32.

Chirot, Daniel (ed.), 1991: *The Crisis of Leninism and the Decline of the Left* (Seattle: Washington University Press).

Clark, Robert P., 1979: *The Basques: The Franco Years and Beyond* (Reno: University of Nevada Press).

Clark, Robert P., 1984: *The Basque Insurgents. ETA, 1952–1980* (Madison: University of Wisconsin Press).

Clausen, Lars (Hrsg.), 1996: *Gesellschaften im Umbruch: Verhandlungen des 27. Kongresses der Deutschen Gesellschaft für Soziologie in Halle an der Saale* (Frankfurt am Main: Campus Verlag).

Coakley, John (ed.), 1993: *The Social Origins of Nationalist Movements* (London: Sage).

Colomé, Gabriel and Lòpez-Nieto, Lourdes, 1998: 'The Spanish political parties from fragmentation to bipolar concentration', in Ignazi and Ysmal, 1998, pp.241–53.

Connor, Walker, 1973: 'The politics of ethnonationalism', *Journal of International Affairs*, 27(1), 1–21.

Conner, Walker, 1977: 'Ethnonationalism in the First World: the present in historical perspective', in Esman, 1977, pp.19–45.

Conner, Walker, 1994: *Ethnonationalism: The Quest for Understanding* (Princeton: Princeton University Press).

Conradt, David *et al.* (eds.), 1995: *Germany's New Politics* (Oxford: Berghahn).

Conradt, David *et al.* (eds.), 2000: *Power Shift in Germany: The 1998 Election and the End of the Kohl era* (Oxford: Berghahn).

Conversi, Daniele, 1997: *The Basques, The Catalans and Spain – Alternative Routes to Nationalist Mobilisation* (London: Hurst and Company).

Cooke, Paul and Grix, Jonathan (eds.), 2000: *German Monitor: East Germany: Continuity and Change* (Amsterdam: Rodopi).

Crawford, Beverly and Lijphart Arend, 1995: 'Old legacies, new institutions, hegemonic norms and international pressures', *Comparative Political Studies*, Special Issue, July 1995, 171–99.

Crawford, Robert, 1982: 'The SNP 1960–74: An Investigation into its Organisation and Power Structure' (Glasgow: University of Glasgow, PhD Thesis, 1982).

Crewe, Ivor and Denver, David (eds.), 1985: *Electoral Change in Western Democracies: Patterns and Sources of Electoral Volatility* (London: Croom Helm).

Cullen, Michael S. (ed.), 1999: *Das Holocaust Mahnmal: Dokumentation einer Debatte* (Zürich: Pendo Verlag).

Curtis, Tony (ed.), 1986: *Wales: The Imagined Nation: Essays in Cultural and National Identity* (Bridgend: Poetry Wales Press).

Daalder, Hans and Mair, Peter (eds.), 1983: *Western European Party Systems: Continuity and Change* (London: Sage).

Dahn, Daniella, 1997: *Westwärts und nicht vergessen* (Berlin: Rowohlt).

Dalton, Russell J., Flanagan, Scott C. and Beck, Paul Allen (eds.), 1984: *Electoral Change in Advanced Industrial Democracies: Realignment or Dealignment?* (Princeton: Princeton University Press).

Dalton, Russell J., 1996: 'A divided electorate', in Smith *et al.*, 1996, pp.35–54.

Dalton, Russell J., 1998: 'A celebration of democracy: the 1998 Bundestag election', *German Politics and Society*, 16(4), 1–6.

Daniels, Philip, 1999: 'Italy: rupture and regeneration', in Broughton and Donovan, 1999, pp.71–95.

Deinert, Rudolf Günter, 1998: 'Die PDS, die rechten Parteien und das Alibi der "Politikverdrossenheit". Die Beweggründer westdeutscher Rechts- und ostdeutscher PDS-Wähler auf dem empirischen Prüfstand', *Zeitschrift für Parlamentsfragen*, 29(3), 422–41.

Dellheim, Judith, 1999: 'Ostdeutschland – Region in Europa, das "Rostocker Manifest" europäisch diskutieren', in *Beiträge zur Wirtschaftspolitik: Globalisierung oder Regionalisierung?* (Berlin: Arbeitsgemeinschaft Wirtschaftspolitik beim Parteivorstand der PDS, 1999), pp.28–47.

De Winter, Lieven and Türsan, Huri (eds.), 1998: *Regionalist Parties in Western Europe* (London: Routledge).

De Winter, Lieven, 1998a: 'The *Volksunie* in Flanders', in De Winter and Türsan, 1998, pp.28–50.

De Winter, Lieven, 1998b: 'Conclusion: a comparative analysis of the electoral, office and policy success of ethnoregionalist parties', in De Winter and Türsan, 1998, pp.204–47.

De Winter, Lieven and Dumont, Patrick, 1999: 'Belgium: party system(s) on the eve of disintegration?', in Broughton and Donovan, 1999, pp.183–206.

Deth, Jan van, Rattinger, Hans and Roller, Edeltrud (Hrsg.), 2000: *Die Republik auf dem Weg zur Normalität? Wahlverhalten und politische Einstellungen nach acht Jahren Einheit* (Opladen: Leske und Budrich).

Detjen, Claus, 1999: 'Auferstanden aus Ruinen – Die PDS als neuer Machtfaktor', *Die Politische Meinung*, 44(1), 5–12.

Dieckmann, Christoph, 1999: *Das wahre Leben im falschen: Geschichten von ostdeutscher Identität* (Berlin: Ch. Links Verlag).

Dietrich, Isolde, 1999: 'Mikrokosmos Kleingarten', *Berliner Debatte INITIAL*, 10(2), 63–73.

Dinkel, Rainer, 1978: 'The relationship between federal and state elections in West Germany', in Kaase and von Beyme, 1978, pp.53–68.

Ditfurth, Christian V., 1998: *Ostalgie oder linke Alternative? Meine Reise durch die PDS* (Köln: Kiepenheuer and Witsch).

Dornberg, John: 'Five years after unification – easterners discover themselves', *German Life*, December1995/January 1996, on http://www.webcom.com /gerlife/maga-zine/1995/9512_01.html

Donovan, Mark and Broughton, David, 1999: 'Party system change in western Europe: positively political', in Broughton and Donovan, 1999, pp.255–75.

Duckenfield, Mark and Calhoun, Noel, 1997: 'Invasion of the western Ampelmännchen', *German Politics*, 6(3), 54–69.

Dümcke, Wolfgang and Vilmar, Fritz (Hrsg.), 1995: *Kolonialisierung der DDR* (Münster: Agenda Verlag).

Dürr, Tobias, 1996: 'Abschied von der "inneren Einheit": Das Lebensgefühl PDS und der alte Westen', *Blätter für deutsche und internationale Politik*, 11, 1349–56.

Duverger, Maurice, 1964: *Political Parties: Their Organisation and Activity in the Modern State* (London: Methuen).

Edinger, Lewis J. and Nacos, Brigitte L., 1998: *From Bonn to Berlin: German Politics in Transition* (New York: Columbia University Press).

Ehrlich, Charles E: 'Federalism, regionalism, nationalism: a century of Catalan political thought and its implications for Scotland in Europe', *Space and Polity*, 1(2), 205–24.

Eisel, Stephan and Graf, Jutta, 2001: *Die PDS und die Bundestagswahl 2002* (Sankt Augustin: Konrad Adenauer Stiftung).

Eith, Ulrich, 1998: 'Voting behaviour in subnational elections: local and state elections in three Länder, 1988–95', in Anderson and Zelle, 1998, pp.201–22.

Eith, Ulrich, 2000: 'New patterns in the East? Differences in voting behaviour and consequences for party politics in Germany', *German Politics and Society*, 18(3), 119–36,

Elkins, David J., 1980: 'The sense of place', in Elkins and Simeon, 1980a, pp.1–30.

Elkins, David J. and Simeon, Richard, 1980a: *Small Worlds: Provinces and Parties in Canadian Political Life* (London: Methuen).

Elkins and Simeon, 1980b: 'Introduction', in Elkins and Simeon, 1980a, pp.x–xvi.

Elklit, Jørgen and Tonsgaard, Ole, 1993: 'The absence of nationalist movements: the case of the Nordic area', in Coakley, 1993, pp. 81–98.

Eltermann, Ludolf K, 1978: 'Zur Wahrnehmung von Kanzlerkandidaten', in Oberndörfer, 1978, pp.465–531.

Ellwein, Thomas and Holtmann, Everhard (Hrsg.), 1999: *50 Jahre Bundesrepublik Deutschland* (Opladen: Westdeutscher Verlag).

Esman, Milton J (ed.), 1997: *Ethnic Conflict in the Western World* (Ithaca: Cornell University Press).

Falkner, Thomas and Huber, Dietmar, 1994: *Aufschwung PDS* (München: Knaur).

Falter, Jürgen W. and Klein, Markus, 1994: 'Die Wähler der PDS bei der Bundestagswahl 1994. Zwischen Ideologie, Nostalgie und Protest', *Aus Politik und Zeitgeschichte*, B51–52, 22–34.

Falter, Jürgen and Schoen, Harald, 1999: 'Wahlen und Wählerverhalten', in Ellwein and Holtmann, 1999, pp.454–70.

Falter, Jürgen W., Schoen, Harald and Caballero, Claudio, 2000a: 'Zur Validierung des Konzepts "Parteiidentifikation" in der Bundesrepublik', in Klein, Jagodzinski, Mochmann und Ohr, 2000, pp. 235–71.

Falter, Jürgen W., Gabriel, Oscar W. and Rattinger, Hans (Hrsg.), 2000b: *Wirklich ein Volk? Die politischen Orientierungen von Ost- und Westdeutschen im Vergleich* (Opladen: Leske und Budrich).

Faulenbach, Bernd, 1999: 'Geteilte Vergangenheit – eine Geschichte? Eine Bestandsaufnahme', in Kleßmann, Misselwitz and Wichert, 1999, pp.15–34.

Ferchland, Rainer *et al.*, 1995: *Ost–West-Wahlanalyse 3. Ergebnisse einer repräsentativen gesamtdeutschen Bevölkerungsbefragung in Zusammenarbeit mit EMNID Bielefeld* (Berlin: Institut für Sozialdatenanalyse e.V. Studie 17).

Fink, Erwin *et al.*, 1999: 'Memory, democracy and the mediated nation: political cultures and regional identities in Germany, 1848–1998', *German History*, 17(2), 258–64.

Flanagan, Scott C. and Dalton, Russell J., 1984: 'Parties under stress: realignment and dealignment in advanced industrial societies', *West European Politics*, 7(1), 7–23.

Flora, Peter, Kuhnle, Stein and Urwin, Derek (eds.), 1999: *State Formation, Nation-Building and Mass Politics in Europe: The Theory of Stein Rokkan* (Oxford: Oxford University Press).

Förster, Peter, 1999: 'Die 25jährigen auf dem langen Weg in das vereinte Deutschland: Ergebnisse einer seit 1987 laufenden Langschnittstudie bei jungen Ostdeutschen', *Aus Politik und Zeitgeschichte*, B43–44, 20–31.

Fraude, Andreas, 1999: 'Die PDS in der Berliner Republik: Die 1. und 2. Tagung des 6. PDS-Bundesparteitages', *Deutschland Archiv*, 2, 172–7.

Freese, Michael, Kring, Wolfgang, Soose, Andrea and Zempel, Jeannette, 1996: 'Personal initiative at work: differences between East and West Germany', *Academy of Management Journal*, 39(1), 37–63.

Friedrich Ebert Stiftung, 1995: *Die PDS: Strukturen, Programm, Geschichtsverständnis* (Potsdam: Landesbüro Brandenburg).

Friedrich Ebert Stiftung, 1997: *Befunde über die PDS: Tagungsdokumentation* (Potsdam: Landesbüro Brandenburg).

Fritze, Lothar, 1995: 'Gestörte Kommunikation zwischen Ost und West', *Deutschland Archiv*, 29(6), 922–8.

Fritze, Lothar, 1997: *Die Gegenwart des Vergangenen. Über das Weiterleben der DDR nach ihrem Ende* (Weimar: Böhlau).

Fritze, Lothar, 1999: 'Paradoxe Zumutungen: Ursachen ostdeutscher Verunsicherungen', in Probst, 1999, pp.39–45.

Fuchs, Dieter, Roller, Edeltraud and Weßels, Bernhard, 1997: 'Die Akzeptanz der Demokratie des vereinigten Deutschlands', *Aus Politik und Zeitgeschichte*, B51, 3–12.

Fücks, Ralf, 1999: 'Risse im Gebälk: Kulturelle Differenzen im vereinigten Deutschland', in Probst, 1999, pp.9–14.

Fulbrook, Mary, 1991: '"Wir sind ein Volk"? Reflections on German unification', *Parliamentary Affairs*, 44(3), 389–404.

Fulbrook, Mary, 1998: *Anatomy of a Dictatorship* (Oxford: Oxford University Press).

Fulbrook, Mary, 1999: 'Verarbeitung und Reflexion der geteilten Vergangenheit seit 1989', in Kleßmann, Misselwitz and Wichert, 1999, pp.286–98.

Fulbrook, Mary, 1999: 'Re-reading recent (East) German history', *German History*, 17(2), 271–84.

Gabler, Wolfgang, 1999: 'Zeichen der Ostalgie: Vom Ampelmännchen zum Zimmerspringbrunnen' in Bender *et al.*, 1999, pp.19–33.

Gabriel, Oscar W. and Troitzsch, Klaus G. (Hrsg.), 1993: *Wahlen in Zeiten des Umbruchs* (Frankfurt am Main: Peter Lang Verlag).

Gabriel, Oscar W. and Niedermayer, Oskar, 1997: 'Entwicklung und Sozialstruktur der Parteimitgliedschaften', in Gabriel, Niedermayer and Stöss, 1997.

Gabriel, Oscar W., Niedermayer, Oskar and Stöss, Richard (Hrsg.), 1997: *Parteiendemokratie in Deutschland* (Opladen: Westdeutscher Verlag).

Gabriel, Oscar W.: 'Parteiidentifikation, Kandidaten und politische Sachfragen als Bestimmungsfaktoren des Parteienwettbewerbs', in Gabriel, Niedermayer and Stöss, 1997, pp.233–54.

Gabriel, Oscar W. unter Mitarbeit von Katja Neller, 2000: 'Einleitung: Wirklich ein Volk? Die politische Orientierungen von Ost- und Westdeutschen im Vergleich', in Falter, Gabriel and Rattinger, 2000, pp.9–40.

Gaiser, Wolfgang *et al.*, 2000: 'Politikverdrossenheit in Ost und West?', *Aus Politik und Zeitgeschichte*, B19–20, 12–22.

Gallagher, Tom, 1993: 'Regional nationalism and party system change: Italy's Northern League', *West European Politics*, 16(4), 616–21.

Gapper, Stuart, 2002: 'The PDS: Eastern European Communist Successor Party or Modern Western European Socialist Party?' (Birmingham: University of Birmingham, PhD Thesis).

Gay, Caroline, 2000: 'Reshaping the Myth: National Memory Management, *Vergangenheitsbewältigung* and the Dialectic of Normality in Post-War West Germany' (Birmingham: University of Birmingham, MPhil Thesis).

Gehring, Uwe W. and Winkler, Jürgen R, 1997: 'Parteiidentifikation. Kandidaten- und Issueorientierungen als Determinanten des Wahlverhaltens in Ost- und Westdeutschland', in Gabriel, 1997, pp.473–506.

Geißler, Raine, 1996: *Die Sozialstruktur Deutschlands: Zur gesellschaftlichen Entwicklung mit einer Zwischenbilanz zur Vereinigung* (Opladen: Westdeutscher Verlag).

Gellner, Ernest, 1987: *Culture, Identity and Politics* (Cambridge: Cambridge University Press).

Gensicke, Thomas, 1998: *Die neuen Bundesbürger: Eine Transformation ohne Integration* (Opladen: Westdeutscher Verlag).

Gensicke, Thomas, 1999: 'Die feinen Unterschiede: Die Deutschen im Blick der Werteforschung', in Probst 1999, pp.132–43.

Gerner, Manfred, 1994: *Partei ohne Zukunft? Von der SED zur PDS* (München: Tilsner Verlag).

Gerner, Manfred, 1996: 'Antagonismen der PDS – Zum Pluralismus der SED-Nachfolgepartei', *Deutschland Archiv*, 29(2), 227–39.

Gerner, Manfred, 1998: 'Widerspruch und Stagnation in der PDS', *Zeitschrift für Politik*, 45(2), 159–81.

Gerner, Manfred, 2000: 'Die SPD–PDS Regierungskoalition in Mecklenburg-Vorpommern. Nagelprobe für die Regierungsfähigkeit der SED-Nachfolgeorganisation', in Hirscher and Segal, 2000, pp.97–108.

Gille, Martina and Krüger, Winfried (Hrsg.), 2000: *Unzufriedene Demokraten: Politische Orientierungen der 16– bis 29jährigen im vereinten Deutschland* (Opladen: Leske und Budrich).

Giordano, Benito, 1999: 'A place called Padania? The *Lega Nord* and the political representation of northern Italy', *European Urban and Regional Studies*, 6(3), 215–30.

Gissendanner, Scott and Wielgohs, Jan, 1997: 'Conference report: Einheit und Differenz – the transformation of East Germany in comparative perspective', *German Politics*, 6(2), 181–9.

Glaab, Manuela, 1999: 'Geteilte Wahrnehmungswelten. Zur Präsenz des deutschen Nachbarn im Bewußtsein der Bevölkerung', in Kleßmann *et al.*, 1999, pp.206–20.

Glaeßner, Gert-Joachim, 1999: *Demokratie und Politik in Deutschland* (Opladen, Leske und Budrich).

Golz, Hans-Georg, 1998: 'Machtwechsel', *Deutschland Archiv*, 31(6), 873–80.

Golz, Lutz and Heller, Peter, 1996: *Jugend im Transformationsprozeß. Untersuchungen zum Sozialisationsprozeß Jugendlicher in der strukturschwachen Region Neubrandenburg* (Berlin: GSFP).

Göschel, Albrecht, 1999a: 'Kulturelle und politische Generationen in Ost und West', *Berliner Debatte INITIAL*, 10(2), 29–40.

Göschel, Albrecht, 1999b: 'Kulturelle und politische Generationen in Ost und West: Zum Gegensatz von wesenhafter und unterschiedlicher Identität', in Probst, 1999, pp.113–31.

Gottman, Jean, 1975: 'The evolution of the concept of territory', *Social Science Information*, 14, 29.

Grabner, Wolf-Jürgen, Heinze, Christiane and Pollack, Detlef (eds.), 1990: *Leipzig im Oktober* (Berlin: Wichern Verlag).

Green, Simon, 1995: 'All Change? The German party system in the aftermath of *Superwahljahr*', *Contemporary Politics*, 1(4), 47–71.

Greiffenhagen, Martin and Greiffenhagen, Sylvia, 1993: *Ein schwieriges Vaterland* (München: List).

Gries, Rainer, 1994: 'Der Geschmack der Heimat. Bausteine zu einer Mentalitätsgeschichte der Ostprodukte nach der Wende', *Deutschland Archiv*, 27(10), 1041–58.

Grix, Jonathan, 1998: *The Role of the Masses in Regime Transformation: Exit, Voice and Loyalty and the Collapse of the GDR* (Birmingham: PhD thesis, University of Birmingham).

Grix, Jonathan, 1999: *Civil Society in East Germany Pre and Post-1989* (Birmingham: Discussion Papers in German Studies, The University of Birmingham, Number 4).

Grix, Jonathan, 2000a: 'The Enquete-Kommission's contribution to research on state–society relations in the GDR', in Barker, 2000, pp.55–66.

Grix, Jonathan, 2000b: 'East German political attitudes: socialist legacies versus situational factors – a false antithesis', *German Politics*, 9(2), 109–24.

Grix, Jonathan and Cooke, Paul (eds.), 2002: *East German Distinctiveness in a Unified Germany* (Birmingham: University of Birmingham Press, 2002, forthcoming).

Guibernau, Montserrat, 1999: *Nations without States: Political Communities in a Global Age* (Cambridge: Polity Press).

Gunlicks, Arthur B., 1996: 'The new constitutions of East Germany', *German Politics*, 5(2), 262–75.

Gustavsson, Sverker and Lewin, Leif: (eds.), 1996: *The Future of the Nation-State* (Stockholm: Routledge).

Gysi, Gregor, 1998: *Nicht nur freche Sprüche* (Berlin: Schwarzkopf and Schwarzkopf).

Gysi, Gregor, 2001: *Ein Blick zurück, ein Schritt nach vorn* (Hamburg: Hoffman and Campe).

Haeger, Gabi, 1998: *Wächst wirklich zusammen, was zusammen gehört? Identität und Wahrnehmung der Intergruppensituation in Ost- und Westdeutschland* (Münster: LIT Verlag, Univ. Diss.).

Haferkamp, Hans (Hrsg.), 1989: *Sozialstruktur und Kultur* (Frankfurt am Main: Suhrkamp).

Hall, Stuart and Gieben, Bram (eds), 1992: *Formations of Modernity* (Cambridge: The Open University).

Hallett, Hugh A. J. and Ma, Yue, 1993: 'East Germany, West Germany, and their *mezziogiorno* problem: a parable for European economic integration', *The Economic Journal*, 103, 416–28.

Hampton, Mary N. and Søe, Christian (eds.), 1999: *Between Bonn and Berlin: German Politics Adrift?* (Oxford: Rowman and Littlefield).

Handler, Richard, 1998: *Nationalism and the Politics of Culture in Quebec* (London: University of Wisconsin Press).

Hanns-Seidel Stiftung, 1995: *Geschichte einer Volkspartei – 50 Jahre CSU, 1945–1995* (München: Hanns-Seidel Stiftung).

Harmel, Robert, 1985: 'On the study of new parties', *International Political Science Review*, 6(4), 403–18.

Harmel, Robert and Robertson, John D., 1985: 'Formation and success of new parties', *International Political Science Review*, 6(4), 501–24.

Harmel Robert and Svasand Lars, 1993: 'Party leadership and party institutionalisation', in *West European Politics*, 16(1), 67–88.

Harvey, David, 1993: 'Class relations, social justice and the politics of difference', in Keith and Pile (eds.), 1993, pp.41–66.

Hay, Colin, 1995: 'Structure and agency', in Marsh and Stoker, 1995, pp.189–206.

Hearl, Derek, Budge, Ian and Peterson, Bernard, 1996: 'Distinctiveness of regional voting: a comparative analysis across the European Community countries (1979–1993)', *Electoral Studies*, 15(2), 167–82.

Hechter, Michael, 1975: *Internal Colonialism: The Celtic Fringe in British National Development, 1536–1966* (Berkeley: University of California Press).

Hechter, Michael, 1985: 'Internal colonialism revisited', in Tiryakin and Rogowski, 1985, pp.17–26.

Hedges, Clive, 1988: 'Problems in combining labour and nationalist politics: Irish nationalists in Northern Ireland', in Johnston, Knight and Kofman, 1988.

Helms, Ludger (ed.), 2000: *Institutions and Institutional Change in the Federal Republic of Germany* (Basingstoke: Macmillan).

Herzmann, Jan, 1993: 'Die ersten freien Parlamentswahlen in der DDR, in Ungarn und in der CSFR', in Gabriel and Troitzsch, 1993, pp.309–18.

Hess, Andreas, 2000: 'Identical with what? Chartering the unknown waters of the concept of identity', *German Politics and Society*, 18(3), 150–56.

Hilsberg, Stephen, 1996: 'Die innere Einheit Deutschlands – eine brauchbare Vision?', *Deutschland Archiv*, 29(4), 607–11.

Hirscher, Gerhard and Segall, Peter Christian (Hrsg.), 2000: *Die PDS: Zustand und Entwicklungsperspektiven* (München: Hanns Seidel Stiftung).

Hoffman, George W., 1977: 'Regional politics and regional consciousness in Europe's mulitnational societies', *Geoforum*, 8(3).

Hoffman, Jürgen and Neu, Viola, 1998: *Getrennt agieren, vereint marschieren?: Die Diskussion über ein Linksbündnis bei SPD/Grünen und PDS* (Sankt Augustin bei Bonn: Konrad Adenauer Stiftung, Interne Studie Nummer 162).

Hoffman, Lutz, 1993: *Warten auf den Aufschwung: Eine ostdeutsche Bilanz* (Berlin: tv Transfer Verlag).

Hogwood, Patricia, 2000: 'After the GDR: reconstructing identity in post-Communist Germany', *Journal of Communist Studies and Transition Politics*, 16(4), 45–67.

Holter, Helmut and Westphal, Christian, 1999: *PDS 2005 – Überlegungen für künftige Strategien der PDS in Mecklenburg-Vorpommern* (Schwerin: PDS Landeszentrale).

Holter, Helmut, 1999: *Die PDS als Zukunftspartei* (Schwerin: PDS Landesverband Mecklenburg-Vorpommern).

Holtmann, Everhard, 1998: 'Funktionen regionaler Parteien und Parteiensysteme – Überlegungen für ein analytisches Konzept', in Benz and Holtmann, 1998, pp.65–76.

Holzer, Anton and Schwegler, Barbara, 1998: 'The Südtiroler Volkspartei: a hegemonic ethnoregionalist party' in De Winter and Türsan, 1998, pp.158–73.

Hoschka, Peter and Schunck, Hermann, 1978: 'Regional stability of voting behaviour in Federal Elections: a longitudinal aggregate data analysis', in Kaase and von Beyme, 1978, pp.31–52.

Hough, Daniel, 1999: *The Creation of a Regional Divide: The PDS as a Regional Actor in Eastern Germany* (Birmingham: Discussion Paper in German Studies, University of Birmingham, Number 15).

Hough, Daniel, 2000a: 'SED to PDS: a case of continuity through change?', in Cooke and Grix, 2000, pp.123–32.

Hough, Daniel, 2000b: 'Societal transformation and the creation of a regional party: the PDS as a regional actor in eastern Germany', *Space and Polity*, 4(1), 57–75.

Hough, Daniel, 2000c: '"Made in Eastern Germany": the PDS and the articulation of eastern German interests', *German Politics*, 9(3), 125–48.

Hough, Daniel, 2001: 'The PDS: A Study in the Development and Stabilisation of an Eastern German Regional Party, 1989-2000', Birmingham: University of Birmingham PhD Thesis.

Hough, Daniel, 2002: 'East German identity and party politics', in Grix and Cooke, 2002, forthcoming.

Hough, Daniel and Grix, Jonathan, 2001: 'The PDS and the SPD's dilemma of governance in the eastern German *Länder*', *Politics*, 21(2), 159–68.

Howard, Marc, 1995a: 'Die Ostdeutschen als ethnische Gruppe? Zum Verständnis der neuen Teilung des geeinten Deutschlands', *Berliner Debatte INITIAL*, 4/5, 119–31.

Howard Marc, 1995b: 'An eastern German ethnicity? Understanding the new division of unified Germany', *German Politics and Society*, 13, 49–70.

Hradil, Stefan, 1995: 'Die Modernisierung des Denkens. Zukunftspotentiale und 'Altlasten' in Ostdeutschland', *Aus Politik und Zeitgeschichte*, B20, 3–15.

Hubble, Nick, 1998: 'The PDS in Erfurt and the Erfurter Erklärung', in Barker, 1998, pp.78–93.

Hudson, Ray and Williams, Allan M. (eds.), 1999a: *Divided Europe: Society and Territory* (London: Sage).

Hudson, Ray and Williams, Allan M., 1999b: 'Re-shaping Europe: the challenge of new divisions within a homogenised political-economic space', in Hudson and Williams, 1999a, pp.1–28.

Huhn, Klaus, 1998: *Der Kandidat* (Berlin: Spotless Verlag).

Huinik, Johannes *et al.*, 1995: *Kollektiv und Eigensinn. Lebensverläufe in der DDR und danach* (Berlin: Akad. Verlag).

Ignazi, Piero and Ysmal, Colette (eds.), 1998a: *The Organization of Political Parties in Southern Europe* (London: Praeger).

Ignazi, Piero and Ysmal, Colette, 1998b: 'Conclusion: Party organisation and power – a southern European model?', in Ignazi and Ysma, 1998a, pp.281–304.

Inglehart, Ronald, 1977: *The Silent Revolution: Changing Values and Political Styles Among Western Publics* (Princeton: University Press).

Innis, Harold, 1951: *The Bias of Communication* (Toronto: University of Toronto Press).

Institut der Deutschen Wirtschaft Köln, 1998: *Zahlen zur wirtschaftlichen Entwicklung der Bundesrepublik Deutschland* (Köln: Institut der Deutschen Wirtschaft).

Ishiyama, John, 1995: 'Communist parties in transition: structures, leaders and processes of democratisation in eastern Europe', *Comparative Politics*, 27(2), 147–66.

James, Peter, 2000: 'The 1998 German Federal Election', *Politics*, 20(1), 33–8.

Jarausch, Konrad H. (ed.), 1997a: *After Unity – Reconfiguring German Identities* (Oxford: Berghahn).

Jarausch, Konrad H., 1997b: 'The German Democratic Republic as history in united Germany: Reflections on public debate and academic controversy', *German Politics and Society*, 15(2), 33–48.

Jeffery, Charlie, 1999: 'Party politics and territorial representation in the Federal Republic of Germany', *West European Politics*, 22(2), 130–66.

Jeffery, Charlie and Hough, Daniel, 1999: 'The German election of September 1998', *Representation*, 36(1), 78–84.

Jenkins, Philip, 1992: *A History of Modern Wales 1536–1990* (London: Longman).

Jesse, Eckhard, 1997: 'SPD and PDS relationships', *German Politics*, 6(3), 89–102.

Jesse, Eckhard, 2000: 'Die Landtagswahl in Sachsen vom 19. September 1999: Triumphale Bestätigung der CDU', *Zeitschrift für Parlamentsfragen*, 31(1), 69–87.

Johnston, Ronald J., 1979: *Political, Electoral and Spatial Systems: Contemporary Problems in Geography* (Oxford: Oxford University Press).

Johnston, Ronald J, Knight, David B. and Kofman, Eleonore (eds.), 1988: *Nationalism, Self-Determination and Political Geography* (London: Croom Helm).

Johnston, Ronald J. *et al.*, 1990: *Regional Geography: Current Developments and Future Prospects* (London: Routledge).

Jung, Matthias and Roth, Dieter, 1998: 'Wer zu spät geht, den bestraft der Wähler – Eine Analyse der Bundestagswahl 1998', *Aus Politik und Zeitgeschichte*, 52, 3–19.

Kaase, Max, 1983: 'Sinn oder Unsinn des Konzepts 'Politische Kultur' für die Vergleichende Politikforschung, oder auch: Der Versuch, einen Pudding an die Wand zu nageln', in Kaase and Klingemann, 1983, pp.144–71.

Kaase, Max, 1994: 'Is there a personalisation in politics? Candidates and voting behaviour in Germany', *International Political Science Review*, 15(3), 211–30.

Kaase, Max and Beyme, Klaus von (eds.), 1978: *Elections and Parties* (London: Sage).

Kaase, Max and Klingemann, Hans Dieter (eds.), 1983: *Wahlen und Politisches System: Analysen aus Anlaß der Bundestagswahl 1980* (Opladen: Westdeutscher Verlag,).

Kalberg, Stephen: 'The far slower and more conflict-ridden path to German social integration: toward a multicausal, contextual and multidirectional explanatory framework', *German Politics and Society*, 17(4), 34–51.

Katz, Richard S. and Mair, Peter (eds.), 1992: *Party Organisations: A Data Handbook on Party Organisations in Western Democracies, 1960–90* (London: Sage).

Kaufmann, Sylvia-Yvonne, 1999: *Die Euro-Falle: Plädoyer für ein soziales Europa* (Berlin: Dietz).

Keating, Michael, 1988: *State and Regional Nationalism – Territorial Politics and the European State* (London: Harverster Wheatsheaf).

Keating, Michael, 1996: *Nations against the State* (New York: St Martin's Press).

Keating, Michael and Jones, Barry, 1991: 'Scotland and Wales: peripheral assertion and European integration', *Parliamentary Affairs*, 44(3), 311–24.

Keith, Michael and Pile, Steve (eds.), 1993: *Place and the Politics of Identity* (London: Routledge).

Keller, Dietmar, 1995: 'Zwischen Anspruch und eigener Blockade', in Brie, Herzig and Koch, 1995, pp.131–45.

Kirchheimer, Otto, 1966: 'The transformation of the western European party systems' in La

Polombara and Weiner, 1966, pp.177–200.

Kitschelt, Herbert, Mansfeldova, Zdenka, Markowski, Radoslaw and Tóka, Gábor, 1999: *Post-Communist Party Systems: Competition, Representation and Inter-Party Cooperation* (Cambridge, Cambridge University Press).

Klein, Dieter, 1998: 'Die PDS zwischen Ideologie und politischer Realität', in Barker, 1998, pp.109–27.

Klein, Markus and Caballero, Claudio, 1996: 'Rückwärts in die Zukunft. Die Wähler der PDS bei der Bundestagswahl 1994', *Politische Vierteljahresschrift*, 37(2), 229–47.

Klein, Markus, Jagodzinski, Wolfgang, Mochmann Ekkehard and Ohr, Dieter (Hrsg.), 2000: *50 Jahre Empirische Wahlforschung in Deutschland* (Opladen: Westdeutscher Verlag).

Kleinfeld, Gerald R, 1995: 'The return of the PDS', in Conradt, Kleinfeld, Romuser and Søe, 1995, pp.221–54.

Kleinfeld, Gerald R., 1999: 'The PDS: between socialism and regionalism', in Hampton and Søe, 1999, pp.137–54.

Kleinfeld, Gerald R., 2000: 'The Party of Democratic Socialism: victory across the east and on to Berlin!', in Conradt *et al.*, 2000, pp.98–113.

Kleßmann, Christoph *et al.* (Hrsg.), 1999: *Deutsche Vergangenheiten – eine gemeinsame Herausforderung* (Berlin: Links Verlag).

Klingemann, Hans D. and Taylor, Charles Lewis, 1978: 'Partisanship, candidates and issues: attitudinal components of the vote in West German Federal Elections', in Kaase and Beyme, 1978, pp.97–136.

Knelangen, Wilhelm and Vorwick, Johannes, 1998: 'Magdeburg ist nicht Weimar. Oder doch? Die Auseinandersetzung über den "richtigen" Umgang mit der PDS', *Gegenwartskunde*, 47(2), 213–21.

Knight, David B, 1982: 'Identity and territory: Geographical perspectives on nationalism and regionalism', *Annals of the Association of American Geographers*, 72(4), 514–31.

Knight, David B., 1985: 'Territory and people or people and territory', *International Political Science Review*, 6(2), 248–72.

Koch, Thomas, 1995: 'Die PDS im Vereinigungsprozeß', in Brie, Herzig and Koch, 1995, pp.181–99.

Koch, Thomas, 1997a: 'Von der "dualistischen Gesellschaft" zur "solidarischen Bürgergesellschaft"?', *Deutschland Archiv*, 30(1), 95–105

Koch, Thomas, 1997b: 'Ostdeutsche Identitätsbildungen in der dualistischen Gesellschaft', *Berliner Debatte INITIAL*, 8(3), 93–108.

Koch, Thomas, 1998: 'Eine Nation – zwei politische Kulturen? Auf der Suche nach einer Formel zur Beschreibung der deutschen Wirklichkeit', *Deutschland Archiv*, 31(4), 624–9.

Koch, Thomas, 1999: 'Parteienwettbewerb und "politisch-kulturelle Hegemonie"', *Berliner Debatte INITIAL*, 10(2), 74–84.

Koch-Baumgarten, Sigrid, 1997: 'Postkommunisten im Spagat: Zur Funktion der PDS im Parteiensystem', *Deutschland Archiv*, 30(6), 864–78.

Korte, Karl-Rudolf, 1994: *Die Chance genutzt? Die Politik zur Einheit Deutschlands* (Frankfurt am Main: Campus Verlag).

Köstlin, Konrad, 1979a: 'Die Regionalisierung von Kultur', in Köstlin and Bausinger, 1979b, pp.25–38.

Köstlin, Konrad und Bausinger, Hermann (Hrsg.), 1979b: *Heimat und Identität: Probleme regionaler Kultur* (Neumünster: Studien zur Volkskunde und Kulturgeschichte Schleswig-Holsteins Band 7).

Krämer, Raimund, 1997: *Transfederal Relations of the Eastern German Länder: The Case of Brandenburg* (Birmingham: Discussion Paper in German Studies, University of Birmingham, Number 9).

Kreikenbom, Henry, 1997: 'Einstellungen der Bürger zu den Parteien', in Gabriel, 1997, pp.167–88.

Kreikenbom, Henry, 1998: 'Nachwirkungen der SED-Ära. Die PDS als Katalysator der Partei- und Wahlpräferenzen in den neuen Bundesländern', *Zeitschrift für Parlamentsfragen*, 1, 24–46.

Krisch, Henry, 1998: 'Searching for voters: PDS mobilisation strategies, 1994–1997', in Barker, 1998, pp.38–53.

Krüger, Paul, 1996: *14 Thesen zum Ost-Profil der CDU* (Neubrandenburg: CDU).

Kunz, Volker, 2000: 'Einstellungen zur Wirtschaft und Gesellschaft in den alten und neuen Bundesländern', in Falter, Gabriel and Rattinger, 2000, pp.509–37.

Küpper, Mechthild, 1999: 'Mit der PDS in die deutsche Einheit? Überlegungen zur Beweglichkeit einer ostdeutschen Partei', in Probst, 1999, pp.54–64.

La Polombara, Joseph and Weiner, Myron (eds.), 1966: *Political Parties and Political Development* (Princeton: Princeton University Press).

Land, Rainer, 1996: 'Staatssozialismus und Stalinismus' in Bisky *et al.*, 1996, pp.186–98.

Lane, Jan-Erik, McKay, David and Newton, Kenneth, 1991: *Political Data Handbook: OECD Countries* (Oxford: Oxford University Press).

Lane, Jan-Erik and Ersson, Svante, 1999: *Politics and Society in Western Europe* (London: Sage).

Lang, Jürgen P. 1995: 'Nach den Wahlen 1994: "PDS-Strategie im Wandel?"', *Deutschland Archiv*, 28(4), 369–80.

Lang, Jürgen P., 1998: *Das Prinzip Gegenmacht: Die PDS und Parlamentarismus* (Sankt Augustin bei Bonn: Konrad Adenauer Stiftung, Interne Studie Nr. 166).

Lang, Jürgen P., Moreau, Patrick und Neu, Viola, 1995: *Auferstanden aus Ruinen? Die PDS nach dem Superwahljahr 1994* (Sankt Augustin bei Bonn: Konrad Adenauer Stiftung).

Lay, Conrad, 1997: 'Der Siegeszug der Ostprodukte – Zur Mentalitäts– und Produktgeschichte der deutschen Vereinigung'. On http://www.oeko-net.de/kommune/kommune1-97/tlay197.html

Laycock, David, 1994: 'Reforming Canadian democracy? Institutions and ideology in the Reform Party project', *Canadian Journal of Political Science*, 27(2), 213–47.

LeDuc, Lawrence, 1998: 'The Canadian Federal Election of 1997', *Electoral Studies*, 17(1), 132–7.

Le Galès, Patrick and Lequesne, Christian (eds.), 1998: *Regions in Europe* (London: Routledge).

Levi, Margaret and Hechter, Michael, 1985: 'A rational choice approach to the rise and decline of ethnoregional political parties', in Tiryakin and Rogowski, 1985, pp.128–46.

Liese, Hans-J., 1995: *Die Politische Parteien in Deutschland: Geschichte, Programmatik, Organisation, Personen, Finanzierung* (München: Günter Olzog Verlag,).

Lijphart, Arend, 1994: *Electoral Systems and Party Systems: A Study of Twenty-seven Democracies* (Oxford: Oxford University Press).

Linneman, Rainer, 1994: *Die Parteien in den neuen Bundesländern: Konstituierung, Mitgliederentwicklung, Organisationsstrukturen* (Münster: Waxmann).

Lipset, Seymour M. (ed.), 1969: *Politics and the Social Sciences* (London: Oxford University Press).

Lipset, Seymour M. and Rokkan, Stein, 1967: *Party Systems and Voter Alignments: Cross-National Perspectives* (London: Macmillan).

Little, John Irvine, 1989: *Ethno-Cultural Transition and Regional Identity in the Eastern Townships of Quebec* (Ottawa: Canadian Historical Association).

Lopez, Cesar Diaz, 1985: 'Centre–periphery structures in Spain: from historical conflict to territorial-consociational accommodation?', in Meny and Wright, 1985, pp.236–72.

Lösche, Peter, 1994: *Kleine Geschichte der deutschen Parteien* (Berlin: Kohlhammer).

Löw, Konrad, 1998: *Für Menschen mit kurzem Gedächtnis: Das Rostocker Manifest der PDS* (Köln: Kölner Universitätsverlag).

Ludwig, Andreas, 1999: 'Objektkultur und DDR-Gesellschaft – Aspekte einer Wahrnehmung des Alltags', *Aus Politik und Zeitgeschichte*, B28, 3–11.

Luft, Christa, 1998: *Abbruch oder Aufbruch? Warum der Osten unsere Chance ist* (Berlin: Aufbau Taschenbuch Verlag).

Maaz, Hans-Joachim, 1991: *Das Gestürtzte Volk oder die verunglückte Einheit* (Berlin: Argon Verlag).

Mahr, Alison and Nagle, John, 1995: 'Resurrection of the successor parties and democratisation in east-central Europe', *Communist and Post-Communist Studies*, 28(4), 394.

Mair, Peter (ed.), 1990: *The West European Party System* (Oxford: Oxford University Press).

Markus, Uwe, 1997: *Im Blickpunkt: Wahlen 1998. Zur Typologie ostdeutscher Wählerzielgruppen* (Berlin: Trafo Verlag).

Marsh, David and Stoker, Gerry (eds.), 1995: *Theory and Methods in Political Science* (Basingstoke: Macmillan).

McDonald, Terry, 1999: 'The Quebec provincial election of 1998', *Representation*, 36(1), 85–96.

McFalls, Laurence H, 1995a: 'Political culture, partisan strategies and the PDS: prospects for an east German party', *German Politics and Society*, 13(1), 50–61.

McFalls, Laurence H., 1995b: *Communism's Collapse, Democracy's Demise? The Cultural Context and Consequences of the East German Revolution* (Basingstoke: Macmillan).

McFalls, Laurence H., 1997: 'Politische Kultur und das deutsch–deutsche Mißverständnis', *Berliner Debatte INITIAL*, 8(4), 20–26.

McFalls, Laurence H., 1998: 'Shock therapy and mental walls: East Germany as a model for post-Communist political culture', in Smith, 1998, pp.143–60.

McFalls, Laurence, 2001: 'Die kulturelle Vereinigung Deutschlands: Ostdeutsche politische und Alltagskultur vom real existierenden Sozialismus zur postmodernen kapitalistischen Konsumkultur', *Aus Politik und Zeitgeschichte*, B11, 23–9.

Mckay, Joanna, 1996: 'The Wall in the ballot box', *German Politics*, 5(2), 276–91.

Mckay, Joanna, 1998: *The Official Concept of the Nation in the Former GDR* (Aldershot: Ashgate).

Mckay, Joanna, 2000: 'The 1999 Berlin Land elections', *German Politics*, 9(1), 123–38.

Meier, Andreas, 1997: *Jugendweihe – JugendFEIER: Ein deutsches nostalgisches Fest vor und nach 1990* (München: Deutscher Taschenbuch Verlag).

Meier, Helmut, Reblin, Bodo and Weckesser, Erhard, 1995: *Die Schwierigkeiten der Ostdeutschen Bundesbürger zu werden* (Dresden: Clara Weg Verlag).

Meining, Stefan, 2000: 'Die Leiche Last der Vergangenheit. Die Aufarbeitung der DDR-Geschichte durch die PDS', in Hirscher and Segal, 2000, pp.139–62.

Meny, Yves, 1987: 'The political dynamics of regionalism: Italy, France and Spain', in Morgen, 1987, pp.1–28.

Meny, Yves and Wright, Vincent (eds.), 1985: *Centre–Periphery Relations in Western Europe* (London: George Allen and Unwin).

Merkl, Peter H, 1992: 'A new German identity', in Smith, Paterson, Merkl and Padgett, 1992, pp.327–48.

Merkl, Peter H (ed.), 1999: *The Federal Republic of Germany at Fifty: The End of a Century of Turmoil* (London: Macmillan).

Meulemann, Heiner, 1997: 'Value changes in Germany after unification', *German Politics*, 6(1), 122–39.

Meuleman, Heiner, 1998: *Werte und Wertewandel. Zur Identität einer geteilten und wieder vereinten Nation* (München: Leske und Budrich).

Minnerup, Günther, 1998: 'The PDS and the strategic dilemma of the German left', in Barker, 1998, pp.209–20.

Misselwitz, Hans-J., 1996: *Nicht länger mit dem Gesicht nach Westen* (Berlin: Dietz).

Mitchell, James, 1991: 'Factions, tendencies and consensus in the SNP in the 1980s', *Scottish Government Yearbook* (Edinburgh: Edinburgh University Press).

Mitter, Armin and Wolle, Stefan, 1993: *Untergang auf Raten: Unbekannte Kapitel der DDR Geschichte* (München: Bertelmann).

Modrow, Hans, 1991: *Aufbruch und Ende* (Hamburg: Konkret).

Modrow, Hans, 1998: *Ich wollte ein neues Deutschland* (Berlin: Dietz).

Möller, Kurt, 1998: 'Extremismus', in Schäfers and Zapf, 1998, pp.188–200.

Moreau, Patrick, 1992: *PDS. Anatomie einer postkommunistischen Partei* (Bonn–Berlin: Bouvier).

Moreau, Patrick, 1996a: 'Der Durchbruch der PDS im 'Superwahljahr 1994' – Demokratie in der Krise', in Oberreuter, 1996, pp.229–48.

Moreau, Patrick, 1996b: 'Mit Lenin im Bauch … ? Die PDS auf der Suche nach einer Berliner Republik von Links', *Politische Studien*, 349, 27–42.

Moreau, Patrick, 1998a: *Die PDS: Profil einer antidemokratischen Partei* (München: Hanns Seidel Stiftung).

Moreau, Patrick, 1998b: 'Eine kurze Geschichte der PDS in der bundespolitischen Parteienlandschaft (1989 – 1997)', in Moreau, Lazar and Hirschner, 1998, p. 277.

Moreau, Patrick and Lang Jürgen, 1994: *Was will die PDS?* (Frankfurt am Main: Ullstein).

Moreau, Patrick and Lang, Jürgen P., 1996a: *Linksextremismus. Eine unterschätzte Gefahr* (Bonn: Bouvier).

Moreau, Patrick and Lang, Jürgen P., 1996b: 'Aufbruch zu neuen Ufern? Zustand und Perspektiven der PDS', *Aus Politik und Zeitgeschichte*, B6, 54–61.

Moreau, Patrick, Lazar, Marc and Hirscher, Gerhard (eds.), 1998: *Der Kommunismus in Westeuropa. Niedergang oder Mutation?* (Landsberg am Lech: Günter Olzog Verlag).

Moreau, Patrick and Neu, Viola, 1994: *Die PDS zwischen Linksextremismus und Linkspopulismus* (Sankt Augustin bei Bonn: Interne Studien 76, Konrad Adenauer Stiftung).

Morgen, Roger (ed.), 1987: *Regionalism in European Politics* (London: Policy Studies Institute).

Mühlberg, Dietrich, 1999: 'Nachrichten über die kulturelle Verfassung der Ostdeutschen', *Berliner Debatte INITIAL*, 10(2), 4–17.

Mühlberg, Dietrich, 2000: 'Kulturelle Differenz als Voraussetzung innerer Stabilität der deutschen Gesellschaft?', *Berliner Debatte INITIAL*, 11(2), 47–58.

Mühlberg, Dietrich, 2001: 'Beobachtete Tendenzen zur Ausbildung einer ostdeutschen Teilkultur', *Aus Politik und Zeitgeschichte*, B11, 30–38.

Müller-Rommel, Ferdinand, 1998: 'Ethnoregionalist parties in western Europe: theoretical considerations and framework of analysis', in De Winter and Türsan, 1998, pp.17–27.

Murswick, Axel (Hrsg.), 1996: *Regieren in den neuen Bundesländern* (Opladen: Leske und Budrich).

Mushaben, Joyce Marie, 1997: 'Auferstanden aus Ruinen: Social capital and democratic identity in the new Länder', *German Politics and Society*, 15(4), 79–101.

Nairn, Tom, 1981: *The Break-up of Britain. Crisis and Neo-Nationalism* (London: Verso).

Naßmacher, Hiltrud, Niedermayer, Oskar and Wollman, Helmut, 1994: *Politische Strukturen im Umbruch* (Berlin: Akad. Verlag).

Neller, Katja, 2000: 'DDR-Nostalgie? Analysen zur Identifikation der Ostdeutschen mit ihrer politischen Vergangenheit, zur ostdeutschen Identität und zur Ost–West-Stereotypisierung', in Falter, Gabriel and Rattinger, 2000, pp.571–602.

Neller, Katja and Gabriel, Oscar W., 2000: 'Die Deutsche Nationale Wahlstudie 1998', in Klein, Jagodzinski, Mochmann and Ohr, 2000, pp. 542–63.

Neu, Viola, 1994: *Das Wählerpotential der PDS Ende 1993* (Sankt Augustin bei Bonn: Konrad Adenauer Stiftung).

Neu, Viola, 1997: 'Party of government in waiting', *German Comments*, April 1997, 20–24.

Neu, Viola, 1998: *Die Potentiale der PDS und der Republikaner im Winter 1997–98* (Sankt Augustin bei Bonn: Konrad Adenauer Stiftung).

Neu, Viola, 1999: *Die PDS 10 Jahre nach dem Fall der Mauer* (Sankt Augustin bei Bonn: Konrad Adenauer Stiftung).

Neugebauer, Gero, 1994: '1994 im Aufschwung Ost: Die PDS. Eine Bilanz', *Gegenwartskunde*, 43(4), 431–44.

Neugebauer, Gero, 1995: 'Hat die PDS bundesweit im Parteiensystem eine Chance?', in Brie, Herzig and Koch, 1995, pp.39–57.

Neugebauer, Gero, 1996: 'Die Position der PDS im Parteiensystem der Bundesrepublik', *PDS Pressedienst*, Number 46, 15 November 1996, p.17.

Neugebauer, Gero, 2000: 'Die PDS zwischen Kontinuität und Aufbruch', *Aus Politik und Zeitgeschichte*, B5, 39–46.

Neugebauer, Gero and Stöss, Richard, 1996: *Die PDS, Geschichte, Organisation, Wähler, Konkurrenten* (Opladen: Leske and Budrich).

Neuwirth, Rebecca A., 1997: 'The long footprints of Communism: PDS on the rise, in *German Life* on http://www.germanlife.com/magazine/1997/9710_02.html

Nevitte, Neil, 1985: 'The religious factor in contemporary nationalist movements: an analysis of Quebec, Wales and Scotland', in Tiryakin and Rogowski, 1985, pp.337–52.

Newell, James L., 1994: 'The Scottish National Party and the Italian *Lega Nord*', *European Journal of Political Science*, 26(2), 135–53.

Newell, James L. and Bull, Martin, 1996: 'The Italian Election of 1996', *Parliamentary Affairs*, 49(4), 616–47.

Newman, Simon, 1994: 'Ethnoregional parties: a comparative perspective', *Regional Politics and Policy*, 4(2), 28–66.

Nick, Harry, 1998: *Alternativen '98? Die Wahlprogramme von SPD, PDS und Bündnis 90/Die Grünen im Vergleich* (Berlin: Diskussionsangebot der PDS, Grundsatzkommission der PDS).

Niedermayer, Oskar, 1995: 'Party system change in East Germany', *German Politics*, 4(3), 75–91.

Niedermayer, Oskar, 1998: 'Die Stellung der PDS im ostdeutschen Parteiensystem', in Barker, 1998, pp.18–37.

Niedermayer, Oskar, 2000: 'Die Wahl zum Berliner Abgeordnetenhaus vom 10. Oktober 1999: Der gescheiterte Versuch einer politischen Wachablösung', *Zeitschrift für Parlamentsfragen*, 31(1), 86–102.

Noelle-Neumann, Elisabeth and Köcher, Renate, 1997: *Allensbacher Jahrbuch der Demoskopie 1993–97* (München: K.G.Saur Verlag).

Norden, John *et al.*, 1995: *Ost–West–Wahlanalyse 2. Ergebnisse einer repräsentativen gesamtdeutschen Bevölkerungsbefragung in Zusammenarbeit mit EMNID Bielefeld* (Berlin: Institut für Sozialdatenanalyse e.V. Studie 16).

Norpoth, Herbert, 1977: 'Kanzlerkandidaten: Wie sie vom Wähler bewertet werden und seine Wahlentscheidung beeinflussen', in *Politische Vierteljahresschrift*, 18, 551–72.

Oberndörfer, Dieter and Schmitt, Karl, 1991: *Parteien und regionale Traditionen in der Bundesrepublik Deutschland* (Berlin: Duncker and Humboldt).

Oberreuter, Heinrich (Hrsg.), 1996: *Parteiensystem am Wendepunkt? Wahlen in der Fernsehdemokratie* (München: Olzog Verlag).

Offe, Claus, 1994: *Der Tunnel am Ende des Lichts – Erkundungen der politischen Transformation im Neuen Osten* (Frankfurt am Main: Campus Verlag).

Offe, Claus, 1996: *Varieties of Transition: The East European and East German Experience* (Oxford: Polity Press).

Olsen, Jonathan, 2000: 'Seeing red: the SPD–PDS coalition government in Mecklenburg West Pomerania', *German Studies Review*, 23(3), 557–80.

Orenstein, Michael, 1998: 'A genealogy of Communist successor parties in east–central Europe and the determinants of their success', *East European Politics and Societies*, 12(3), 472–99.

Orridge, Andrew W. and Williams, Colin H., 1982: 'Autonomist nationalism: a theoretical framework for spatial variations in its genesis and development', *Political Geography Quarterly*, 1(1), 19–39.

Ostrowski, Christine and Weckesser, Ronald, 1996: 'Ein Brief aus Sachsen', *Neues Deutschland*, 8 May 1996, p.1.

Ostrowski, Christine, 1999: *Ossi's PDS-Gesetze* (Dresden: Projekt Piccolo).

Owen Smith, Eric, 1994: *The German Economy* (London: Routledge).

Padgett, Stephen and Burkett, Tony, 1986: *Political Parties and Elections in Western Germany: The Search for a New Stability* (London: C.Hurst and Company).

Padgett, Stephen, 1992: 'The new German economy' in Smith *et al.*, 1992, pp.187–207.

Padgett, Stephen (ed.), 1993: *Parties and Party Systems in the New Germany* (Aldershot: Dartmouth).

Padgett, Stephen, 1995: 'Superwahljahr in the new *Länder*: polarisation in an open political market', *German Politics*, 4(2), 75–94.

Padgett, Stephen, 1999: 'The boundaries of stability: the party system before and after the 1998 Bundestagswahl', *German Politics*, 8(2), 88–107.

Patton, David F., 1998: 'Germany's Party of Democratic Socialism in comparative perspective', *East European Politics and Societies*, 12(3), 500–526.

Patton, David, 2000: 'The rise of Germany's Party of Democratic Socialism: "Regionalised Pluralism" in the Federal Republic?', *West European Politics*, 23(1), 144–60.

Patton, David, 2000: 'A comparative perspective on the Bundestag elections', in Conradt *et al.*, 2000, pp.239–52.

Patzelt, Werner J., 1998: 'Kommentar zum Beitrag von Everhard Holtmann. Die vergleichende Untersuchung von Landesparteien', in Benz and Holtmann, 1998, pp.77–88.

Pau, Petra, 1996: 'Die PDS auf dem Weg in die BRD' in Bisky *et al.*, 1996, pp.119–25.

Payne, Stanley G., 1975: *Basque Nationalism* (Reno: University of Nevada Press).

PDS: 'Programm zur Vertretung ostdeutscher Interessen', in Beinert, 1995, pp.244–249.

Phillips, Ann L., 1995: 'An island of stability – the German political party system and the elections of 1994', *West European Politics*, Special Issue, July 1995, 219–29.

Pickel, Andreas and Wiesenthal, Helmut, 1997: *The Grand Experiment: Debating Shock Therapy, Transition Theory and the East German Experience* (Oxford: Westview Press).

Pickel, Gert, 1998a: 'Und nochmals – Die PDS als Repräsentant der Ostdeutschen? Soziale Benachteiligung und Wahlverhalten in den neuen Bundesländern', in Pickel, Pickel and Walz, 1998, pp.97–112.

Pickel, Gert, 1998b: 'Eine ostdeutsche 'Sonder'-Mentalität acht Jahre nach der Vereinigung? Fazit einer Diskussion um Sozialisation und Situation', in Pickel, Pickel and Walz, 1998, pp.157–77.

Pickel, Gert, Walz, Dieter and Brunner, Wolfram, 2000: *Deutschland nach den Wahlen. Befunde zur Bundestagswahl 1998 und zur Zukunft des deutschen Parteiensystems* (Opladen: Leske und Budrich).

Pickel, Susanne, Pickel, Gert and Walz, Dieter (Hrsg.), 1998: *Politische Einheit – Kultureller Zwiespalt? Die Erklärungen politischer und demokratischer Einstellungen in Ostdeutschland vor der Bundestagswahl 1998* (Frankfurt am Main: Peter Lang,).

Pintaris, Sylvia, 1996: *Macht, Demokratie und Regionen in Europa: Analysen und Szenarien der Integration und Desintegration* (Marburg: Metropolis Verlag).

Plasser, Fritz *et al.* (Hrsg.), 1999: *Wahlen und politische Einstellungen in Deutschland und Österreich* (Frankfurt am Main: Peter Lang Verlag,).

Poguntke, Thomas, 1999: 'Das Parteiensystem der Bundesrepublik Deutschland: Von Krise zu Krise?', in Ellwein and Holtmann, 1999, pp.429–39.

Pollack, Detlev, 1997: 'Das Bedürfnis nach sozialer Anerkennung. Der Wandel der Akzeptanz von Demokratie und Marktwirtschaft in Ostdeutschland', *Aus Politik und Zeitgeschichte*, B13, 3–14.

Pollack, Detlev, 1999: 'Trust in institutions and the urge to be different: on attitudinal change in eastern Germany', *German Politics*, 8(3), 81–102.

Pollack, Detlev and Pickel, Gert, 1998: 'Die ostdeutsche Identität – Erbe des DDR-Sozialismus oder Produkt der Wiedervereinigung?', *Aus Politik und Zeitgeschichte*, B41–42, 9–23.

Pollack, Detlev and Pickel, Gert, 2000: 'Besonderheiten der politischen Kultur in Ostdeutschland als Erklärungsfaktoren der Bundestagswahl 1998 und die Rückwirkungen der Bundestagswahl auf die politische Kultur Ostdeutschlands' in van Deth, Rattinger and Rolle, 2000, pp.117–44.

Probst, Lothar, 1998a: *Die PDS: Zur Anatomie einer postkommunistischen Partei* (Schwerin: Unpublished paper given at a Konrad Adenauer Stiftung sponsored conference on 10 March 1998).

Probst, Lothar, 1998b: *Die PDS in Rostock: Eine Lokalstudie über die Anatomie einer postkommunistischen Partei*, in Barker, 1998, pp.54–77.

Probst, Lothar, 1998c: 'Ost–West-Differenzen und das republikanische Defizit der deutschen Einheit', *Aus Politik und Zeitgeschichte*, B41–42, 3–8.

Probst, Lothar (Hrsg.), 1999a: *Differenz in der Einheit: Über die kulturellen Unterschiede der Deutschen in Ost und West* (Berlin: Ch. Links).

Probst, Lothar, 1999b: 'Ost–West-Unterschiede und das kommunitäre Erbe der DDR', in Probst, 1999a, pp.15–27.

Probst, Lothar, 2000: *Die PDS – von der Staats- zur Regierungspartei: Eine Studie aus Mecklenburg-Vorpommern* (Hamburg: Verlag Dr. Kovac).

Pulzer, Peter, 1993: 'Political ideology', in Smith, Paterson, Merkl and Padgett, 1993, pp.303–26.

Putnam, Robert D., 1993: *Making Democracy Work: Civic Traditions in Modern Italy* (Princeton: Princeton University Press).

Raento, Pauliina: 'Political mobilisation and place-specificity: regional nationalist street campaigning in the Spanish Basque country', *Space and Polity*, 1(2), 191–204.

Ragin, Charles: 'Ethnic political mobilisation: the Welsh case', *American Sociological Review*, 44(4), 619–34.

Raschke, Joachim, 1994: 'SPD und PDS. Selbstblockade oder Opposition?', *Blätter für deutsche und internationale Politik*, 12, 1453–64.

Rattinger, Hans and Maier, Jurgen, 1998: 'Der Einfluß der Wirtschaftslage auf die

Wahlentscheidung bei den Bundestagswahlen 1994 und 1998', *Aus Politik und Zeitgeschichte*, B52, 45–54.

Rausch, Thomas, 1999: 'Zwischen Freiheitssuche und DDR-Nostalgie: Lebensentwürfe und Gesellschaftsbilder ostdeutscher Jugendlicher', *Aus Politik und Zeitgeschichte*, B45, 32–8.

Rawkins, Phillip, 1985: 'Living in the house of power: Welsh nationalism and the dilemma of antisystem politics', in Tiryakin and Rogowski, 1985, pp.294–314.

Rehberg, Eckhardt, 1996: *Identitätsgewinn im Aufbau Ost: Diskussionspapier zur Werte- und Strategiedebatte 'CDU 2000' in Mecklenburg-Vorpommern* (Schwerin: CDU Fraktion, Landtag Mecklenburg-Vorpommern).

Reich, Jens, 2000: 'Zehn Jahre deutsche Einheit', *Aus Politik und Zeitgeschichte*, B1-2, 28–32.

Reissert, Bernd and Schaefer, Günther F., 1985: 'Centre–periphery relations in the Federal Republic of Germany', in Meny and Wright, 1985, pp.104–24.

Ringer, Fritz, 1997: *Max Weber's Methodology. The Unification of the Cultural and Social Sciences* (Cambridge, USA: Harvard University Press).

Ritter, Claudia, 1996: 'Politische Identitäten in den neuen Bundesländern', in Wiesenthal, 1996, pp.141–87.

Ritter, Claudia, 1997: 'Identitätspolitik in Ostdeutschland', *Identitäten in Europa. Welt Trends. Internationale Politik und vergleichende Studien*, 15, 64–78.

Ritter, Gerhard A. and Niehuss, Merith, 1991: *Wahlen in Deutschland – 1946 – 1991* (München: Verlag C. H. Beck).

Roberts, Geoffrey K, 1991: '"Emmigrants in their own country": German reunification and its political consequences', *Parliamentary Affairs*, 44(3), 373–404.

Rochon, Thomas R., 1985: 'Mobilizers and challengers: toward a theory of new party success', *International Political Science Review*, 6(4), 419–40.

Rochtus, Dirk, 1995: 'Die Zählebigkeit der ostdeutschen Identität – Ein Erklärungsversuch aus flämischer Sicht', *Deutschland Archiv*, 28(8), 842–4.

Rochtus, Dirk *et al.*, 1996: *Wer ist die PDS?: Zwei Beiträge zu Programm und Profil einer postkommunistischen Partei* (Bremen: Institut für kulturwissenschaftliche Deutschlandstudien, Universität Bremen, Heft 10).

Roesler, Jörg, 1997: 'Zwischen High-Tech und Mezzogiorno. Ostdeutschlands ungewisse Zukunft', *UTOPIE Kreativ*, 83, 34–41.

Roesler, Jörg, 1998: 'The Party of Democratic Socialism in the German unification process', in Smith, 1998, pp.51–74.

Roewer, Helmut, 2000: 'Die PDS in Thüringen: Ein Spaziergang durch die politische Landschaft im Freistaat', in Hirscher and Segall, 2000, pp.89–96.

Rohrschneider, Robert, 1999: *Learning Democracy: Democratic and Economic Values in Unified Germany* (Oxford: Oxford University).

Rokkan, Stein, 1970: *Citizens, Elections, Parties* (Oslo: Universitetsforlaget).

Rokkan, Stein and Urwin, Derek W. (eds.), 1982: *The Politics of Territorial Identity* (London: Sage).

Rokkan, Stein and Urwin, Derek W., 1983: *Economy, Territory, Identity: The Politics of Western European Peripheries* (London: Sage).

Rokkan, Stein, Urwin, Derek, Aarebrot, Frank H., Malaba, Pamela and Sande, Terje, 1987: *Centre–Periphery Structures in Europe: An ISSC Workbook in Comparative Analysis* (Frankfurt/Main: Campus).

Roller, Edeltrud, 1999: 'Shrinking the welfare state: citizens' attitudes towards cuts in social spending in Germany in the 1990s', *German Politics*, 8(1), 21–39.

Rose, Richard and Haerpfer, Christian, 1997: 'The impact of a ready-made state: East Germans in comparative perspective', *German Politics*, 6(1), 100–121.

Rose, Richard, Mishler, William and Haerpfer, Christian, 1998: *Democracy and its Alternatives: Understanding Post-Communist Societies* (Oxford: Blackwell).

Rose, Richard and Page, Edward C., 1995: *German Responses to Regime Change: Culture, Class, Economy or Context?*, (Glasgow: Centre for the Study of Public Policy, Studies in Public Policy 244, University of Strathclyde).

Rose, Richard and Urwin, Derek W. 1975: 'Persistence and change in western party systems since 1945', *Political Studies*, 18(3), 287–319.

Rose, Richard and Urwin, Derek W., 1990: 'Persistence and change in western party systems since 1945', in Mair, 1990, pp.185–94.

Rosenthal, David H., 1991: *Post-war Catalonian Poetry* (Lewisberg: Bucknell University Press).

Ross, Chris, 1996: 'Nationalism and party competition in the Basque Country and Catalonia', *West European Politics*, 19(3), 488–506.

Roth, Dieter, 1990: 'Die Wahlen zur Volkskammer in der DDR. Der Versuch einer Erklärung', *Politische Vierteljahresschrift*, 31, 369–93.

Rudolph, Joseph R. and Thompson, Robert J.(eds.), 1989: *Ethnoterritorial Politics, Policy and the Western World* (London: Lynne Rienner).

Rüther, Günther, 1995: *Politische Kultur und innere Einheit in Deutschland* (Sankt Augustin bei Bonn: Konrad Adenauer Stiftung).

Ruzza, Carlo E. and Schmidtke, Oliver, 1993: 'Roots of success of the *Lega Lombarda*: mobilisation dynamics and the media', *West European Politics*, 16(1), 1–23.

Sartori, Giovanni, 1968: 'The sociology of parties: a critical review', in Stamme, 1968, pp.1–25.

Sartori, Giovanni, 1969: 'From the sociology of politics to political sociology', in Lipset, 1969, pp.65–100.

Sartori, Giovanni, 1976: *Parties and Party Systems: A Framework for Analysis – Volume 1* (Cambridge: Cambridge University Press).

Scarrow, Susan E., 1991: 'Politicians against parties: anti-party arguments as weapons for change in Germany', in *European Journal of Political Research*, 29(3), 297–317.

Scarrow, Susan E., 1998: 'Political parties and the changing framework of German electoral competition', in Anderson and Zelle, 1998, pp.301–22.

Schäfers, Bernhard, 1998: *Sozialstruktur und sozialer Wandel in Deutschland* (Stuttgart: Ferdinand Enke Verlag).

Schäfers, Bernard and Zapf, Wolfgang (Hrsg.), 1998: *Handwörterbuch zur Gesellschaft Deutschlands* (Opladen: Leske and Budrich).

Scherer, Klaus-Jürgen, 1998: 'Die SPD und die PDS', in Barker, 1998, pp.182–193.

Schmidt, Ute, 1998: 'Sieben Jahre nach der Einheit: Die ostdeutsche Parteienlandschaft im Vorfeld der Bundestagswahl 1998', *Aus Politik und Zeitgeschichte*, B1-2, 37–53.

Schmitt, Karl, 1991: 'Parteien und regionale politische Traditionen. Eine Einführung', in Oberndörfer and Schmittt, 1991, pp.5–16.

Schmitt, Karl, 1998: 'The social bases of voting behaviour in unified Germany', in Anderson and Zelle, 1998, pp.33–54.

Schmitt, Karl, 2000: 'Die Landtagswahlen in Brandenburg und Thüringen vom 5. und 12. September 1999: Landespolitische Entscheidungen im Schlagschatten der Bundespolitik', *Zeitschrift für Parlamentsfragen*, 31(1), 43–68.

Schneider, Peter, 1999: 'Walls in our minds: history brought Germany's two halves together, but the future lies in celebrating diversity', *Central European Economic Review*, 7(9), 16–34.

Schreck, Erich, 1996: 'Die PDS in der Parteienlandschaft', *Deutschland Archiv*, 29(2), 471–2.

Schröder, Klaus, 1992: 'Die blockierte Vereinigung: Gemeinsamkeiten und Unterschiede der

Deutschen in Ost und West', *Gegenwartskunde*, 3, 297–308.

Schultze, Rainer-Olaf, 1995: 'Wiedersprüchliches, Ungliechzeitiges und kein Ende in Sicht: Die Bundestagswahl vom 16. Oktober 1994', *Zeitschrift für Parlamentsfragen*, 26(2), 325–52.

Schulz, Wilfried, 1998: 'Keine linke Alternative – Die Ebenen und Abgründe der PDS', *Deutschland Archiv*, 31(5), 801–3.

Schumann, Siegfried, 1997: 'Formen und Determinanten der Protestwahl', in Gabriel, 1997, pp.401–21.

Schweigler, Gebhard Ludwig, 1975: *National Consciousness in Divided Germany* (London: Sage).

Segall, Peter Christian *et al.*, 1999: *Die PDS im Wahljahr 1999: 'Politik von links, von unten und von Osten'* (München: Akademie für Politik und Zeitgeschehen, Hanns Seidel Stiftung e. V).

Segall, Peter Christian and Schorpp-Grabiak, Rita, 1999: *Die PDS vor den Europawahlen* (München: Akademie für Politik und Zeitgeschehen, Hanns Seidel Stiftung e. V).

Segert, Astrid, 1998: 'Problematic normalisation – eastern German workers eight years after unification', *German Politics and Society*, 16(3), 105–24.

Simeon, Richard and Elkins, David J., 1980: 'Provincial political cultures', in Elkins and Simeon, 1980, pp.31–76.

Smith, Anthony D., 1979: 'Towards a theory of ethnic separatism', *Ethnic and Racial Studies*, 2(1), 21–37.

Smith, Gordon, 1972: *Politics in Western Europe* (London: Heinemann Educational Books).

Smith, Gordon, 1992: 'The "new" party system', in Smith *et al.*, 1992, pp.77–102.

Smith, Gordon, Paterson, William E., Merkl, Peter H. and Padgett, Stephen (eds.), 1992: *Developments in German Politics* (Durham: Duke University Press).

Smith, Gordon *et al.* (eds.), 1996: *Developments in German Politics II* (Basingstoke: Macmillan).

Smith, Patricia J. (ed.), 1998: *After the Wall: Eastern Germany since 1989* (Boulder: Westview).

Smolicz, Jerzy J., 1981: 'Core values and cultural identity', *Ethnic and Racial Studies*, 4(1), 75–90.

Smolicz, Jerzy J., 1988: 'Tradition, core values and intercultural development in plural societies', *Ethnic and Racial Studies*, 11(4), 387–410.

Soares do Bem, Arim, 1998: *Das Spiel der Identitäten in der Konstitution von 'Wir' Gruppen: Ost- und westdeutsche Jugendliche und in Berlin geborene Jugendliche ausländischer Herkunft im gesellschaftlichen Umbruch* (Frankfurt am Main: Peter Lang GmbH, Europäischer Verlag der Wissenschaften).

Solga, Heike, 1995: 'Die Etablierung einer Klassengesellschaft in der DDR: Anspruch und Wirklichkeit des Postulats sozialer Gleichheit', in Huinink *et al.*: *Kollektiv und Eigensinn. Lebensverläufe in der DDR und danach* (Berlin: Akad. Verlag).

Späth, Lothar, 1998: *Blühende Phantasien und harte Realitäten: Wie der Umschwung Ost die ganze Republik verändert* (München: Econ and List Taschenbuch Verlag).

Spellerberg, Annette, 1997: 'Lebensstil, soziale Sicherheit und Lebensqualität in West- und Ostdeutschland', *Aus Politik und Zeitgeschichte*, B13, 25–37.

Spittman, Ilse, 1994: 'PDS – Anwalt der Ostdeutschen?', *Deutschland Archiv*, 27(6), 673–4.

Spittman, Ilse, 1996: 'Vertrauensverlust', *Deutschland Archiv*, 29(6), 841–4.

Spöhrer, Jochen, 2000: *Zwischen Demokratie und Oligarchie: Grüne und PDS im Deutschen Bundestag* (Baden-Baden: Nomos Verlagsgesellschaft).

Staab, Andreas, 1997: 'Testing the West: consumerism and national identity in eastern Germany', *German Politics*, 6(2), 139–49.

Staab, Andreas, 1998: *National Identity in Eastern Germany – Inner Unification or Continued Separation?* (Westport, Connecticut: Praeger).

Stammer Otto (ed.), 1968: *Party Systems, Party Organisation and the Politics of the New Masses* (Berlin: Institut für Politische Wissenschaft an der Freien Universität).

Statistisches Bundesamt, 1996: *Statistisches Jahrbuch 1996 für die Bundesrepublik Deutschland* (Wiesbaden: Metzler and Poeschel).

Statistisches Amt der DDR, 1990: *Statistisches Jahrbuch der DDR* (Berlin: Statistisches Amt der DDR).

Steinbach, Peter, 1998: 'Deutschland vor und seit der Wende – Von der Kenntnis zur Anerkennung der Verschiedenheiten', in *Aus Politik und Zeitgeschichte*, B51, 24–30.

Steinitz, Klaus, 1998: *Aufschwung Ost? Ergebnisse, Probleme, Perspektiven* (Berlin: Helle Panke e.V., Pankower Vorträge, Heft 13).

Stognienko, Michael, 1999: 'Der Krieg in den Köpfen: Wie der Kosovo-Einsatz die Deutschen trennt und eint', in Probst, 1999, pp.73–8.

Stöss, Richard and Niedermayer, Oskar, 2000: 'Zwischen Anpassung und Profilierung: Die SPD an der Schwelle zum neuen Jahrhundert', *Aus Politik und Zeitgeschichte*, N5, 3–11.

Strom, Kaare, 1990: 'A behavioural theory of comparative political parties', *American Journal of Political Science*, 34(2), 565–98.

Sturm, Eva, 2000: *'Und der Zukunft zugewandt'? Eine Untersuchung zur Politikfähigkeit der PDS* (Opladen: Leske und Budrich).

Tarchi, Marco, 1998: 'The *Lega Nord*', in De Winter and Türsan, 1998, pp.143–57.

Thierse, Wolfgang, 1999: 'Vorwort' in Cullen, 1999, pp.9–13.

Thierse, Wolfgang, 2000: *Zwischen Mauerfall und deutscher Einheit: 10 Jahre danach – bleibt der Osten anders?* (Schwerin: Schweriner Gespräche, Landeszentrale für politische Bildung Mecklenburg-Vorpommern).

Thomas, Michael, 1998: 'Paradoxien in der deutschen Transformationsdebatte', *Berliner Debatte INITIAL*, 9(2), 104–16.

Thompson, Wayne C., 1996: 'The Party of Democratic Socialism,' *Communist and Post-Communist Studies*, 29(4), 435–52.

Tiryakin, Edward J. and Rogowski, Ronald (eds.), 1985: *New Nationalism of the Developed West* (Boston: Allen and Unwin).

Tong, Yanqu, 1995: 'Mass alienation under state socialism and after', *Communist and Post-Communist Studies*, 28(2), 215–37.

Ugarte, Beatriz Acha and Pérez-Nievas, Santiago, 1998: 'Moderate nationalist parties in the Basque Country', in De Winter and Türsan, 1998, pp.87–104.

Unger, Frank, 1995: 'Adieu PDS? Plädoyer für eine neue Parteienlandschaft der Linken in der Berliner Republik', in Beinert, 1995, pp.81–8.

Urwin, Derek W., 1982: 'Perspectives on the conditions of regional protest and accommodation', in Rokkan and Urwin, 1982, 425–36.

Urwin, Derek W., 1983: 'Harbinger, fossil or fleabite? 'Regionalism' and the west European party mosaic', in Daalder and Mair, 1983, pp.221–56.

Urwin, Derek W., 1985: 'The price of a kingdom: territory, identity and the centre–periphery dimension in western Europe', in Meny and Wright, 1985, pp.151–70.

Urwin, Derek W., 1998: 'Modern democratic experiences of territorial management: Single houses, but many mansions', *Regional and Federal Studies*, 8(2), 81–110.

Uschner, Manfred: *Die Roten Socken* (Berlin: Dietz).

Veen, Hans-Joachim, 1997a: 'Innere Einheit – aber wo liegt sie? Eine Bestandsaufnahme im siebten Jahr nach der Wiedervereinigung Deutschlands', *Aus Politik und Zeitgeschichte*, B40–41, 19–28.

Veen, Hans-Joachim, 1997b: '"Inner Unity" – Back to the Community Myth? A Plea for a Basic Consensus', *German Politics*, 6(3), 1–15.

Veen, Hans-Joachim *et al.* 1998: *Analyse der Bundestagswahl vom 27. September 1998* (Sankt Augustin bei Bonn: Konrad Adenauer Stiftung,).

Veen, Hans-Joachim and Graf, Jutta: *Rückkehr zu traditionellen Werten?* (Sankt Augustin bei Bonn: Konrad Adenauer Stiftung, 1997).

Veen, Hans-Joachim and Wilamowitz-Moellendorff, Ulrich von, 2000: *Das Wahljahr 1999: Trends und Perspektiven* (Sankt Augustin bei Bonn: Konrad Adenauer Stiftung).

Veen, Hans-Joachim and Zelle, Carsten, 1994: *Zusammenwachsen oder Auseinanderdriften?* (Sankt Augustin bei Bonn: Konrad Adenauer Stiftung).

Vester, Michael, 1995: 'Milieuwandel und regionaler Strukturwandel in Ostdeutschland', in Vester, Hoffman and Zierke, 1995, pp.7–50.

Vester, Michael, Hoffman, Michael and Zierke, Irene (eds.), 1995: *Soziale Milieus in Ostdeutschland. Gesellschaftliche Strukturen zwischen Zerfall und Neubildung* (Köln: Bund).

Wagenknecht, Sahra, 1996: *Die PDS: Zwischen Antikapitalismus und Sozialdemokratie* (Hamburg: Rote Hefte 2, JUKO (Junge KommunistiInnen)).

Wagenknecht, Sahra, 1998: *Kapital, Crash, Krise … Kein Ausweg in Sicht?* (Bonn: Pahl-Rugenstein Verlag).

Wagenknecht, Sahra and Brie, Andre, 1996: '*Wie macht sich die PDS nicht überflüssig?*' (Berlin: Neues Deutschland, ND im Club – Streitgespräch: Ein Tonbandprotokoll).

Wagstaff, Peter (ed.), 1994: *Regionalism in Europe* (Oxford: Intellect).

Walz, Dieter, 1997: 'Einstellungen zu den politischen Institutionen', in Gabriel, 1997, pp.147–66.

Walz, Dieter and Brunner, Wolfram, 1997: 'Das Sein bestimmt das Bewußtsein (Oder: Warum sich die Ostdeutschen als Bürger 2. Klasse fühlen)', *Aus Politik und Zeitgeschichte*, B51, 13–19.

Weber, Max, 1968: *Economy and Society: An Outline of Interpretive Sociology*, edited by Günther Roth and Claus Wittich (New York: Bedminster Press).

Weidenfeld, Werner (Hrsg.), 1993: *Deutschland: Eine Nation – Doppelte Geschichte* (Bonn: Verlag Wissenschaft und Politik).

Weihrich, Margit, 1999: 'Alltägliche Lebensführung im ostdeutschen Transformationsprozeß', *Aus Politik und Zeitgeschichte*, B12, 15–26.

Weins, Cornelia, 1999: 'The East German vote in the 1998 General Election', *German Politics*, 8(2), 48–71.

Weizsäcker, Richard von, 1999: *Zwischen Mauerfall und deutscher Einheit: Zehn Jahre danach – die ungleichen deutschen Geschwister* (Schwerin: Schweriner Gespräche, Landeszentrale für politische Bildung Mecklenburg-Vorpommern).

Welsh, Helga A, Pickel, Andreas and Rosenberg, Dorothy, 1997: 'East and West German identities – united and divided?', in Jarausch, 1997, pp.103–36.

Werz, Nikolaus, 1998: 'Vor den Wahlen: Ein Stimmungsbericht aus dem Nordosten', *Gegenwartskunde*, 47(1), 7–13.

Werz, Nikolaus, 1998: 'Politische parteien', in Werz and Schmidt, 1998, pp.85–100.

Werz, Nikolaus and Schmidt, Jochen (Hrsg.), 1998: *Mecklenburg-Vorpommern im Wandel – Bilanz und Ausblick* (München: Günther Olzog Verlag).

Weßels, Bernhard, 2000: 'Gruppenbindungen und Wahlverhalten: 50 Jahre Wahlen in der Bundesrepublik' in Klein, Jagodzinski, Mochmann and Ohr, 2000 pp. 129–55.

Wiesenthal, Helmut (Hrsg.), 1996: *Einheit als Privileg* (Frankfurt am Main: Campus).

Wiesenthal, Helmut: 'Post-unification dissatisfaction, or why are so many east Germans unhappy with the new political system', *German Politics*, 7(2), 1–30.

Wiesenthal, Helmut, 1999: *Die Transformation der DDR* (Gütersloh: Verlag Bertelsmann Stiftung).

Williams, Colin H., 1999: 'Nationalism and its derivatives in post-1989 Europe', in Hudson and Williams, 1999, pp.79–106.

Wittich, Dietmar, 1996a: 'Zur Soziologie der Umwandlung der SED in die PDS' in Bisky *et al.*, 1996, pp.175–85.

Wittich, Dietmar, 1996b: *Alltagsleben und soziale Situation in der DDR und in der Wendezeit in Mecklenburg-Vorpommern* (Schwerin: PDS Fraktion im Landtag Mecklenburg-Vorpommern).

Woderich, Rudolf, 1997: 'Gelebte und inszenierte Identitäten in Ostdeutschland', *Identitäten in Europa. Welt Trends. International Politik und vergleichende Studien*, 15, 79–98.

Wolf, Herbert, 1995: *Woher kommt und wohin geht die PDS?* (Berlin: Grundsatz Kommission der PDS).

Wolinetz, Steven, 1990: *Parties and Party Systems in Liberal Democracies* (New York: Routledge).

Yoder, Jennifer A., 1999a: *From East Germans to Germans? The New Postcommunist Elites* (London: Duke University Press).

Yoder, Jennifer A., 1999b: 'Truth without reconciliation: an appraisal of the Enquete Commission on the SED dictatorship in Germany', *German Politics*, 8(3), 59–80.

Zelle, Carsten, 1997: *Ostalgie? National and Regional Identifications in Germany after Unification* (Birmingham: Discussion Paper in German Studies, University of Birmingham, Number 10).

Zelle, Carsten, 1998a: 'Factors explaining the increase in PDS support after unification', in Anderson and Zelle, 1998, pp.223–46.

Zelle, Carsten, 1998b: 'Soziale und liberale Wertorientierungen: Versuch einer situativen Erklärung der Unterschiede zwischen Ost- und Westdeutschen', *Aus Politik und Zeitgeschichte*, B41-42, 24–36.

Zelle, Carsten: 'Socialist heritage or current unemployment: why do the evaluations of democracy and socialism differ Between East and West Germans', *German Politics* 8(1), 1–20.

Zentralinstitut für sozialwissenschaftliche Forschung, 1996: *Endbericht des Kommission für die Erforschung des sozialen und politischen Wandels in den neuen Bundesländern e. V. (KSPW) Projekt 'Kreisparteien': Organisation, Politik und Vernetzung der Parteien auf Kreisebene in den fünf neuen Bundesländern* (Berlin: Freie Universität, Zentralinstitut für sozialwissenschaftliche Forschung).

Ziblatt, Daniel F.: 'Putting Humpty-Dumpty back together again', *German Politics and Society*, 16(1), 1–29.

Znaniecki, Florian, 1963: *Cultural Sciences* (Urbana: University of Illinois).

Newspapers

Berliner Morgenpost.
Bild am Sonntag.
Die Welt.
Die Zeit.
Frankfurter Allgemeine Zeitung.
Junge Welt.
Leipziger Volkszeitung.
Neues Deutschland.

Rheinischer Merkur.
Schweriner Volkszeitung.
Spiegel.
Süddeutsche Zeitung.
Tageszeitung.
The Economist.
The Independent.
This Week in Germany.
Wochenpost.

Index